Globalizing the Lower Rio Grande

European Entrepreneurs in the Borderlands, 1749–1881

Kyle B. Carpenter

Number 2 in the Randolph B. "Mike" Campbell Series

University of North Texas Press
Denton, Texas

©2024 Kyle B. Carpenter

All rights reserved.
Printed in the United States of America.

10 9 8 7 6 5 4 3 2 1

Permissions:
University of North Texas Press
1155 Union Circle #311336
Denton, TX 76203-5017

The paper used in this book meets the minimum requirements of the American National Standard for Permanence of Paper for Printed Library Materials, z39.48.1984. Binding materials have been chosen for durability.

Library of Congress Cataloging-in-Publication Data

Names: Carpenter, Kyle B., 1985- author.
Title: Globalizing the Lower Rio Grande : European entrepreneurs in the borderlands, 1749-1881 / Kyle B. Carpenter.
Other titles: Randolph B. "Mike" Campbell series ; no. 2.
Description: Denton, Texas : University of North Texas Press, [2024] | Series: Randolph B. "Mike" Campbell series ; no. 2 | Includes bibliographical references and index.
Identifiers: LCCN 2024016811 (print) | LCCN 2024016812 (ebook) | ISBN 9781574419450 (cloth) | ISBN 9781574419559 (ebook)
Subjects: LCSH: Globalization--Texas--Lower Rio Grande Valley--History--19th century. | Business enterprises, Foreign--Texas--Lower Rio Grande Valley--History--19th century. | Colonial companies--Texas--Lower Rio Grande Valley--History--19th century. | Settler colonialism--Texas--Lower Rio Grande Valley--History--19th century. | Europeans--Texas--Lower Rio Grande Valley--History--19th century. | Entrepreneurship--Texas--Lower Rio Grande Valley--History--19th century. | Transnational history--Texas. | Lower Rio Grande Valley (Tex.)--Economic conditions--19th century.
Classification: LCC F392.R5 C37 2024 (print) | LCC F392.R5 (ebook) | DDC 327.764/400934--dc23/eng/20240418
LC record available at https://lccn.loc.gov/2024016811
LC ebook record available at https://lccn.loc.gov/2024016812

Globalizing the Lower Rio Grande is Number 2 in the Randolph B. "Mike" Campbell Series.

The electronic edition of this book was made possible by the support of the Vick Family Foundation. Typeset by vPrompt eServices.

For Arlo

. . . that one most perilous and long voyage ended, only begins a second; and a second ended, only begins a third, and so on, for ever and for aye. Such is the endlessness, yea, the intolerableness of all earthly effort.

—Herman Melville, *Moby Dick*

Contents

List of Maps and Images vii

Acknowledgments ix

Introduction 1

Part 1 **Searching for Profit in Settler Colonialism** **13**

Chapter 1 The Spanish Context: Setting European Foundations in the Rio Grande Borderlands, 1749–1821 15

Chapter 2 The Beales Colony Experiment 43

Chapter 3 British and French Borderlands Entrepreneurs in the Republic of Texas 67

Part 2 **Networks, Modernity, and Economic Expansion** **93**

Chapter 4 Constructing Transnational Entrepreneurial Networks 95

Chapter 5 Walking in Tall Cotton 125

Chapter 6 Railroaded in the Rio Grande Borderlands 149

Epilogue 173

Endnotes 179

Bibliography 215

Index 239

List of Maps and Images

1. Rio Grande Borderlands, 1855   9
2. Mapa de la Sierra Gorda, 1792   19
3. Nuevo Santander, 1795   27
4. Humboldt Carte du Mexique, 1811   32
5. Map of Texas, 1835   58
6. John C. Beales's River Grant, 1834   61
7. Texas Land Grants, 1842   81
8. Levee Street, Brownsville, Texas, 1865   102
9. Elizabeth Street, Brownsville, Texas, 1865   131
10. Rio Grande Railroad Locomotive   161
11. Map of the Railroad System of Texas on September 1, 1883   168

Acknowledgments

In writing this book, I learned a lot about debts: financial, social, and otherwise. An acknowledgements page cannot come close to repaying these folks, but it is at least something to offset the accruing interest.

This work could not have been accomplished without the guidance and wisdom of Neil Foley, along with Ariel Ron, Erin Hochman, and Alicia Dewey. I owe all these folks an immense amount of gratitude for their encouragement and constructive feedback. Additionally, numerous faculty across an array of institutions helped make this book a reality. At Southern Methodist University, Ken Andrien, Sabri Ates, Kate Carté, John Chávez, Ed Countryman, Crista DeLuzio, Brian Franklin, Andrew Graybill, Jo Guldi, Ken Hamilton, Jill Kelly, Tom Knock, Alexis McCrossen, Dan Orlovsky, Sherry Smith, and Laurence Winnie deserve my thanks. At the University of Texas at Arlington, Patryk Babiracki, Stephanie Cole, Imre Demhardt, John Garrigus, and Sam Haynes contributed important input into the development of the ideas of this book. Sam Haynes's support throughout my entire academic career has been unflagging. He deserves more than these two sentences in an acknowledgement. I am grateful to Terri Hernández at the University of Houston, Richard Bell at the University of Maryland, Jonathan Bean at Southern Illinois University, Miguel Ángel González Quiroga, Scott and Mark Grayson, and Federico M. Garza Martínez.

I have been fortunate enough to be granted funding from sundry centers and institutions. I am deeply indebted to the Clements Center for Southwest Studies and, more specifically, Ruth Ann Elmore, who aided me from the beginning of this project through its completion. Her deep well of optimism and willingness to support everyone who comes to her door has always amazed me. Additionally, the Niemi Center at the Cox School of Business provided significant funding for me to pursue research for this project and supported me in the writing process. I need to thank Robert Lawson and Liz Chow for their help at the Niemi Center. The Dedman College Interdisciplinary Institute provided an important fellowship. Finally, the Institute for Humane Studies gave me generous research and conference funding.

The friendship and intellectual support of colleagues has been a constant blessing. Roberto Andrade, Jonathan Angulo, Camille Davis, Margi Evans, Braunshay Pertile, Ashton Reynolds, Tim Seiter, Josh Tracy, Pat Troester, and Joel Zapata have all my thanks. Andrew Klumpp still reads every draft I send him and politely eviscerates it so that my writing will be legible for the public.

Several archivists lent their expertise in the research process. They include Joan Gosnell and Terre Heydari at the DeGolyer Library at SMU, Ben Huseman and Sara Pezzoni in the Special Collections and Archives at UTA, Catherine Best at the Briscoe Center for American History, Shelby Gonzalez at the Texas A&M–Corpus Christi Special Collections, Leslie Stapleton at the Bexar County Archives, Bailey Smith and Carmen Martinez at the South Texas Archives, and Veronica Martinez at the Corpus Christi Public Library Special Collections.

I have been lucky enough to be a part of one of the most collegial departments at the University of Arkansas Rich Mountain. Krystal Thrailkill deserves special mention for her unwavering support no matter the harebrained ideas I bring to her door. We have the best faculty and staff. The college is too large to list everyone, but I want to thank you all.

Finally, my family carried the weight of this project from beginning to end. Mick, you and George make every day better than the last one. I love you this much.

Introduction

In April of 1837, Joseph Crawford, the British vice-consul at Tampico, Mexico, traveled north to the Rio Grande to compile a report about the conditions and prospects of British trade at the port of Matamoros. He noted that more than two-thirds of all the goods that entered Mexico at the Rio Grande came from British manufacturers. The vice-consul believed Matamoros, with its location inland, trade connections with Monterrey, and healthy climate, could become a significant center for trade if foreigners had more guarantees for their property. The threats of Indigenous attack and corrupt government officials far from the center of Mexican authority restrained the expansion of trade. However, those conditions applied to everyone in the region, giving nobody a sense of advantage. He did not know what the future held for the prospects of British commercial interests on the Rio Grande, but there was a growing community of European merchants in the city vying for the borderlands market. Crawford also heard news of a British settlement that had recently been established upriver, as well as a growing number of British entrepreneurs taking residence in towns all along the Rio Grande. He suggested that the British Foreign Office appoint a consular agent at Matamoros to give British borderlands entrepreneurs in the region all the advantages to succeed, stating, "That our commercial interests and the residents would be bettered by having a prudent consular agent here, there is no doubt."[1] Crawford believed that a state agent on the Rio Grande could spur trade and influence Mexican authorities to protect commerce. He imagined the Rio Grande becoming an important center of trade and wanted to ensure a strong British presence there.

The British were not alone in their optimistic perception of the prospects of the Rio Grande. Europeans' interest in expanding their footprint in the region was not new in 1837. Spain and its Indigenous allies had made the first incursions almost a century earlier in 1747. Led by a military officer with commercial designs for the region, the Spanish project for settlement promoted the borderlands' economic potential. Spain succeeded in founding six villas on the Lower Rio Grande. However, the enterprise stagnated as political and economic decline wracked the Spanish Empire at the turn of the century.

After Mexico achieved its independence in 1821, the region was contested among Indians, Mexicans, Anglo-Americans, and Europeans.[2] Those Europeans, primarily from Great Britain, France, and German principalities, attempted to extend formal control to parts of the borderlands in hopes of exploiting an untapped market.[3] British entrepreneurs tried and failed to establish settlements on the Rio Grande in the 1830s and 1840s. French entrepreneurs attempted similar projects in the 1840s, drawing German-speaking investors and emigrants into their schemes. At the same time, merchants and clerks from all over Europe poured into the broader borderlands region to extract natural resources and exploit its trading potential. They constructed vast networks that connected the Rio Grande to ports all over the Atlantic. European-born entrepreneurs openly competed with Anglo-Americans and, on occasion, undermined US commercial domination of the region. All these activities inspire significant questions. What opportunities did Europeans imagine finding in the borderlands and how did reality frustrate their imaginations?

What actions did European-born entrepreneurs take to seize and maintain their hold on the market in the Rio Grande borderlands? Most significantly, how does shifting the perspective from the American point of view change the way we look at the borderlands in the nineteenth century?

Globalizing the Lower Rio Grande tackles these questions and more. It argues that the Rio Grande borderlands became the focus of intense commercial modernization projects initiated by both state agents and individual businessmen from all over Europe. These borderlands entrepreneurs wanted to transform the Rio Grande borderlands from a regional crossroads into a hub of the Atlantic economy. In doing so they pushed back against US expansion and tried to remake the region according to European precepts. However, their efforts to create rapid change were often stymied by roadblocks, including the region's environmental conditions, European notions of ethnic and cultural superiority, and continual eruptions of violent conflict. European-born entrepreneurs met success in their ventures on occasion, but, overall, most of the enterprises they set out to establish ended in loss, a subsequent migration, or a complete shift in business model. By elucidating the many ways European-born entrepreneurs attempted to reform the Rio Grande borderlands into the commercial utopia they imagined, I hope to ultimately show just how contingent American imperial expansion remained in the nineteenth century. Europeans' consistent and evolving approaches preempted Anglo-American efforts and sometimes actively worked to subvert American designs.

European-born entrepreneurs had a persistent presence in the Rio Grande borderlands. From the era of Spanish settlement in the mid-eighteenth century, European colonizers encouraged European-born migrants to move to the region. They succeeded in drawing in hundreds of entrepreneurial immigrants in each of their successive attempts.[4] By 1860 the European-born population of the

US counties on the northern bank of the Rio Grande totaled 6.5 percent of the total population. In comparison, US-born residents comprised about 15 percent while Mexican-born inhabitants occupied an almost 80 percent majority. Even as they made up a significant portion of the non-Mexican population, European denizens of the Rio Grande borderlands dominated skilled labor positions within society. Almost half of the entire European-born community partook in mercantile activity as either merchants or clerks. Europeans had a significant presence in borderlands communities, where they influenced all aspects of society and culture.[5]

After traveling to the borderlands, entrepreneurial migrants faced political, cultural, and economic conditions that diverged from their European understandings of hierarchies of power, interethnic social interactions, and systems of exchange and ownership. They entered the borderlands with expectations that there existed an impersonal governing system like those they left in Europe. Often, they found limited or even no government authority. They expected a centralized state and found a space dominated by local rulers. European-born entrepreneurs quickly realized that Native Americans tended to wield the most power and controlled the most territory. Powerful Indigenous groups had vastly different conceptions of exchange than European understandings of ownership and transactions. Additionally, the new markets that European borderlands entrepreneurs sought to create contained Mexicans who were often more interested in maintaining the lifestyles they developed under the Spanish regime than speculating for profits. Furthermore, Anglo-Americans steeped in Jacksonian democracy defied European notions of hierarchy and propriety. These diverse worldviews mixed through porous ethnic boundaries in the Rio Grande borderlands, challenging Europeans to react in individual ways.[6]

In response, European-born entrepreneurs strove to transform the physical and cultural characteristics of the region to suit their expectations. They built relationships across cultural boundaries, played North American states against one another, and attempted to draw European states into protecting their interests on the American frontier. They all practiced some form of "borderlands entrepreneurialism," which I define as entrepreneurs attempting, with various degrees of success, to pull this far-flung frontier into Atlantic markets. Some examples of these strategies included settlement schemes to boost European populations, importing a glut of manufactured goods to create a sense of uniformity, and distributing easy credit to create dependent relationships. They were entrepreneurs because they took on significant risk to enrich themselves on the margins of the global market. Their activities varied greatly. Merchants, writers, doctors, soldiers, diplomats, adventurers, and more all had enough faith in the borderlands market to risk their time, bodies, and monetary investments there.

Scholars have used the term *entrepreneur* as flexibly as I do here. Alfred Chandler variously describes them as distributors, sellers, or enterprise creators. Shino Konishi defines them as imperial adventurers, and Frank Knight marks the entrepreneur as an individual who tackles incalculable conditions to make estimates, pass judgements, and take control. The borderlands entrepreneur had to be all these things and more.[7]

Studying European-born borderlands entrepreneurs who moved to the Rio Grande borderlands offers a new lens through which to analyze the rapid changes that affected the region in the nineteenth century. Primarily, it provides a perspective of individuals who moved to a new place and actively tried to understand it so that they might better succeed in their ventures. In that acclimation process, some became frustrated with the social, cultural, and political conditions in the borderlands such that they attempted to reshape their localities to meet their own ends. Others adapted quickly to the conditions they faced and entered kinship relationships with borderlanders. Still others became so disillusioned that they fled the borderlands altogether. All their accounts demonstrate how individual Europeans actively tried to impose their notions of modernity on this region of the world.[8]

While it is true that studying such a broad group of people like European-born entrepreneurs presents certain complications, I argue that their shared European mindset and entrepreneurial spirit make them an ideal slice of borderlands society to investigate. By the end of the eighteenth century, an increasing number of Europeans decided that they were modern and living in modern societies. Entrepreneurs were particularly enmeshed in processes of emulating and spreading modern notions that included freedom of commerce and creating uniformity. European-born entrepreneurs all also shared the entrepreneurial anxieties of taking on tremendous financial and personal risks half a world away from their European homes in the North American borderland.[9]

While their shared mindset, experiences, and goals allow for these seemingly diverse peoples to be grouped, what made European borderlands entrepreneurs different from Mexicans or Anglo-Americans in the Lower Rio Grande? Primarily, I let them tell me themselves. If individuals documented that they were of a European national heritage or wrote about Anglo-Americans and Mexicans as distinct others, I took their word for it. However, it was not always easy to define each individual. Their identities remained fluid. In certain conditions their identities might shift, then shift again as circumstances changed. Rather than be discouraged by these shifting identities, I recognized that as the nature of the borderlands. Individuals leveraged whatever was most useful at the time. Another marker I used to define them as distinct from Anglo-Americans and Mexicans was the social and business networks they built. Borderlands entrepreneurs entered the borderlands market often at great financial risk to themselves. They needed associates they could trust. Usually, they engaged with other Europeans of similar ethnicity and worked in direct competition with Anglo-Americans and Mexicans, which clearly set them as a group apart.[10]

Historians have tended to ignore the significant European presence on the US southwestern frontier.[11] The most cited economic history of borderlands reinforced notions of American expansion and market dominance.¹² The long-accepted periodization of the US-Mexico borderlands also obscured the history of European influence in the region. Mexican independence, the Texas Revolution, and the US-Mexico War mark transition points away from European dominance toward American control. However, new trends in borderlands historiography are pushing the boundaries of periodization and highlighting themes of cooperation and interdependence among diverse cultural groups.¹³ By centering the focus on European-born entrepreneurs, *Globalizing the Lower Rio Grande* offers a new lens to build on that scholarship. As migrants Europeans had to cooperate with local groups to succeed. In their relationships they attempted to transfer their norms and institutions to the frontier. They also actively connected the region to global ideas and markets beyond the United States. From the Spanish Imperial period to the Porfiriato and Gilded Age, Europeans continuously affected the Rio Grande borderlands.

I began asking questions about the European-born population in the borderlands while doing research for an article on the Galveston Bay and Texas Land Company. The executives of that company invested significant amounts of money advertising in Europe and even transported an entire ship full of Czech and German-speaking Europeans to Galveston Bay. I wanted to know what happened to those folks after they left the port. Further research demonstrated to me that there were Europeans all over the frontier region between the United States and Mexico. German, French, English, and Irish colonies dotted the landscape. Entrepreneurs from Europe opened shops in every settlement along the Rio Grande. They married Mexican women and connected to local networks, which they then tied to complex webs of transatlantic exchange. They were the proverbial "ants," to borrow loosely from Bruno Latour, moving items and ideas back and forth across the Atlantic.¹⁴ In doing so they established the "patterns of local economic intensification [that] were the leading motors for change" in the region.¹⁵

European borderlands entrepreneurs tried to make a modern market out of the Rio Grande borderlands. Their primary motive was to create a place that demanded European manufactures in exchange for raw materials to produce more manufactured goods. By the nineteenth century, the textile economy drove their market orientation. Europeans adopted both formal and informal strategies through settlement projects and mercantile competition. The European trade in cotton and animal hide enticed entrepreneurs to the borderlands. The region became a major cattle producer and thus a source for the hide thongs that drove textile machines. They wanted to trade finished textiles for borderlands hides to complete the loop. European successes upset the expectations of the Anglo-American commercial elite who assumed the Rio Grande would become a part of the American market with only Mexico as a competitor.[16]

The evidence base demonstrating the significance of European-born entrepreneurs in the Rio Grande borderlands over this long period is quite broad. I rely most heavily on family and personal papers, travelogues and journals, business records, government documents, and political and commercial correspondence.[17] Personal papers show what impact European-born entrepreneurs had on the region and offer insights into projects that failed or succeeded. They document colonizing schemes and mercantile enterprises from their inception to the point when they floundered, demonstrating interconnectedness and change over time. Successive entrepreneurs used their forebears' records to inform them on their next venture. I also utilize government documents from the United States, Mexico, Spain, England, and France.[18] Government documents reveal how state agents viewed the Rio Grande borderlands and the European-born entrepreneurs working there. Using customs records, foreign office dispatches, broadsides, and congressional investigations, I piece together the economic and political connections among European-born entrepreneurs, their social and business networks, and the goals European states had for the region.[19]

My analysis proceeds along three interrelated geographic levels within which Europeans operated. At the broadest level is

Introduction

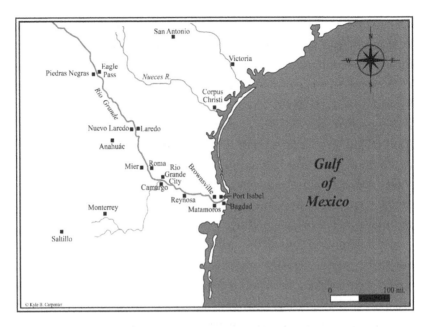

The Rio Grande Borderlands in 1855. Map by Alex Mendoza.

the portion of the Atlantic World spanning Europe, North America, the Caribbean, and especially the Gulf of Mexico. Regionally, the Rio Grande borderlands is the space where European-born entrepreneurs focused the intensity of their programs. The region is bounded in the north by San Antonio, in the southeast by Corpus Christi, in the south by Brownsville/Matamoros, in the southwest by Monterrey, and in the west by Piedras Negras / Eagle Pass, and includes Laredo / Nuevo Laredo, Roma, Camargo, Reynosa, and other borderland communities. Mexican historians have long argued in favor of the study of the geographic region between San Antonio and Monterrey.[20] Finally, the local cities, towns, and villas mark the narrowest of my geographic focus.[21]

I conceive of the region as a borderland from 1749–1881 for several reasons. Spain entered the region in 1749 and, until the end of the US-Mexico War in 1848, the Rio Grande borderland was contested among several imperial powers, including Spain, Mexico, the United States, the Comanche Empire, Britain, and France. They all failed to extend permanent authority over the region, which allowed for local freedom of social and economic movement. After the Treaty of Guadalupe Hidalgo in 1848, the Rio Grande borderlands became a bordered land on paper. The United States and Mexico had treaties and maps that showed their respective states' control extended to the Rio Grande. For the most part, that control was illusory. Individuals in the borderland still had an incredible amount of local freedom of social and economic movement. Though the language changed to define commercial movement across the boundary at the Rio Grande as "illicit trade" or "smuggling," state agents had little recourse to stop it. Attempts to control the movement of people across the national boundary were virtually nonexistent. Geographic distance from government centers, the continued presence of powerful Indigenous groups, and the significant power of strong local elites severely limited centralized state authority. European-born entrepreneurs in the region mark one of the many multicultural subjects who took advantage of the fluidity of the region to implement their own schemes. Until the railroads obliterated the distance between state centers and the Rio Grande in 1881, the region remained a borderland.[22]

The book is divided into six chapters that analyze particular events to illustrate how European-born entrepreneurs and state agents continually attempted to make the Rio Grande borderlands into their own modern hub of Atlantic trade. Chapter 1 examines how José de Escandón settled the region in the name of Spain. It focuses on the blended networks of Indigenous and Spanish colonists who worked together to carve out an existence in the harsh climate of the Lower Rio Grande and how Escandón utilized commerce to settle the region. Chapter 2 connects the Mexican state to growing interest in Europe for northern Mexican lands and markets in the 1820s. Mexico encouraged Europeans to move to its northern frontier with favorable land and immigration policies. However, nearly every political and economic strategy Mexican officials and European entrepreneurs employed seemed to fail in the face of the rising power of the Comanche and

American empires. By examining one single European-led colonization venture, Englishman John Charles Beales's colony at Dolores, I argue that expectations for the Rio Grande borderlands were so unrealistic that the colony lasted only a few years. Chapter 3 examines the role of European states and state agents, many of whom earned land grant contracts from the government of the Republic of Texas. They actively attempted to harness the power and authority of European states to build settlements for European-born immigrants to push back against Anglo-American expansion.

The second half of the book focuses more on the informal ways that European-born entrepreneurs attempted to extend their control of the Rio Grande borderlands. Chapter 4 compares how two different European mercantile networks worked to gain a foothold in the region after the US-Mexico War. They connected the local to global in ways that supported European borderlands entrepreneurs. Chapter 5 examines the role of European-born entrepreneurs in the cotton trade during the US Civil War. The outbreak of the Civil War created new tensions as rapid political change forced entrepreneurs to compromise their loyalties and moral principles to earn the profits and power they desired. Chapter 6 explores the competition between Anglo-American railroad development and Europeans who wanted their own railroad lines. By 1881 Anglo-Americans were able to harness the full power of the United States and Mexican governments to crush their European competition and embark on an era of US domination that effectively erased the remnants—and the history—of their European-born competition.

PART 1

Searching for Profit in Settler Colonialism

PART 1

Chapter 1

The Spanish Context
Setting European Foundations in the Rio Grande Borderlands, 1749–1821

As one of the first Europeans to seek his fortune in the Rio Grande borderlands, José de Escandón fundamentally changed the way Spain interacted with the region. His primary goal, to create settled towns in a region that had been largely occupied by mobile Indigenous people for centuries, was meant to satisfy his superiors in the government of New Spain who wanted the *indios bárbaros* Christianized and congregated for productive labor.[1] Achieving this goal would also provide Escandón personal opportunities for agricultural and commercial wealth heretofore unavailable on New Spain's northern frontier. He sought to capitalize by acquiring large tracts of arable land and creating a mercantile monopoly. Escandón worked within the structures of the Spanish Empire to achieve his entrepreneurial ambitions. His initial efforts to build the region through diplomatic, commercial, and military force set the foundation for future transformational efforts led by Europeans in the Rio Grande borderlands.

When José de Escandón set out on reconnaissance of the Rio Grande borderlands in the mid-eighteenth century, one of his primary strategies was to find local Indigenous groups and ingratiate himself to them. Escandón, a colonel in the Spanish army and renowned Indian fighter, presented himself to the leaders of each Indigenous band he came across to offer provisions and tobacco to any willing to participate in discussion of future Spanish settlement. Indigenous people along the Rio Grande, often in constant conflict with one another for the limited resources in the region, engaged Escandón in cautious negotiations. Other Indigenous groups resisted Spanish incursions and attacked Spanish settlers, killing some and capturing those they did not kill. In these cases Escandón and his military cohort countered with sorties of their own to "pacify" the region. Pacification often resulted in chaining Indigenous people and marching them to work in enslavement in Central Mexico.[2]

As made clear by Escandón's actions, Spanish expansion to the Rio Grande borderlands often required that settlers build alliances with Indigenous people. By 1749 incorporating Indians into the Spanish imperial project had become an important institution for how the empire expanded. The Bourbon Reforms that swept through New Spain in the eighteenth century shifted the focus of imperial expansion from conquest and exploitation to settlement and cooperation. The Bourbons wanted to defend the empire cheaply and efficiently. Creating Indigenous allies to build frontier populations and aid in defense thus served their administrative goals. Not only did the networks built between Spanish and Indians help create Spanish legitimacy on its frontiers, but it also formed the foundations of important infrastructures that allowed Spain to expand. Seeking personal wealth and promoting imperial expansion, Escandón sought to merge Spanish and Indigenous institutions and infrastructures to settle the Rio Grande borderlands.[3]

Comercio libre, or free trade, was also a key piece of reform designed to tie the Spanish Empire more tightly together. English merchants probed establishing a trading post on the Gulf Coast, and French merchants traveled through northern New Spain seeking to network with Indigenous traders. Spain had to adapt to keep their competitors out. Seeking personal wealth and promoting imperial expansion, Escandón sought to impose European notions of impersonal exchange onto Indigenous people and Indigenous institutions to expand trade and exchange to settle the Rio Grande borderlands, solidifying Spanish control of the region.[4]

In some ways Escandón acted as a European borderlands entrepreneur who traveled to the Rio Grande borderlands to remake it into a new outlet for Atlantic trade. However, the Spanish imperial structure and competing interests tempered Escandón's successes in transforming the borderlands. His military subordinates chafed at his leadership decisions and the power he wielded. Spanish settlers challenged his land policies and agreements with Indigenous people. Religious orders, threatened by Escandón's trust in secular institutions, lobbied to have him replaced. All these groups came together to successfully undermine Escandón's commercial program, ensuring his plan was only partially implemented.

As the Spanish looked to expand New Spain northward, the Spanish Empire went through a series of reform movements. The most important imperial reorganization for the Rio Grande borderlands was the Bourbon Reforms. Born out of constant warfare in Europe and Indigenous revolts in the Americas, the Bourbon Reforms began in the early eighteenth century with the goals of modernizing the empire through efficient and pragmatic policies that included reorganizing the imperial army and divesting religious orders of rural Indigenous parishes. The Bourbon Reforms also sought to curb smuggling by loosening trade restrictions to utilize market transactions for imperial gain. Expansions in free trade encouraged more entrepreneurial activity. The settlement of the Rio Grande borderlands reflected the changes in the modern, reform-oriented Spanish Empire.[5]

By the mid-eighteenth century, the Bourbon-appointed leadership in New Spain sought to settle the land adjacent to the northwestern Gulf of Mexico, a region called the Seno Mexicano. A vast swath of land, the Seno Mexicano ranged from the Nueces River in the north all the way south to the Panuco River and the northeastern boundaries of Querétaro. Due to its size, varied topography, and unpredictable climate, Spain had initially left the area virtually unsettled until the region posed security issues for its empire. Primarily, France and England had begun to make probing inroads along the Gulf Coast. Spain feared that if either of those competing empires gained a foothold, it would lose the region. Additionally, the Seno Mexicano had become a refuge for *indios bárbaros* who resisted Spanish priests and for soldiers who occupied the northern frontier.[6]

Before the Bourbons took over the Spanish imperial project, there remained two institutional frameworks on Spain's northern frontier that preceded Escandón's colonization scheme: the mission and the presidio system. Missions marked the first institution to expand northward because they were cost-effective and maintained the goal of acculturating Indigenous populations to make them productive Spanish subjects who would defend the empire. Using missions also helped Spanish authorities justify their conquest by claiming they were spreading the gospel. Andrés de Olmos led the first mission to the Seno Mexicano in the mid-sixteenth century. A scholar of Indigenous languages, Olmos brought Nahuatl-speaking people to the region around Tampico, where he began studying the languages of nearby people to attempt to Christianize and Hispanicize the nomadic people who lived there. Though he died of illness in Tampico without making significant inroads with the people along the Rio Grande, his effort provided an example of utilizing Indigenous allies to expand imperial control through missionaries.[7]

It took over a century after Olmos died for the Franciscans to return their attention to the Rio Grande borderlands as incidents of Indigenous violence exploded across New Spain's frontier. Drought and Comanche expansion pushed the Lipan Apache from eastern New Mexico and the Texas Plains down to the Rio Grande and below. Poor rainfall accumulations drove the Lipans to seek lands with better access to freshwater. Additionally, the Comanche began to exert increasing power on the Southern Plains by the end of the seventeenth

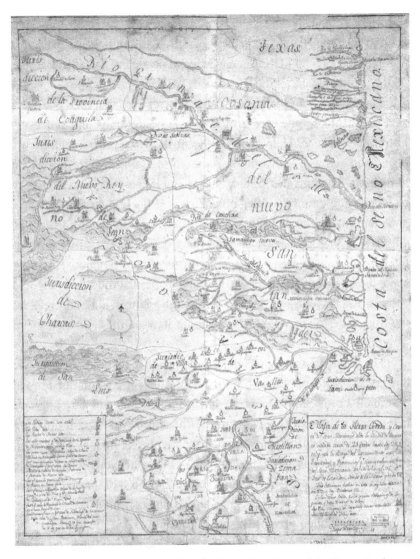

Mapa de la Sierra Gorda, 1792. José de Escandón, *Mapa de la Sierra Gorda y Costa del Seno Mexicano desde la Cuidad de Queretaro*, 1747, Library of Congress, https://www.loc.gov/item/2007632265/.

century, pushing southward into Apache territories. As the Lipan Apache moved to seek well-watered land and to avoid the Comanche onslaught, they challenged the Coahuiltecans for the limited resources in the Rio Grande borderlands. To stem the violence that creeped southward, Spanish missionaries from Querétaro set out to proselytize and turn the raiding Indians into settled agriculturalists. The first mission to take hold in the Seno Mexicano opened at San Juan Bautista on the southern bank of the Rio Grande in 1699.[8]

The friars at San Juan Bautista quickly realized that their Christian zeal could not soothe the turmoil in the borderlands and requested military assistance. Help came in the form of the presidios, a highly developed defense network of stone forts connected by troops on horseback. The presidio system became a key part of Spain's strategy to defend the empire's outer boundaries, stifle Indigenous violence, and stem incursions into Spanish territory from competing European empires. To help presidios achieve success, soldiers came from frontier populations that had an interest in their own defense. Having a stake in the place they defended helped ensure that the soldiers would commit to protecting the frontier. Through the mission and presidio, the Spanish Crown sought to strengthen its hold on the periphery of its empire.[9]

The plan of using missions and presidios to hold the frontier did not always work, as can be seen through the exploits of French merchant Louis Saint-Denis. In 1713 Saint-Denis and a small band of French explorers traveled through northern New Spain building alliances and opening trade connections with Karankawa bands and other Indian groups along the Gulf Coast. They also navigated a large portion of the Lower Rio Grande and moved south of the river before the captain at the presidio San Juan Bautista found out about it. Saint-Denis eluded presidio scouts for months while he explored the Rio Grande, gained intelligence about the Spanish frontier, and made valuable commercial contacts with Indigenous people. Spanish officials responded by filing reports that the French had colonial designs on Spanish territory. They believed Saint-Denis was only the first of a wave of French settlers to overtake the Gulf Coast. Some even worried the French might drive all the way from the Gulf to New Mexico. This prompted the newly installed Bourbon leadership to reconsider Spanish policies regarding the Seno Mexicano.[10]

The Spanish Context

Saint-Denis revealed the limitations of the mission and presidio systems to secure the frontier from imperial incursions. In fact his mercantile operations demonstrated that the French had commercial advantages over Spain and that trade could successfully penetrate Spain's frontier line. French traders ingratiated themselves into Indian customs, learned Indigenous languages, and generally engaged in trade as level partners. French merchants accepted the importance of building kinship relationships with Indigenous people all over their imperial claims in North America, and Saint-Denis's expedition applied French knowledge of Indian trade when it entered the Rio Grande borderlands. Most importantly, the French did not have the same restrictions on Indian trade that Spain did. The Spanish actively avoided trading guns or ammunition to Indians in fear of those weapons being turned on them. The fact that the French willingly exchanged weapons made them attractive trade partners for Indigenous people. The frustrations with and fears of French commercial expansion influenced Spanish policy in the Seno Mexicano.[11]

Saint-Denis's expedition also coincided with a new monarchy in Spain. The Bourbon government emerged victorious in the War of the Spanish Succession in 1713 and took over the Spanish Crown from the Hapsburgs. The Bourbon regime sought to modernize the Spanish imperial structure, including military commitments and economic growth. The mission and presidio represented the outdated methods of the old regime. Bourbon administrators wanted to tighten Spain's trade system to make New Spain more profitable for the empire. Administrators believed that by cutting military expenditures, creating bureaucratic oversight, and encouraging internal trade, Spain's American colonies would produce considerably more wealth than before. The margin of the empire along the Rio Grande seemed to be a perfect place to implement new imperial changes. The Bourbon regime just had to find an agent to execute the new course of action.[12]

After years of deliberation and politicking, the job of settling the Seno Mexicano eventually fell to Colonel José de Escandón. Born in Santander in Spain, Escandón made his home in Querétaro, the center of New Spain's commercial society. The Marqués de Altamira handpicked Escandón for the job because of the colonel's previous accomplishments in pacifying the Sierra Gorda. Another reason Escandón received his commission was that he spurned both the mission and presidio systems as impotent, believing that commerce and settled agriculture were the keys to long-term success. Escandón embraced the notion that open trade would lead to the permanent settlement of the Seno Mexicano but also had the martial ability to use force in case commerce failed to control Indigenous groups.[13]

Seeing the success of French commercial expeditions into the Rio Grande borderlands spurred Bourbon officials to embrace the notion that commerce would better secure the frontier than missions or presidios. For example, the Marqués de Altamira noted in a letter to the viceroy of New Spain that if the Seno Mexicano was settled with large communities instead of presidios or missions, trade would naturally expand between Coahuila and Nuevo León. All the people on the frontier would benefit, which would result in a population dedicated to conserving the Spanish presence in the region. The Marqués de Altamira also believed that commerce would pacify the Indigenous population of the Seno Mexicano. Altamira wrote, "The souls of the Gentiles and the apostates to the security and extension, not only of those borders, but all those who have plots of land, will be free with the open traffic of trade."[14] Prominent members of the Spanish Empire were pushing to expand internal trade as a key to solving the frontier problem.

Bourbon policymakers listened to men like the Marqués de Altamira. Rather than send out more missionaries or build more presidios, the Bourbon reformers opted to acculturate *indios bárbaros* into Spanish society through market mechanisms. By mobilizing the wage system, reformers hoped to utilize Indigenous labor and Europeanize Indians. In practice the wage system turned into debt peonage, in which Indians were advanced wages and spent years working off the interest. For those Indians who failed to embrace Spain's enticements of peace, trade, work, and economic growth, the Crown endowed the military with the power to eradicate them through whatever means necessary. By the mid-eighteenth century, the Seno Mexicano became the focus for Spain's new colonization program.[15]

Escandón had the challenge of implementing the dual Bourbon reform policy of the velvet glove backed by the iron fist. Civilian villas rather than military establishments lay at the heart of Escandón's strategy, making the settlers he recruited the most important group of the entire project. They needed to be convinced to leave their homes and trek hundreds of miles across largely unmapped and rugged landscape to build towns from the ground up in a territory they knew to be inhabited by Indians who might violently defend against incursions. Escandón and the Spanish state had to build value into the venture to get enough volunteers who would be willing to exert such efforts. The first key to recruiting settlers was to draw them from the northern territories around Coahuila, Nuevo León, and San Luis Potosí so they were already familiar with the land and living at considerable distance from central New Spain. Escandón and the Marqués de Altamira demanded support from the authorities of those provinces to ensure settlers had access to the supplies needed to settle in the borderlands.[16]

Tlaxcalans made up a significant portion of the settled population in New Spain's far north. From the end of the sixteenth century, Tlaxcalans and other Nahuatl-speaking people aided Spain in settling its northern frontier. Nearly half of the towns and villas established in Nuevo León were founded by Tlaxcalan migrants. Many of the settlers that Escandón recruited came from the former Tlaxcalan settlements.[17]

Potential settlers, Tlaxcalan or not, needed material encouragement to leave the relative security of established settlements and enter the unsettled lands. Escandón offered settlers who traveled to the Rio Grande borderlands promises of land allotments for both farming and pasturing that exceeded anything they could attain farther south. Each family who decided to join the expedition received up to two hundred pesos to purchase supplies and offset the costs that would burden potential settlers. Escandón combined initial cash payments with prospects in land and property to convince people to settle on the frontier. With these inducements the first two settlements on the Rio Grande, Camargo and Reynosa, began with more than forty families apiece in the spring of 1749.[18]

With townsites established, Escandón turned his attention to the potential for lucrative entrepreneurial success. In his report to the viceroy of New Spain, Escandón made a point to highlight the commercial advantages of the Rio Grande borderlands. The salt lagoons that dotted the areas north and south of the Rio Grande drew his attention. Downplaying the lack of freshwater, he focused on the quality of the salt that the lagoons produced and the ease of extracting it in copious quantities. Enterprising individuals in Nuevo León already made semiannual trips to the region to gather salt to sell in the south, but Escandón saw that the trade in salt from the Rio Grande borderlands could be expanded significantly and with remarkable success.[19]

Salt was one of the most important commodities in the world in the eighteenth century. It preserved food, aided in the domestication of cattle, and remained an essential ingredient to silver mining. From before 2000 BCE, humans had used salt to cure and preserve fish and meat. Having salt deposits in the Rio Grande borderlands meant that potential settlers would be able to keep proteins in storage for lean times. The largest deposit, La Sal del Rey, sits on about one square mile of land north of the Rio Grande. Other small lagoons dot the region of the Lower Rio Grande. These deposits supplied salt to people north and south of the Rio Grande for centuries. With the region's lack of freshwater and semiarid climate, Escandón likely envisioned that the people would encounter times of drought in which they would have to rely on salted food to get through.[20]

Not only did salt aid in food preservation, but also the Rio Grande's salt lagoons and rolling grasslands contributed to the creation of a successful cattle industry. Describing the terrain around the Rio Grande as "very flat, with the exception of some low rolling hills and it is of beautiful quality for all kinds of planting and raising livestock due to producing the best pasturage I have ever seen in as far as I have traveled," Escandón clearly anticipated the ranching culture that would develop around the river.[21] Settlers who chose the area could produce enough livestock to not only sustain themselves but also to export beef on the hoof, wool, and hide in great quantity. Established saltworks from Rio Grande lagoons would allow for the long-term storage of surplus meat and the production of quality, exportable hide. The salt deposits in the Rio Grande borderlands offered the possibility of a sprawling cattle industry for New Spain's frontier.[22]

Salt in the Rio Grande borderlands also meant that the region had a ready export commodity to ship south in exchange for necessary finished goods and hard currency. By the mid-eighteenth century, Spanish silver drove the entire Atlantic economy. San Luis Potosí and Zacatecas had grown into key producers of silver for Spain and the entire Western world, but silver production relied upon the patio process for extracting silver from its ore. The patio process required significant quantities of salt mixed with mercury and copper sulfate to create the chemical reaction to free silver from its compounds. For decades the Spanish had to ship tons of salt from Guadalajara or even the Yucatán to San Luis Potosí and Zacatecas. If the Rio Grande borderlands could produce efficient saltworks, it would make the silver mining ventures more profitable and add to the economic stability of the new borderland settlements.[23]

Despite the boon of salt, Escandón anticipated problems. The biggest obstacle Escandón saw for the commercial success of the Rio Grande borderlands was the lack of roads and ports necessary to ship goods into and out of the region. The development of transportation infrastructure became key to his mission to settle the Seno Mexicano. Escandón called for roads to be constructed from every settlement in the borderlands that would build upon the already existing system of Indigenous pathways and connect with the key thoroughfares developed in

Coahuila and Nuevo León. The idea was to shorten distances between way stations to make it more difficult for Indian raiding parties to plunder trading caravans. New roads also allowed for the rapid movement of Spanish troops to counter the speed of Indigenous attacks. Commercially, the road system expanded communications on New Spain's northern frontier, allowing for greater interconnectedness among the villas to build a regional market. Escandón set his entire enterprise to building roads to quash Indigenous unrest and quickly jump-start commerce in the borderlands.[24]

The Nueces Strip, an area of land between the Nueces River and the Rio Grande, became a consistent frustration for Escandón. It proved to be a northern boundary for his roadbuilding project. Due to the desertlike conditions there and the power the Apache wielded near the Nueces's headwaters, the costs of building additional roads from the Rio Grande villas to San Antonio de Béxar outweighed the benefits. Regardless of the difficulties, Escandón pushed his subordinates to establish a villa near the Nueces delta and develop a safe road connecting the Nueces to the Rio Grande that included stops with access to freshwater. The man he put in charge, Captain Pedro Paredes, set out with fifty families to accomplish the mission. Paredes found his task impossible, as there was just not enough water between the Nueces and Rio Grande. The already-established Indigenous pathways provided better access to freshwater than any road the Spanish could build. He told Escandón as much and abandoned the venture. Eventually, a small community named Dolores developed in the Nueces Strip about twenty miles north of the Rio Grande, but it collapsed within a decade. Escandón could not crack the Nueces Strip.[25]

With the Nueces Strip cutting off northern extensions, Escandón wanted to open as many connections with the population centers in central New Spain as he could. He became increasingly preoccupied with establishing ports to connect the coast of the Seno Mexicano to the bustling port of Veracruz. However, barrier islands, shallow estuaries, and constantly shifting sandbars made the Gulf Coast of

The Spanish Context

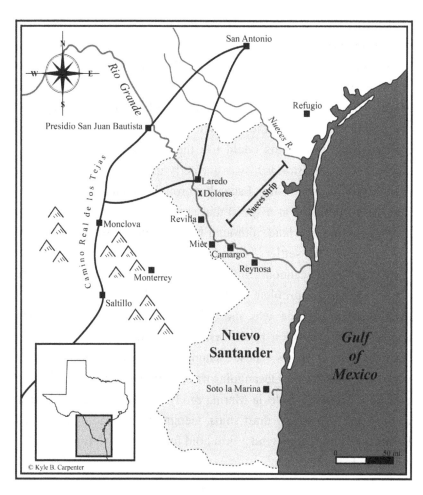

Nuevo Santander in 1795. Map by Alex Mendoza.

the Rio Grande borderlands a treacherous place for ships. He took his time exploring the coast to choose the best possible location for portage. Eventually, Escandón and his advisors decided the area near modern-day Soto la Marina to be the most favorable. Though it could only accommodate galleys and smaller ships, it remained the most sensible location for a port in all the Seno Mexicano. As early as 1609, leaders in Coahuila and Nuevo León had looked to the area around Soto la Marina to build a port. They just had trouble covering the overland distance to the coast. Escandón's road projects eliminated that problem. The harbor at Soto la Marina remained imperfect, though. Deposits from the delta of Río Soto la Marina constantly pushed water from the harbor into inland lagoons, decreasing the depth of the channel. Without regular maintenance, only shallow draft boats could use the port. Escandón's personal galley, the *Conquistadora*, was perfectly designed for the shallow harbor. With his small ship, Escandón brought much-needed supplies into the borderlands at a speed that could not be matched by mule trains traveling overland, although he could not move goods in the bulk quantities the settlers needed.[26]

Even with Escandón's infrastructure projects, the Rio Grande borderlands had a problem with friction of distance. Travel to and from the Rio Grande was inefficient. Overland travel remained unpredictable. Monsoon rains washed out roads. Heat and drought dried up watering holes. These changing conditions made lumbering mule trains vulnerable. Oceangoing travel would have been much more effective. However, Soto la Marina rarely saw much traffic because of the need for shallow draft ships. Geographical conditions limited Escandón's ability to extend a firm hold for the Spanish Empire in the Rio Grande borderlands.[27]

✪ ✪ ✪ ✪ ✪

By 1757 Escandón had finished the first stage of his plan to settle the Seno Mexicano. The region became the internal province of Nuevo Santander, of which Escandón was named governor. In the decade after the establishment of the first settlements along the Rio Grande, the Spanish and their Indigenous partners created a total of twenty towns in Nuevo Santander. The new road system and small port led to an upsurge of productivity. As Escandón anticipated, salt exports and cattle raising became the primary economic activities for the settlers. His plan to settle the region through commerce came to fruition without significant complications, though the scale was more limited than he had hoped.[28]

After eight years of allowing Escandón the freedom to do as he saw fit, the viceroy of New Spain decided that he needed to assess Escandón's progress. The Marqués de las Amarillas sent an envoy to investigate the settlements in Nuevo Santander in 1757. Following instructions, the leader of the inspection team, José Tienda de Cuervo, focused on Nuevo Santander's demographics, subsistence, transportation, and mineral wealth. All his investigations and depositions painted a picture of an isolated colony that was growing rapidly but needed sustained trade with other regions and land reform to survive and prosper.[29]

Northern New Spain's burgeoning population struck Tienda de Cuervo as he toured the region. The population growth in the Rio Grande borderlands occurred for several reasons. Natural increase provided for a key source of growth. For example, in Camargo's first year of existence, the census of the town showed that seventy-two families settled there with twenty percent of the heads of household listed as *indio* or *mestizo*.[30] By 1757, during the time of Tienda de Cuervo's visit, the population had grown by seventeen families, with most of those created through intermarriage. Many of the older children of the original settlers married one another to help build a tight-knit, highly networked community. *Indio* and *mestizo* families blended in Camargo, helping it to grow to one of the most stable settlements in the Rio Grande borderlands.[31]

Other contributors to the rapid population increase included in-migration of entrepreneurs from neighboring Nuevo León and Coahuila. Revilla and Mier drew hundreds of migrants from Monterrey and Saltillo who sought to take advantage of the land for cattle and the salt deposits nearby. The first settlers of both towns came from Monterrey, and they recruited heavily in their former hometowns to bring more settlers to the Rio Grande. Also, being the closest Rio Grande settlements to Coahuila and Nuevo León made Revilla and Mier more attractive to potential migrants.[32]

A final source of early population growth came from nearby Indians trickling into the new towns. The towns offered better protection from the intermittent raiding that still occurred in the region. During the 1750s and 1760s, the Comanche on the Texas Plains were going through a political evolution. Several bands of the Eastern Comanche broke away from the main body to push their territory farther south and east. Initially, this aided the formation of Spanish villas near the Lower Rio Grande because the Comanche avoided attacking settlements that might result in casualties. While that would change in the 1770s and 1780s, the division of the Eastern Comanche gave the Spanish an era of respite from concentrated raids.[33]

The area around Mier was particularly attractive to Indians who lived near the Rio Grande because of its location near an important ford in the river. However, some of the Indian families may not have chosen to settle in Mier voluntarily. With the growing saltworks near the town, owners needed labor to work it and transport it. It is probable that town leaders forcibly congregated a few Indigenous families to exploit their labor. The need for labor often resulted in settlers of the villas using debt or even physical captivity to draw local Indigenous workers. In the two years between 1755 and 1757, seven Indian families moved to and settled in Mier. The total population of the town grew by 106 people during those same two years. Indigenous migration combined with natural increase to create a steady growth rate in the population of the Rio Grande borderlands.[34]

The growing population needed greater access to trade and markets. Tienda de Cuervo focused a significant portion of his time trying to find a better harbor to open Nuevo Santander to trade within the Spanish Gulf of Mexico but failed to find anything that met with his satisfaction. He interviewed Escandón and the governor's most trusted helmsman, Bernardo Vidal Buzcarrones, about the best possible place to construct a new and bustling port. Both men suggested investing in improving Soto la Marina, but Tienda de Cuervo found the location to be inadequate with too many sandbars and too shallow shipping lanes. He commandeered Escandón's galley and had

Buzcarrones take him up and down the coast for a week looking for a better harbor. When he found none, he classified the coast as too expensive to trouble with. Tienda de Cuervo concluded that founding a sustainable port on the Seno Mexicano was going to require dredging and constant maintenance. The inspector left Escandón with his small dock and lone galley at Soto la Marina without recommending royal support for port construction. The state left Escandón on his own to manage oceangoing transport.[35]

Even though Tienda de Cuervo could not find a suitable harbor to expand sea trade to the borderlands, he recognized that Spain had to open more effective trade routes to the Rio Grande borderlands if Escandón's experiment was going to succeed. Cattle raising had quickly become the primary subsistence activity on the frontier because of the excellent pasturage and salt deposits. Cattle also reigned because, contrary to Escandón's initial reports, it was nearly impossible to grow surplus crops in the region. Rains came sporadically, often in monsoon conditions, leaving sown fields either flooded or dried out with drought. The settlers recognized that creating irrigation canals from the Rio Grande would require changing the entire landscape. The depth of the riverbed was so low that water only ever rose to the level of the surrounding land in times of flood. No irrigating canal dug by hand could be constructed from the river to water surrounding lands. This meant that when the borderlanders needed produce, they had to trade for it. At Mier buyers from Monterrey exchanged their surplus maize for mules, wool, hides, and salt. The same trade occurred at Camargo, Reynosa, and Revilla with agricultural settlements farther south.[36]

The soaring demand for essentials like corn and flour combined with arduous overland travel to the centers of exchange deflated the value of the goods produced in the borderlands. Even with Escandón's expanded road system, caravan transport remained costly, leaving the people in the Rio Grande borderlands to live at a deficit in the 1750s. Salt became the most important form of exchange for borderlanders. In the best of market conditions, two fanegas of salt bought a fanega of

Humboldt Carte du Mexique, 1811. J. B. Porison and Alexander von Humboldt, *Carte du Mexique et pays limitrphes situes au nord et a l'est: dressee d'apres la grande carte de lat Nouvelle Espagne de Mr. A. de Humboldt et d'autres materiaux*, 1811. Courtesy of Special Collections, University of Texas at Arlington Libraries.

corn.[37] In years of extended drought conditions, the price of corn might rise to be sixteen times more than salt. Tienda de Cuervo recognized that further integrating the borderlands into the greater market of New Spain would lower costs and improve the lives of the settlers.[38]

The inspector looked to Laredo, the last settlement established under Escandón as a model for how to better integrate the borderlands. The town's founder had complete knowledge and acceptance that acquiring crops would have to come through overland trade. Laredo's founder, Tomás Sanchez de la Barrera y Garza, chose a location near the Camino Real that connected San Antonio de Béxar to Nuevo León and Coahuila. He and the Laredo settlers relied on the road to acquire the necessary foodstuffs to supplement their ranching subsistence, connecting to trade centers both north and south. In fact the growing trade and transportation through Laredo contributed to the abandonment of the Dolores townsite. Tienda de Cuervo found the entire system self-sustaining and applauded it for not costing the Crown anything. However, he still believed trade to be too isolated among just the townspeople and encouraged more use of the Camino Real, an imperial highway that connected Saltillo to Béxar. The people of the Rio Grande borderlands needed to market their goods in as many places as possible.[39]

In response to Tienda de Cuervo's report, Escandón set to work building more infrastructures to allow Nuevo Santander to continue its growth. The most labor-intensive task he set was to construct a new road from Tampico to Monterrey. With this new east-west highway, villas to the north and south could more quickly move their products to either offload in the growing commercial center of Monterrey or transport north or south along the Camino Real. Escandón acknowledged the wisdom inherent in Tienda de Cuervo's report and took initiative to turn the report into an action plan.[40]

Parts of Tienda de Cuervo's report foreshadowed some of the problems that would grow to undermine the new province. Political maneuverings and disputes over land began to erode the delicate bonds Escandón had built on the Rio Grande that connected him to his military subordinates and the settlers. A member of the initial expedition to the Seno Mexicano wrote a scathing critique of Escandón's leadership and the founding of Nuevo Santander. Shortly after the province officially came into existence, Escandón removed Sergeant Major Antonio Ladrón de Guevara from his post as captain of the town of Santander for "reasons of health." Furious for his removal, Ladrón de Guevara wrote his own report to Tienda de Cuervo criticizing the placement of each settlement in the colony. He argued that a key component in the failure of the Rio Grande towns to be agriculturally self-sufficient came from Escandón's poor decision-making and pursuit of personal profit. According to one of his subordinates, blame for the borderlands' isolation rested solely on Escandón.[41]

The settlers, too, began to turn on Escandón in the second decade of Nuevo Santander's existence. Politics and questions over land combined to lead the settlers to protest the governor's rule. Politically, Escandón had appointed his most capable military officers to leadership positions in each newfound town. Initially, this proved appropriate because all the townspeople oversaw their own defense, and it made sense to make a military leader also the civic leader in the early years of establishment. The military officer in charge could quickly mobilize a militia and strategize with confidence to defend against attack from *los indios bárbaros*. As the roots of the colony took hold, the settled families began to challenge the military leadership. They wanted to hold the political power in their villas and not remain beholden to military control. Borderlanders resisted an authority they came to view as autocratic and demanded a more civilian-oriented government.[42]

The settlers also grew restless about their land grants. From the commencement of Escandón's venture, settlers were promised grants for personal ownership of land. Even so, until 1767 most lands were held in common, or *ejido*. Individual families were allotted parcels on which to graze their cattle, but the land remained collective. Since Escandón refused to distribute title to individual owners, the land was unsaleable. He argued that if he assigned individual titles, the colonists would desert the towns to live on their own land. Without title, the settlers argued, no individuals could profit on the improvements they made to the land. Tienda de Cuervo received complaints about the practice of collective land use in 1757 and tensions grew to the boiling point a decade later, particularly in Camargo. There, the population had grown significantly since 1749. The original families worried that their promised grants would be parceled off to the newcomers instead of awarded to them. The first families felt entitled to the land Spain had promised and turned against their governor, Escandón, as the representative of a policy that hindered economic development. With the growing complaints about land distribution and political leadership, the viceroy recalled Escandón and sent a new inspection team to Nuevo Santander to attempt to satisfy the settlers.[43]

The Crown stepped in to assert its power in the Rio Grande borderlands in 1767 with a royal commission headed by Juan Armando de Palacio and José de Ossorio de Llamas. Primarily, the commission was sent to rectify complaints about Escandón's failure to distribute lands to private owners. Palacio and Ossorio organized, surveyed, and distributed land to the settlers for private use and ownership. Sizes of the allotments were determined by how long a settler or his family had been living in Nuevo Santander. Those who had lived there longer than six years received two leagues of pastureland and twelve *caballerías* of farmland.[44] Those who lived there between two and six years also got two leagues of pastureland but only six *caballerías*. Finally, new migrants to the region only gained the two leagues of pasture without any farmland. In a decade, from 1767–1777, nearly all the land in the Rio Grande borderlands shifted from communal to private ownership.[45]

As egalitarian as this land distribution seemed on paper, landownership consolidated quite quickly to the most wealthy and powerful families while Indigenous people tended to be exploited. The best illustration of this can be seen at Reynosa, where two families emerged to develop huge ranches and consolidate political and economic power. When New Spain announced it would grant title to individual landowners, Captain Juan Hinojosa and his son-in-law, José María de Ballí, applied for their portion of land north of the Rio Grande. Moreover, realizing the extent of lands to the north, both men made claims farther east, where no other colonists had applied. Using Hinojosa's familiarity with the Spanish bureaucratic system through his service in the army, he and Ballí acquired title to thirty-seven leagues of land beyond the standard allotment for first families.[46] Most of the lands they acquired had been seasonal gathering grounds for Coahuiltecans. The cattle the Hinojosas and Ballís set loose would disrupt the ecology and make gathering nearly impossible. Thus, the consolidation of private landholdings marked another point where settlers turned upside-down the lives of Indigenous people.[47]

The Ballís and Hinojosas continued to intermarry, developed strong ties to one another, and created one of the most influential family networks on the Rio Grande. Through claims issued to the Crown, purchases, and further marriage consolidation, the Hinojosas and Ballís came to hold most of the best lands around Reynosa, cutting out Indigenous people and small holders. Similar processes occurred throughout the Rio Grande borderlands, as close family networks and vast landholdings came to replace association with Escandón as markers of local power. Families like the Hinojosas and Ballís undermined Escandón through their accumulation of wealth and power.[48]

The clergy stationed in the Rio Grande borderlands also challenged Escandón's rule as governor. They argued that the missions retained very little power in the region. In fact few of the settlements along the Rio Grande had a priest. The priest at Camargo had to travel to nearby parishes to perform baptisms, marriages, and funerals. To get attention for their plight, the priests argued that they could not effectively evangelize the "*yndios bárbaros*."[49] They claimed that Escandón had worked against the church at every turn in favor of his fanaticism for civilian settlement and promotion of commerce. Missionaries complained of declining Indian populations at the missions. They blamed Escandón when it was likely the result of an array of consequences from labor coercion to outmigration. An avalanche of complaints from borderlands soldiers, settlers, and clergy led to a full imperial investigation of Escandón.[50]

In 1769 Escandón faced inquiry and trial about his conduct in Nuevo Santander. His private business dealings became the central focus of Spain's investigation into the governor. He had received forty thousand pesos from Mexico City each year to ensure the smooth functioning of the colony. This amount was supposed to be spread across the colony to pay soldiers, supply the garrisons, build roads, and generally improve the colony. Testimony from clergy, soldiers, and civilians indicated Escandón improperly used the Crown's funds.

They claimed that the governor embezzled the money to increase his own personal wealth at the expense of the province. Escandón had to defend himself by showing exactly how he distributed the funds. Because he was practically the sole merchant in the region importing goods through Soto la Marina, all those who earned their wages eventually purchased goods from Escandón with those same wages. He distributed the funds every year, and throughout the year much of the money returned to Escandón through trade. Escandón argued that rather than embezzlement, it was legitimate business transactions that contributed to his wealth. Though he died before the conclusion of the trial, his son satisfactorily proved that his father's business was legitimate, and that the governor utilized the funds as the state intended him to. The man Spain sent to the borderlands to encourage civilian-centered commercial expansion became the scapegoat of military, clerical, and civilian leaders who felt threatened by Escandón's commercial agenda.[51]

Concurrently with the movement against Escandón, New Spain's borderland along the Lower Rio Grande faced increased Indigenous power. Rather than sending salt, beef, and leather southward, borderlanders increasingly sent reports of the destruction of Spanish saltworks and ranches. The Bourbon leadership adhered to the policies of using trade to try to draw the Comanche into the Spanish Empire. However, the policy relied heavily on the act of gift giving. The Rio Grande borderlands lacked the resources to satisfy the powerful Indigenous groups who resided in the region. With the Spanish being unable to offer material incentive, raiding increased drastically. The increase in raiding further disrupted trade, creating a violent cycle of economic decline. By the 1780s the colony became noticeably more isolated from central New Spain. The region lost its most important merchant and military leader. Roadways flooded out or became overgrown because travelers feared Indigenous attack. The small port at Soto la Marina sat largely unused because no commercially minded successor replaced Escandón. Trade floundered because travel was so difficult.[52]

The viceroy of New Spain sent yet another inspection team to assess the situation. Led by Félix María Calleja, the investigation recognized that a major shift in power had taken place on New Spain's northern frontier. The eastern half of the Comanche Empire had spread down to the Rio Grande, challenging the Spanish for supremacy in the region. The standard practices of trade and gift giving that the Spanish used to achieve relative peace with the Coahuiltecans and Apache failed to assuage Comanche raiding parties. In addition to stealing cattle to grow their own herds, the Comanche destroyed ranches to assert their power over the region. The Comanche forced New Spain to consider a new strategy in the Rio Grande borderlands.[53]

Calleja formed a new plan for New Spain based on the results of his inspection. He traveled throughout the Rio Grande borderlands taking oral histories from the residents and trying to figure out exactly how life on the frontier worked. The inspector used all the evidence he acquired to produce a two-part report, one that focused on the economic conditions of Nuevo Santander and another that outlined the territory's military conditions. Calleja's report vindicated Escandón by approving the founder's economic methodology. Expanding commerce and improving transportation infrastructure remained central to Calleja's strategy for reinvigorating the borderlands. Additionally, he offered radical suggestions for combating the powerful new Indians in the region.[54]

Changing how borderlanders interacted with Indians became the central focus for Calleja. Essentially, Calleja wanted to blockade the Comanche to keep them from getting any manufactured products, thus crippling their ability to make war. He believed that cutting off supply would create such a demand among the Indians for European goods that they would change their lifestyle. Calleja wrote in his report, "The effect of the generous policy has been to convert the gifts into necessities of life, multiplying the robberies to satisfy the new demands. We would do better to guide them in the road to fulfilling those demands without crime."[55] He believed that by forcing Indians to engage in regular European-style market transactions,

The Spanish Context

they would change their warlike nature to become allies rather than enemies.

To achieve his goal of Europeanizing the Comanche, Calleja proposed further market integration between the frontier and Mexico City. Trade had to be expanded and given priority. The best way to expand commerce in the borderlands was to build more roads. Transportation infrastructure had declined significantly in the two decades since Escandón's death. The road network Escandón worked so diligently to build had been devastated by the annual monsoon cycle. Water erosion washed out tracks and made transportation of goods impossible in spots. With improved roads Calleja believed that more merchants would venture into the borderlands to exploit a waiting market, thus lowering prices and facilitating the movement of goods.[56]

Good portage again became an issue because it had largely gone unresolved since the province's founding. Calleja called for a free and open port to be constructed on the Gulf Coast. The new port would be a hub for Atlantic goods to be imported on the cheap and transferred to Spanish merchants who would control the distribution to Indians in market transactions. A free and open port would also lead to an explosion of settlement, something Calleja desperately wanted. If the borderlands were peopled with more Europeans, marauding Indians would be overwhelmed into changing their lifestyle to match the majority population in the region. However, the location of the much-needed port remained a mystery.[57]

The Spanish never had the opportunity to open a reliable port, improve roads, or expand commerce in the Rio Grande borderlands because the Mexican War of Independence broke out a few years after Calleja's report. Road systems remained the lifeblood of the borderlands' subsistence but often fell into horrible disrepair. For example, one of the roads from the Rio Grande delta to Monterrey became known as the *camino de viborero* because rattlesnakes and other vipers were regularly encountered along the highway. Rather than beat back the snakes and use this faster route, travelers chose to adhere to the river road that ran through Reynosa and Camargo. Lack of use and constant flooding led to parts of the snake road being submerged in marshland and left impassible. Missing ports and inconsistent road maintenance demonstrate how Spain left the construction of commerce in the Rio Grande borderlands incomplete.[58]

As Indigenous power increased, the settled people of the Rio Grande borderlands turned away from the blending of Indigenous and Spanish. With the lack of ports and deteriorating roads, the population of the region stagnated. If residents wanted to expand their families, they had to look inward. Prominent Spanish families tended to only marry other prominent families. Families who owned large tracts of land wanted to consolidate their wealth. Limiting marriage to other wealthy families remained the easiest way to achieve that end. Indians became more segregated and separated. In 1789 Laredo and other Rio Grande towns developed a separate and distinct Indian census. This shift from inclusion to exclusion made building kinship bonds with the right families essential to any outsider who moved to the region.[59]

The strength of the Comanche also inhibited the blending of Spanish and Indigenous people on Spanish terms. Comanche bands in Texas built alliances with Tenewas, Kiowas, and Tawakonis. Former threats to Comanche power became threats to the Spanish and their allies. The Comanche became so powerful that they could control negotiations with the Spanish. Borderlanders had to adjust to a Comanche way of life or risk destruction. Many on the frontier were taken captive and incorporated into Comanche bands. During the Mexican War of Independence, New Spain's frontier became even weaker, allowing the Comanche to further solidify their power.[60]

The era of promise brought about through Escandón's calculated settlement program quickly faded. The rapid rise of the Comanche Empire north of the Rio Grande combined with local elites interested in maintaining their regional authority contributed to a period of stagnation. The political crises that wracked the Spanish Empire in the nineteenth century further isolated the region. The mission to create vibrant and sustained commercial activity on New Spain's northeastern frontier stalled. However, the example highlights foundational conditions for building commerce in the Rio Grande borderlands. Primarily, it required the full support of state agents and the backing of military forces. Escandón's biggest accomplishments came when he had the backing of New Spain's leadership and his military subordinates. His enterprise essentially disappeared when he lost their support. Additionally, any commercial venture had to account for Indigenous power. Making connections with Indigenous people and building bonds produced peace and encouraged exchange. Finally, the environmental aspects of the region created risk. Facilitating agriculture and maintaining transportation infrastructure had to be pursued with full knowledge of the area's drought and monsoon cycles. Disregarding any of these vital conditions opened entrepreneurial activity to failure.

Escandón's settlement of the Rio Grande borderlands was also foundational in more obvious ways. Reynosa, Camargo, Revilla, Mier, and Laredo proved to be long-lasting population centers. The success of these towns demonstrated the possibility of creating something new and productive in this region of the world. The generations of families who resided there would interact and influence European borderlands entrepreneurs who moved to the Lower Rio Grande in the nineteenth century.

After achieving its independence, Mexico inherited all the problems Calleja outlined in his report on the northern borderlands. Mexico also took on a significant amount of debt from the colonial era. Taking all this together, Mexican officials had to creatively figure out how to grow the settled population of its borderlands without investing much money in defense or infrastructure projects. Instead of looking to the Indigenous population like the Spanish had, Mexico turned to the aid of foreigners, Anglo-American and European, to invest in the Mexican frontier to finish building the Rio Grande borderlands.

Chapter 2

The Beales Colony Experiment

In late October 1833, Dr. John Charles Beales of Norfolk, England, hustled around New York City recruiting colonists to join him on his mission to settle his contracted land grant in the Rio Grande borderlands of northern Mexico, an area of land of about eight million acres between the Nueces River and the Rio Grande. He bounced from boarding-house to boarding-house along Broadway trying to convince European migrants who had just landed in the city that their prospects in Mexico exceeded what they would attain in the United States. Finding the most success with entrepreneurial Europeans, Beales pieced together a motley group of fifty-nine English, Irish, and German migrants willing to attempt an expedition that would take them another two thousand miles by sea and then more than two hundred miles overland in the wet, cold winter.[1]

Beales successfully recruited colonists to travel with him to the Rio Grande borderlands because he was able to claim legal support from Mexico, financial support from an American investment group, and the potential for economic success. Beales carried with him a contract he signed with the state of Coahuila y Texas that described the land in which the colonists would settle and promised that the Mexican government would regulate the colony.² He also held $4,000 he received in New York from a recently formed land company and promised as much funding as the colony needed to succeed.³ Finally, Beales offered huge swaths of land to prospective colonists in a region that he described as a paradise for agricultural development.⁴ The prospective colonists took Beales at his word because of the evidence he produced in the forms of contracts and cash. The entire project seemed a legitimate enterprise.

When the English doctor and his troupe of migrants from Europe entered northern Mexico, they found themselves wholly unprepared for the rigors of life in the borderlands. The colony, named Dolores, was located about eighteen miles north of the Rio Grande on Las Moras Creek in the western corner of the Rio Grande borderlands. The big, bulky carts the colonists used to transport their meager belongings from the Gulf to the foothills of the Sierra Madre proved ill-fitted to the terrain, and much of what they brought was lost on the road. The colonists were also surprised to learn of the threat Indians posed to their venture. Beales's recruits did not know they were entering Comanche and Apache lands until they arrived in Texas, and fear of attack became a constant worry. Though they built limited defenses and hired what few Mexican soldiers were willing to tag along, a catastrophic Indian raid remained both a real and imagined threat that undermined the settlers' morale. Furthermore, the fortunes of the venture rested on the shoulders of Beales's ability to lead the construction of a brand-new settlement in the arid wilderness of Northern Mexico. Underfunded and with limited supplies, little in the way of defense, and poor management, it is little surprise that the colony failed.⁵

Beales's case marks an excellent example of where Mexican state interests intersected with European borderlands entrepreneurship and American land speculation in the Rio Grande borderlands. For Mexican officials, Beales brought European colonists to Northern Mexico. Whether they settled in Beales's colony or anywhere else in the vast borderlands proved a win for the Mexican policy of peopling the region with settlers who had no allegiance to the United States and who might "modernize" the few Mexicans living there. Mexico also hoped the European settlers would combat Comanche and Apache raiding in northern Mexico. For European-born entrepreneurs, the venture brought them to the borderlands for relatively little expense. Finally, American speculators funded Beales's project hoping to use Beales to regain access to Texas land after Mexico passed the Law of April 6, 1830, which closed American migration to northern Mexico. At these intersections among Mexican government policies, American speculations, and European entrepreneurial interests, Indians expressed their authority through trade and violence that sometimes undermined and sometimes provided new opportunities for gain for all involved. Taken together, the three-year lifespan of Beales's colony provides insight into how politicians and entrepreneurs imagined they could modernize and capitalize on the Rio Grande borderlands.[6]

Deeper inspection into Beales's example also provides valuable insight into the conditions of settling the Rio Grande borderlands during the Mexican period. Beales's failure highlights the contingencies of settling the borderlands. Other Europeans, Anglo-Americans, and Mexicans also took on the responsibilities of empresario contracts. Some succeeded and some failed. The conditions of their empresario grants and the decisions they made demonstrate key differences with Beales—namely, they highlight the importance of geography and making local connections.[7]

Mexico granted Beales his contract in a time when Mexico sought to eliminate American immigration. Mexican officials believed Europeans to be more desirable as colonists and Beales's venture represents the result of that belief. Further, the colony was founded in a place that would become highly contested between Mexicans and Americans in the Nueces Strip. Entrepreneurs on both sides of the Atlantic believed the Rio Grande to be the next great waterway in the Americas, one that would rival the Mississippi River.[8] Beales and his colonists were some of the first European-born men and women since Escandón to attempt to capitalize on the Rio Grande's potential and connect the region to modern global markets.[9]

European-born colonists, Mexican government officials, and American speculators all had expectations that wildly diverged from reality regarding Beales's enterprise. The promise of free land and cheap access to developing markets drew European borderlands entrepreneurs to northern Mexico, although they found the land to be arid and markets largely inaccessible. Mexican government officials believed European industriousness would reform the nation's northern frontier into a settled agricultural space oriented toward Atlantic markets, while American speculators thought the European colonists would improve the land and transfer it from Mexican stewardship to American private ownership. In practice, the entrepreneurial Europeans struggled mightily to make the colony succeed. As the colony broke down and the joint venture dissolved, the colonists had to rely on themselves to avert complete disaster as the Mexican government and American investors abandoned them to Indigenous authority.

At the dawn of Mexican independence in the 1820s, much of the Rio Grande borderlands remained virtually unknown to Mexicans, Americans, and Europeans. Though Mexico laid claim to the entire territory, lands north and west of Laredo fell within the Comanche Empire, and the Comanches defended incursions into their space with ruthless tenacity. In fact Comanches proved to be one of the biggest concerns for Mexico as the state attempted to consolidate its inhabitants into citizens. Declaring all the settled people of Mexico as citizens regardless of European or Indigenous ethnicity, Mexican leaders hoped to convert the highly mobile Comanche bands into settled people who would both defend and develop the nation's northern frontier, or at least bring an end to the regular conflict and hostilities that marked the borderland. The Comanche and their allies clearly understood that they held all the power on the plains north of the Rio Grande and continued to live the way they saw fit, raiding Rio Grande settlements for horses, cattle, and captives to sell in Santa Fe or San Antonio.[10]

Additionally, Mexico's leadership needed a secondary method to bring its notion of sedentary productive agriculture and commerce to a reality, and it harnessed a scheme that Spain initiated in the waning days of its empire: the empresario system. The empresario system was a contractor program in which individuals would promote settlement of certain regions in exchange for land. This arrangement delegated the work of marketing and settling northern Mexico to entrepreneurs, called empresarios, willing to undertake such hardships for the prospect of future rewards in the choicest and most profitable tracts they could acquire. While the empresario system remained imperfect in many ways, it succeeded in drawing hundreds of families to settle lands not under agricultural development.[11]

For the individual accepting the contract, the process of colonization proved expensive, time-consuming, and arduous. The most successful and famous empresario was Stephen F. Austin. Austin inherited his empresario contract from his father, Moses, and proceeded to colonize the region around the Brazos River. He diligently surveyed, mapped, and dispensed legal title to all the colonists who entered the lands upon which he was contracted to settle. He fully committed to the project, investing everything he had into it, and settled in the colony himself to oversee its development. Importantly, he made key connections within Mexican towns with prominent families. In doing so Austin hooked his colony into well-established trade and communication networks that allowed for its proliferation. His success earned him several leagues of quality, arable land to do with what he would. Notably, he became famous for his achievements as a Mexican empresario in both the United States and Europe, providing hope and unrealistic perceptions about an individual's prospects in the borderlands.[12]

From the Mexican perspective, the growing number of Americans who resisted Mexican laws and declarations became a primary drawback of the empresario system. One of the earliest causes for Mexican anxiety over American colonization in Texas came out of Nacogdoches in 1826. Haden Edwards, an empresario with a grant that covered a large portion of East Texas, attempted to evict longstanding Mexican inhabitants of his grant if they did not pay him $520 for title to their lands. Confused at their predicament, the Mexican families residing in East Texas appealed to the state of Coahuila y Texas for relief. After a long series of correspondence, Mexico canceled Edwards's contract and expelled him from Texas. Infuriated, Edwards declared his colony in revolt, naming it the independent Fredonian Republic. He and his brother Benjamin Edwards initiated a voluminous propaganda campaign to recruit Cherokees and other Americans to their cause. They failed in their recruiting mission and fled to Louisiana when a militia approached Nacogdoches. However, Edwards's campaigning rang loud in Mexico, spurring worry in Mexico City.[13]

Edwards's rebellion prompted leaders in Mexico City to seek a clearer understanding of what was happening in Texas. In 1827 Mexican general Manuel Mier y Terán headed a commission of scientists and artists from Mexico and Europe to survey the northern boundary of Mexico that the United States and Spain had agreed upon in the 1819 Adams-Onís Treaty. The commission was also tasked to explore the northern territories and report on conditions therein. While there, the general witnessed the problems caused by the American population that dominated the area. He found that many of those who resided in Texas loathed the Mexican government and believed it was a "republic that consists only of ignorant mulattoes and Indians."[14] He wrote extensively to Mexico City explaining the American problem in Texas and suggested policy shifts to achieve greater Mexican authority in that territory. One of his suggestions included expanding European colonization in Texas to offset American colonization. Mier y Terán's complaints and suggestions regarding the northern territories resulted in changes to the empresario system in 1830.[15]

Mier y Terán sent his report of conditions in Texas back to Mexico City by the end of 1829. It brought swift action from leadership in

Mexico City in the form of an executive decree. Known as the Law of April 6, 1830, the decree most famously banned further immigration into Mexico from the United States. It also suspended empresario contracts not already fulfilled and declared an end to the importation of slaves into Mexico. Most importantly for Beales, the decree encouraged further colonization of northern Mexico by Mexicans and Europeans.[16]

Officials in Mexico City deemed European immigration preferable as they noticed the positive outcomes of European colonization in Texas. Four Irish empresarios had received contracts to populate lands along the Nueces River, and two Irish colonies emerged. The colony of Refugio developed under the partnership of James Power and James Hewetson, while the colony of San Patricio grew under the guidance of John McMullen and James McGloin. The Irish proved to be exactly what Mexico wanted for its northern frontier: pioneering Europeans who worked through astounding obstacles to develop settled agriculture in an otherwise sparsely populated sector of Mexico's northern frontier. To further satisfy Mexico, most of the Irish colonists were practicing Catholics whom Mexican officials believed would act as a buffer against Protestant American expansion into the Rio Grande borderlands. The gambit paid off, as most of the Irish colonists embraced Mexican culture, married Mexican spouses, adopted the Spanish language, and opened new trade routes between the trans-Nueces and the rest of Mexico. The early successes of the Irish colonies drove Mexico to seek more Europeans willing to take empresario contracts in the Rio Grande borderlands.[17]

With Mexico searching for new European-born empresarios, John Charles Beales found himself swept into three separate empresario contracts. The first contract Beales received came from his wife, María Dolores Soto y Saldaña. Soto y Saldaña came from a prominent family in Michoacán.[18] She had been recently widowed when she met Beales. Her dead husband, Richard Exter, had been a successful merchant and speculator. He earned an empresario contract to populate the western plains of Texas, which he set out to do. Exter, also born in England, organized a land company with a partner in Baltimore and raised nearly $400,000 in investments before he perished at sea in 1829. After Exter's death the contract transferred to his widow, Soto y Saldaña, who encouraged her new husband, Beales, to execute it.[19]

When Beales went to have the Exter contract transferred to his name, he found an entire network of Mexican speculators attempting to take over suspended contracts from American empresarios. Because of this, he engaged a ready partner in his brother-in-law, Fortunato Soto, whose position as a captain in the Mexican army lent more credence to Beales's appeals for contracts. In addition to securing the Exter contract, Beales and Soto joined a network of Mexicans to acquire the contract for Benjamin Milam's grant that abutted the western portion of Austin's lands. Though more accessible than Exter's grant, these lands also remained isolated and largely uncharted. The mixed company of Mexican and English empresarios failed to introduce any colonists into either of Beales's first two contracts, but their failure put him on track to his Rio Grande grant. Trial and error became a theme for Beales as an empresario.[20]

The last grant Beales received drove him to make the effort to settle it with European-born colonists. On a map his third empresario contract looked to be the most lucrative. Bound north and south by the Nueces River and the Rio Grande, respectively, the lands looked seemingly well watered with river access to the Gulf of Mexico. In addition to the possibility of river transport, the old Camino Real that connected San Antonio de Béxar to Mexico City ran through the grant, offering the prospect of access to markets both north and south. Further, Beales entered his Rio Grande contract with another European-born partner, a Scotsman named James Grant. Though Fortunato Soto remained an important partner for his enterprise on the Rio Grande, Beales chose to abandon the Mexican speculation group in favor of a more European one.[21]

Grant had made a somewhat successful name for himself in northern Mexico before his partnership with Beales. In the late 1820s, he settled in Parras, Coahuila, married a Mexican woman, María

Guadalupe Reyes, and declared himself a Mexican citizen. While there, Grant acted as an agent for a British mining company and established his own furnace and cotton mill on his land, hoping to capitalize on the region's iron ore deposits. His successful ventures earned him a positive reputation in the state of Coahuila as a "man of progress" and one who might succeed as an empresario. Mexican officials hoped Grant would bring his modernizing principles and industrious attitude into the empresario system.[22]

Beales and Grant shared important parallels. Both men left the British Isles to seek their future in Mexico, both married into Mexican families, and both sought opportunity in Mexico's vast northern lands through the state-sponsored empresario program. These men not only speculated on real estate, but they also took a chance on the Mexican state leading them to profit. They represented a growing group of European-born entrepreneurs turning to northern Mexico as the future for rapid economic growth.[23]

Once they acquired the Rio Grande contract, Beales and Grant set out to have it explored so that a suitable town could be established for them to boost and sell to prospective colonists. By the terms of the contract, the empresarios only had four years to settle eight hundred families on their prescribed grant to receive their rewards in surplus lands. They hired Beales's close friend and fellow Englishman, William Henry Egerton, into the partnership to organize a party to quickly survey the land for settlement.[24] The exploration sapped most of the empresarios' monetary resources since it required a military escort and at least one engineering specialist to properly choose a site that would sustain a rapidly growing population. Egerton chose a location on Las Moras Creek about eighteen miles north of where it spilled into the Rio Grande. He hurriedly relayed a message to Beales that a suitable townsite existed.[25]

Egerton's report included subtle details about Beales's grant that presaged the problems inherent in colonizing the arid land between the Nueces River and Rio Grande. In his investigation Egerton found that the land in the Nueces Strip lacked water. He seemed worried that there were no streams or rivers in the area. "The land is flat, and rich in pasturage, but rather deficient in water, there being no considerable streams between the Nueces and the Rio Grande."[26] Even the banks of the Rio Grande provided little optimism, as Egerton found bad soil and limited access to water. However, Egerton produced a glowing report about the lands around Las Moras Creek. Egerton called it, "a pretty stream gently winding its way through a very pleasant country."[27] There, the water seemed perpetual and the soil a rich dark loam.

Egerton's report was ambiguous. At times he talked of quality soils and sufficient timber. At other points he complained of sandy wastes bereft of any trees. Beales's lands contained both. The problem was that a reader could not assume which conditions dominated the region. Egerton's report cooled Grant's enthusiasm for the project. He pursued other opportunities in Texas and ceded full power of attorney of the Rio Grande contract to Beales. With the loss of a major partner and rapidly depleting cash reserves, the venture threatened to fail before it even began.[28]

Beales did not panic at the loss of his primary partner but took the initiative and got creative. Likely building upon the model Richard Exter left behind with his conglomeration of investors in Baltimore, Beales sailed for New York to find financial backers for the Rio Grande colony. It did not take him long. Western lands were a hot commodity in the financial centers of the United States prior to the Panic of 1837, with investors dumping thousands of dollars on lands they would never see. With empresario contracts offering millions of free acres of land for merely enticing colonists to the area, northern Mexico became a speculator's dream world. The primary driver for the demand in southwestern lands was the growing Atlantic cotton economy. Between 1829 and 1835, due to the explosion of textile manufacturing in northwest England, the price of cotton nearly doubled, driving more planters to seek more land. Many Southern planters were willing to expand beyond the borders of the United States to find whatever lands they could for cotton production. The Rio Grande borderlands were directly in the pathway of the great land rush that was overtaking the US South. However, the Mexican government had just blocked American migration into northern Mexico with the Law of April 6, 1830. Savvy speculators in New York recognized an opportunity to invest huge amounts of capital to get ahead of Southern planters to profit on the land boom. Beales's appearance in New York came at the perfect time for him to convince several investors to consider his project.[29]

Beales enticed his investors by offering up to five-eighths of all the land he acquired, which drew the interest of many monied land men. The most infamous speculator to invest in Beales's land company scheme was Samuel Swartwout, a New York merchant who was Aaron Burr's personal assistant during the Burr Conspiracy. Part of his responsibility in the conspiracy included seeking British assistance in a scheme to create an independent government in Mexico. Swartwout had contacts in the British foreign ministry, and one of his close associates, Charles Williamson, worked as a land agent for a group of powerful British investors.[30] Williamson shared his strategies for land speculation with anyone who seemed interested. It is likely that Swartwout saw the future of land speculation in northern Mexico and learned the business from Williamson. Swartwout continually invested in Texas land projects, including the Galveston Bay and Texas Land Company and Beales's Rio Grande and Texas Land Company, of which he took out a full one-eighth stake. The Law of April 6 may have blocked the movement of Anglo-American immigrants into Mexico, but not American dollars.[31]

Swartwout was one of many New York speculators who invested in Beales's grant. Other prominent names and powerful New York landmen included Peter Gerard Stuyvesant, Francis Salmon, and William Burrowe.[32] These men from distinguished New York families looked to northern Mexico as a haven for investment. Decades before the boom in railroad investment, monied businessmen in the United States' eastern financial centers saw the future in the expansion of the cotton economy westward. They all believed the land in Beales's grant would yield exponential profits on their investments. Having done no investigation of the Nueces Strip, nor having created a detailed plan for settlement, they were sure to be disappointed.[33]

After spending only a few months in New York City, Beales became the principal agent of the Rio Grande and Texas Land Company, a brand-new consortium whose directors contracted a ship and placed advertisements for prospective colonists in New York, South Carolina, and England.[34] The company also laid out $4,000 for Beales to utilize in setting up the colony's first town. To make sure the empresario did not take too much latitude with the company's finances, the executive board of directors placed Thomas A. Power, an Irishman, as their own agent to catalog the colony's progress and track Beales's spending. With this newfound financial support, the empresario began recruiting immediately.[35]

The formation of the Rio Grande and Texas Land Company added a complicated layer to Beales's venture. By law and the terms of his contract, American colonists were unacceptable targets for populating the grant, but the law said nothing about American dollars. It seemed that if American investors profited from the sale of lands to European or Mexican tenants, then everybody got what they wanted. Mexico colonized its northern frontier with more European colonists, European-born entrepreneurs earned cheap land near the Rio Grande for new farms and businesses, and American land speculators regained access to the market in Mexican land. With his cash reserves and nearly sixty European-born recruits taken from New York boarding-houses, Beales set out for the Rio Grande.

✺ ✺ ✺ ✺ ✺

Two of the colonists, Eduard Ludecus and Sarah Horn, provided records of their experiences. When combined with Beales's company journal, they reveal keen insights into the ordeal of attempting to form a settlement in the Rio Grande borderlands far away from New York or Mexico City. They also show how drastically expectations differed from reality. Ludecus, a 27-year-old from the Saxe-Weimar duchy who quit a mercantile business to homestead on the Missouri River in the United States, joined up with Beales in New York. He wrote a running narrative of letters home that his family had published and distributed throughout the German principalities.[36] Additionally, Sarah Horn, a poor Englishwoman who married a small-time commission merchant before traveling across the Atlantic with her family, related a gripping tale about her harrowing experience in the Rio Grande borderlands.[37] Taken together, all three narratives show the entrepreneurial nature of the colonists and the shock they experienced when they entered the borderlands.

Recruiting Ludecus as a colonist proved a significant victory for Beales. The former German merchant came with a mark of upper middle-class social standing. Eduard's father, Wilhelm, was the ducal court secretary to Karl August, the Duke of Saxe-Weimar, which provided the family with enough money and clout to have Eduard educated at the Wilhelm-Ernst-Gymnasium to prepare him for a career in commerce. From there Eduard Ludecus landed a job with a commercial firm in Braunschweig under the guidance of a Herr Becher. Apparently bored by the mere buying and selling of wool, Ludecus kept up on his study of English and saved his money to set out on his own adventure to America, but he did so without ever burning any bridges. Becher provided Ludecus letters of introduction to all the merchants he knew in America, including the German consul in New York City and a relative, F. M. Becker, from whom Ludecus procured further letters to commercial contacts in New Orleans and Matamoros. In Ludecus Beales found a man he could view as a social equal, a man who could communicate with both the German and English-speaking colonists, and a man who could possibly exploit his network of well-funded merchants who might invest in the venture to ensure its success. He just had to commit to keeping Ludecus happy.[38]

Recruiting Sarah Horn and her family provided a different benefit for Beales. Since he focused his recruiting on boardinghouses, most of those he convinced to travel to the borderlands were single men and women. The Horns, on the other hand, remained a fully intact family of four. By the terms of his empresario contract, the Mexican government sought settlement of families specifically. Having the Horns and a couple other families like them would boost his numbers and make it easier to claim his bounty from Mexico to pay off his investors.[39]

Beales had become a talented salesman of the land on the Rio Grande he had never seen. The promise of free land became his strongest pitch. To Ludecus Beales promised 177 acres of farmland and an additional lot in town for the German to build his home. He also promised regular steamboat arrivals from New Orleans to the colony through Matamoros. To crank the pressure up, Beales made the offer time dependent. Ludecus only had one day to decide if he would accept or miss the boat to the Rio Grande. Even though he thought it might be too good to be true, Ludecus took the offer. Similarly, Sarah Horn's husband, John Horn, became enticed by Beales's offer of land and regular steamboat traffic on the Rio Grande. As a failing commission merchant who had taken a job clerking in New York, John Horn almost certainly found Beales's offer to be exactly what he was looking for when he and his family moved to America. Ludecus and the Horns would soon find that the sales pitch did not match the reality of Beales's colony.[40]

Furthermore, both Ludecus and the Horns believed that the colony was well funded and had the full backing of the Mexican government. Beales captivated Ludecus's attention with his explanation of the creation of the land company and an exaggeration of the financial layouts he had. According to Ludecus, Beales said that "an association of wealthy people was formed, to whom he assigned his grant for fifty thousand dollars."[41] Ludecus believed that Beales set out to establish a colony with a small fortune. Correspondingly, Sarah Horn believed the Mexican government would have more of a presence in the construction of a colony in Texas. In her account she cited Beales's contract and the urgency with which he undertook to

fulfill it because Mexico was tracking the colony's development.⁴²
Advertising his colony with the lure of free land, financial stability,
and government support, Beales took his first wave of colonists to set
sail for the Texas coast.

Problems arose as soon as the colonists were on the boat, as tensions
about supplies bubbled to the surface. Beales had promised to
provision and transport a team of German-speaking laborers to the
borderlands in exchange for six months of work for the colony.
The Englishman in charge of distributing food aboard ship unevenly
distributed rations in favor of the English passengers, often taking
far more than needed and depleting necessary supplies. Before the
enterprise even reached the Texas coast, the people Beales put in
charge caused shortages that increased costs on what Beales would
find to be an extremely limited budget.⁴³

When the ship reached the Texas coast at Aransas Bay in early
December 1833, the passengers were surprised to see no permanent
settlements or even anyone to help them unload the ship. The captain
and crew merely lowered their goods into the shallows and left the
colonists with Beales and Thomas A. Power, an Irish-born accountant
the company board placed on the expedition to protect their investment,
as their only guides through the borderlands. Having no real means to
travel overland other than the carts and wagons they brought from New
York, they first had to procure oxen and mules to carry their goods,
which took a full two weeks. While a few men traveled to Goliad to
replenish supplies and buy the proper beasts of burden, the colonists
were left to sleep in tents on the cold, wet, windy beaches.⁴⁴

When they finally left the coast, their entrepreneurial morale
sank significantly, as did their carts and wagons in the mud. Two carts
broke on the very first day they had taken to the road. To make
matters worse, the colonists had just been informed that Indians
controlled most parts of the country, and they would have to defend
themselves with only the few hunting rifles and pistols they had

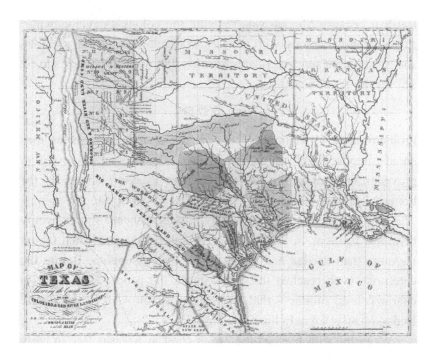

Map of Texas, 1835. Jean-Jacques Konen, *Map of Texas Shewing the Grants in Possession of the Colorado and Red River Land Compy*, Brussels, 1835. Courtesy of Special Collections, University of Texas at Arlington Libraries.

carried with them. However, they had no idea how to differentiate between friendly and aggressive Indians. Colonists like Sarah Horn began to fear anyone they met on the road. Trust in the venture began to evaporate as everyone realized how unprepared they were for the rigors of the borderlands.[45]

Conditions did not improve when the party reached San Antonio, as the lack of supplies, financial strains, and Indigenous power became obvious. The provisions Beales brought to Texas had been nearly wiped out. The road from the coast had also worn out the oxen and carts they had to purchase back at Goliad. In fact the colonists lost four horses and twenty oxen in the 150 miles they traveled. Beales spent the last of the money he had hiring teamsters in San Antonio to escort them the remainder of the journey to the Rio Grande to avoid the same losses.

The Beales Colony Experiment

He also took out an additional loan of a thousand pesos so that they would have at least some money while on the road.[46]

To further decrease morale, the party found a man about five miles outside of San Antonio who had been attacked by Indians. Beaten and shot several times, he was attempting to crawl back to San Antonio to report his attack. In the mid-1830s Mexico's relations with the Lipan Apache were at a nadir. To avoid continuing hostilities with the Comanche, Northern Mexicans chose to make war on the Lipans throughout the 1820s. While this opened a brief time of peace with the Comanche, travelers in Northern Mexico became open targets for Lipan Apache violence. It also did not ensure full protection from Comanche bands who still took advantage of the opportunity in vulnerable people on the road. Seeing this man's condition outside San Antonio draped a pall of foreboding over the colonists about their fortunes.[47]

In March 1834, after nearly four months in Texas, the expedition finally reached the Rio Grande. The disappointment among the colonists was palpable. As Ludecus approached the river, he recognized the dismal state of the land and described the area in elegant detail: "We were still doubtful that there was a river in our vicinity when we saw it hardly a hundred paces in front of us. The sight of it, its murky, sandy water and its bare banks with only fifteen- to twenty-foot-high cane and willows growing there made a very depressing impression on me and on all the others too. Everything is bleak and dead in its vicinity. Nature seemed to have died there."[48] All of the entrepreneurs in the party also realized at first look at the Rio Grande that it was not likely a navigable waterway. The dream that Beales had sold to the colonists of growing bountiful crops on cheap lands to transport downriver shriveled on the dusty banks of the Rio Grande. Life in the borderlands was going to be harder than any of them had imagined.

Shortly after they found the Rio Grande and turned toward the prospective townsite, Beales and the colonists came into a small camp of Shawnee hunters trapping animals along the river. Finding a

Scotsman among them, Beales and several of the English colonists tried to engage the Shawnee in trade. They quickly shifted from colonists worried about their own survival to fur traders looking to strike up business connections among the local Indigenous populations. Beales and the Shawnee struck a deal. The Shawnee would trade some of their furs to Beales and the other mercantile-minded Europeans, but the colonists had to agree to allow the Shawnee to accompany the traveling party to Las Moras. The offer proved mutually beneficial as the Indians would join into a larger group to be able to hunt farther north, taking them deeper into hostile lands. The colonists gained their local knowledge in finding the best ford across the Rio Grande and Indigenous allies in a place where they had none. Their entrepreneurial attitude allowed for them to build local connections with a small band of Shawnee. They needed to make more connections with Indigenous people in this place where Indian power reigned, and Mexican state power was extremely limited.[49]

The limitations of Mexican state power can be seen in the militia Beales had to hire to protect colonists as they founded their first town. Mexico would not pay for the necessary troops to escort the enterprise from the Rio Grande to the townsite. Instead, Beales had to sacrifice purchasing more food supplies at Presidio del Rio Grande to pay for the guards to see after the security of the town. Short on corn and out of flour, Beales presumed they would all subsist through individual gardens and hunting wild game. However, they still had seventy miles to cover to reach the place Egerton had scouted. Once they finally arrived, they found that the townsite was quite isolated, as the nearest Mexican settlement, San Fernando, was almost thirty-five miles south and required fording the Rio Grande to get there. Though Las Moras Creek produced a modest number of trees and vegetation, the colonists were forced to use grass and cane to build their shelters. They also relied on thistle and branches to build their defenses against the possibility of a Comanche raid. Other than the assurance that the creek was fed from a spring not likely to dry up, the colonists faced mean conditions from the beginning.[50]

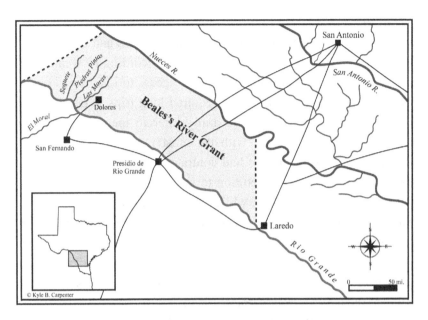

John C. Beales's River Grant on the Rio Grande in 1834. Map by Alex Mendoza.

When Beales, his colonists, their escort of soldiers, and the Shawnee band reached the townsite, which Beales named Dolores after his wife, they all set to work building a means for subsistence. For the Europeans that meant trying to scratch productive farms out of second-rate land. As noted in Egerton's report on the grant, water proved a significant demand for all the colonists. The colonists at Dolores threw all available labor at digging a ditch from Las Moras Creek to begin irrigating gardens, though Ludecus noted that the company planned on charging everyone a fee to draw from the creek to water their lots. The unrelenting sun compounded the lack of water. All their initial crops shriveled and turned yellow after sprouting. None of the colonists knew the techniques of dryland farming. They all brought their notions of farming from northern Europe, where rainfall was rarely scarce. The colonists lost an entire year's worth of crop because they lacked the essential knowledge of the region's growing conditions.[51]

In the face of crop failures, diminishing supplies, and excruciating labor, the town fractured quickly along class and ethnic lines. Physically, the town lots were distributed according to wealth and social standing. The best lots had water access to Las Moras Creek while the less desirable holdings required long trips to get water or significant irrigation ditches to draw water to their lands. Beales claimed the finest location with the most fertile-looking soil that seemed to irrigate itself. He had contracted with German and Irish carpenters prior to the expedition to build his home and demanded it be constructed with stone, which was undertaken with great effort. The next best lots went to Egerton and the other Englishmen of high social standing who Beales brought with him. Ludecus, another German, Power, and Captain Soto were the only non-English settlers to receive lots on the creek. Other than Soto, none of the Mexican soldiers seem to have been granted land.[52]

Politically, Dolores split along ethnic lines. By law the colonists had to elect an ayuntamiento, or town council, with four official posts to gain recognition from Mexico as a legitimate settlement. Beales, naturally, pursued the position of alcalde, or town mayor, because of his status as empresario. Though the colonists had begun to turn on Beales for misleading them, no other challenger rose with enough support to assert a claim to the position. The colonists elected Egerton as regidor, or first officer under the alcalde, and another Englishman, Victor Pepin, as regidor *segundo*. The last position, *syndico*, went to Ludecus as the Germans got one of their own into an official position. As any problems crept up in town, individuals turned to their own ethnic representatives to settle disputes, creating an atmosphere of distrust and resentment. The Irish, who grew fed up with the English leadership, eventually joined the Germans to seek assistance from Ludecus.[53]

Aside from ethnic tensions, the biggest problem in town was clearly its economic woes. Beales had blown through the $4,000 the Rio Grande Land Company had allotted before the party had even gotten to San Antonio de Béxar. There, to purchase extra supplies, oxen, and repair broken carts, he took out an additional $1,000 loan on the company's credit just to get to the Rio Grande. Still thinking that Mexico would provide easy credit to its empresarios, he sent Captain Soto to Monclova with promissory notes to acquire a loan from the Coahuila y Texas state government, but Soto returned with only an official letter welcoming the colonists to the state. Thus, when the colonists began building Beales's house, he had no money to provision them.[54]

To remedy the supply problem, Beales made the most fateful decision for the future of Dolores: he left. After being elected alcalde and distributing written title to lands to all the colonists, he announced he was traveling to Matamoros to draw another loan after only residing in the colony for two weeks. He planned to have an agent return to Dolores with the money while he sailed back to New York to restart the recruitment process again with a new contingent of colonists. It was up to Egerton to oversee the building of the colony until Beales returned.[55]

Beales's decision to leave demonstrated to the colonists that the empresario cared more about satisfying his investors than the people he convinced to move to the Rio Grande borderlands. Beales met the bare necessities of his contract by ensuring the colonists made it to his grant and providing them title to their lands. Unlike Stephen F. Austin, Beales made little individual effort to build connections with nearby Mexican towns or establish any sense of community among the people of his colony. He left the colonists to fend for themselves, which they did, making decisions that would benefit them individually, regardless of the fate of Dolores. Further, by prioritizing recruiting efforts over the foundational maintenance of the town, Beales sought to reach the goals of the contract to receive his reward in land. Only through that reward would the Rio Grande and Texas Land Company become profitable. Beales was more incentivized to inflate the population in his grant than to oversee the successful settlement of it.[56]

With the colony clearly failing and the sense of community fracturing, individuals began seeking their own entrepreneurial gains. Seeing an opportunity in the town's economic hardships, Soto took all the saleable items he owned, including his wagon, oxen, and horses, and pawned them in San Fernando for food goods and basic supplies. He then opened a small mercantile house in Dolores to sell these necessary items to the colonists for exorbitant prices. He took promissory notes that Egerton distributed to prop up the town's economy at face value because he knew that they would be redeemable through his brother-in-law and the Rio Grande Land Company. While he did make a neat profit for himself, Soto's venture was much more successful at breeding unrest and resentment among the colonists. Ludecus vented his frustration: "One was not able to pay them their daily wages and was thus denying them any opportunity to obtain groceries more economically than in San Fernando."[57]

As weeks went by without any infusion of supplies or money, the laborers of the Dolores quit working. Furious, Egerton tried to hold them to the job based on contracts they signed with Beales. Ludecus intervened, claiming that Beales broke the contract first by not providing adequate supplies. To further complicate the issue, the few Mexican militiamen Beales hired to guard the town became restless from not receiving additional pay. Fear of an Indian raid, deteriorating defenses, and declining foodstuffs put everyone on edge. After days of bickering and hard feelings, many of the Germans, including Ludecus, Power, and other Irish laborers, packed up and left.[58]

✪ ✪ ✪ ✪ ✪

A short while after Ludecus boarded a ship in Matamoros to leave northern Mexico for good, the Horn family prepared to leave Dolores. Unlike the Germans who left due to ethnic and economic complaints, the Horns and other English colonists fled out of fear of Indian power. About forty miles from Dolores, a party of Comanche warriors descended on a rancho, killing everyone and burning all the buildings. When news of the attack reached Dolores, the Horns panicked. The town was largely defenseless, and if Comanche bands ranged as close as forty miles, it seemed only a matter of time before they raided the failing settlement. Sarah, her husband, John, and their two sons left with a group of about ten other English to make for Matamoros. They never made it. Rather than take the road that ran along the Rio Grande, the English party traveled northeast to the Nueces, hoping to avoid Mexican troops heard to have been gathering on the Rio Grande. This fateful decision led them directly to a Comanche raiding camp. The Horns and their party were attacked, all the men killed, and the women and children taken captive.[59]

When the Horns left Dolores, the Indigenous politics of the Rio Grande borderlands had shifted considerably from when the Horns landed at Aransas. The tenuous peace between the Comanche and northern Mexicans fell apart. The Lipan Apache no longer posed a threat to Comanche power, meaning the Comanche no longer needed northern Mexicans to fight them. Further, the influx of Americans into East Texas brought more American goods into Texas. The Comanche began to openly trade with Americans for everything they needed, including rifles and ammunition. The Comanche had few reasons to remain at peace with Mexico. Mexican ranches and small settlements in the Rio Grande borderlands became targets of raiding. The rancho destroyed forty miles from Dolores marked only one of several raids in the region that year. The Comanche would eventually lay waste to the abandoned remnants of Dolores.[60]

By 1836 rebellion erupted in northern Mexico as Zacatecas and Coahuila y Texas pronounced against the Mexican central government, drawing the ire of President Santa Anna and the Mexican Army. With Mexican troops marching through the borderlands to fight the Americans who had declared Texas independent, all empresario contracts went on hold. The few remaining Dolores colonists evacuated, leaving the town to Indigenous power.

However, Beales's case demonstrates how Mexican state policies and Anglo-American speculating drew European borderlands entrepreneurs into the Rio Grande borderlands. When Mexican law excluded Anglo-Americans from empresario contracts, Europeans became the locus for Mexican state agents and speculators as a substitute to create settlements in the borderlands. Mexican officials believed that European empresarios would fulfill their contracts independent of state assistance. American speculators stepped in to fill the financial void in hopes of taking a cut of the land rewards. Both sides were disappointed. Beales assumed far more state protection and monetary support than he received. Diverging assumptions contributed to the project's failure.[61]

In the case of Beales's colony, European-born entrepreneurs found themselves caught between Mexico's need to colonize its northern frontier and American greed for Mexican land. Thinking they were taking advantage of Mexico's generous land policies and the financial windfalls that American investment brought, European colonists undertook the task of building a colony on the very edges of the borderlands. There they found Indigenous power dominated any support they might receive from Mexico or the United States. Regardless of what Mexicans, Americans, or Europeans wanted the Rio Grande borderlands to be, the Indians had the power.

The Beales colony was not the last time European-born entrepreneurs attempted to settle the Rio Grande borderlands with migrants from Europe. When the Republic of Texas proclaimed its independence, its leaders fell back on the empresario system to populate its frontier. The French took particular interest in the Rio Grande borderlands to compete with the English and American empires in North America. This led European empires to take a more active role in the region.

Chapter 3

British and French Borderlands Entrepreneurs in the Republic of Texas

The French Imperial aide-de-camp in New York, A. Rullmann, took an interest in Texas in the late 1830s. He likely read some of the innumerable emigrant's guides to Texas and followed the Texas Revolution in New York newspapers.[1] As a result Rullmann began to imagine settling in Texas. He continued to follow the situation in Texas after the rebellion against Mexico and saw an opportunity after the Jackson administration came out against annexation. The Republic of Texas needed political and economic assistance from outside the United States to survive. Why not French help? Rullmann took advantage. He created a settlement contract between himself and the Texas secretary of state that read like a Mexican empresario contract. Texas would allot Rullmann massive tracts of land, and he would settle French families in Texas in exchange for land for himself.[2] Rullmann argued "that the safest guarantee for the performance of the settlement is my personal interest."[3] He made it clear that his station in the French imperial system and influence across the Atlantic would lead to instant settlement and a flourishing French colony.

Rullmann stirred up an idea in Sam Houston's presidential administration. The early years of Houston's republic did not begin auspiciously. The Republic of Texas had to maintain its tenuous claim to independence in the face of dire economic conditions and constant threat of Mexican and Indigenous incursions. Could the old Mexican empresario system help fix Texas? Houston rebooted the program and signed a slew of colonization contracts, most with European borderlands entrepreneurs. By trying to settle Europeans in the Rio Grande borderlands between the Nueces River and the Rio Grande, Texas attempted to draw in European finance and create a buffer zone between itself, Mexico, and the Comanche Empire.[4]

When Houston's second-term administration began to grant empresario contracts in the Rio Grande borderlands, European-born entrepreneurs scrambled to get one. A diverse set of empresarios from all over Europe wanted to colonize the region and profit from their ventures. The French and British particularly took interest in acquiring contracts to grants between the Nueces River and the Rio Grande. They viewed the Rio Grande borderlands as a place with the potential to provide entrepreneurial success and support political ends for their imperial states. Like Rullmann, they thought the blend of individual self-interest and state support would guarantee success.[5]

Driven largely by their imaginations for the future of Texas, European borderlands entrepreneurs carried unrealistic dreams that they would create an agricultural and commercial utopia on the Rio Grande. This new generation of European-born empresarios attempted to harness the power and authority of their own states rather than trusting North American states. Thus, as their entrepreneurial activities expanded in the region, so too did European state interest. European borderlands entrepreneurs played the politics of diplomacy to keep Texas hooked to Europe in their attempts to gain personal wealth. Like Rullmann, other Europeans believed their connections to European state-building apparatuses would lead to thriving colonies in the borderlands.

Two case studies, one involving French empresarios Alexander Bourgeois d'Orvanne and Armand Ducos and another involving the

British empresario William Kennedy, reveal attempts to increase European state presence in the Rio Grande borderlands to protect speculative ventures. Though Bourgeois, Ducos, and Kennedy did their research to learn from previous mistakes—namely, the Beales colony disaster—these European-born empresarios of the Texas Republic also failed to fulfill their contracts. Their projects foundered because they often accepted misinformation as fact and tied the prospects of their enterprises to the geopolitics of the Atlantic World. Because they were agents of their respective states, Bourgeois, Ducos, and Kennedy could not disconnect their political and economic agendas. However, due to their abilities to draw European interest in the region, these borderlands entrepreneurs demonstrate exactly how Europeans tried and failed to make the Rio Grande borderlands a center for modernization and trade during the lifespan of the Republic of Texas.

After the battle of San Jacinto in April 1836, Texas nominally became an independent state. Mexico continued to assert its sovereignty over the territory and threatened military action, but the capture of Santa Anna assured the Anglo-American Texans that, for a time, they could act independently. Almost immediately Texas sought annexation to the United States. By September the people of Texas voted overwhelmingly to enter the United States. However, they were rebuffed. Texas's adherence to chattel slavery and the spreading crisis of the Panic of 1837 cooled support for annexation in the United States. Texas was on its own. Amid the threat of Mexican reconquest and the economic decline the Panic of 1837, Texas leaders, particularly Sam Houston, looked to Europe for political and financial support.[6]

During the same span after San Jacinto, the British and French had become disillusioned with Mexico. Still saddled with millions of dollars of debt and constant political unrest in a time of global economic slowdown, Mexico failed to live up to the lofty economic expectations Europeans had for it. For example, two-thirds of the Mexican mining companies formed in London after Mexico's independence collapsed by 1830. Additionally, British investors plunged millions of pounds into Mexico that yielded little to no return. French entrepreneurs had similar experiences, and both the British and French came to feel duped by Mexican promoters and government officials. To compound European disappointment, the successful Texas rebellion ripped away a huge chunk of northern Mexico and put it in the hands of Anglo-Americans who sought to create their own slaveholders' republic on the Gulf of Mexico. Both the British and the French had already adopted policies against chattel slavery, and neither empire wanted to see the spread of the United States into Texas. Rather than stand by and watch the United States reap all of Texas's economic benefits, the British and French tried to capitalize on the disruption that Texas independence caused. They both moved to gain influence in Texas to open economic inroads and political discussions about slavery.[7]

Texas officials courted any European diplomat or merchant interested in the new Republic. Texas leaders understood that population growth was essential to the republic's success. More people in Texas increased the value of Texas's most abundant resource: land. While the Panic of 1837 spurred thousands of US-born migrants to move to Texas, few settled in the Rio Grande borderlands. The Texas Congress created a new empresario program that gave the president the power to designate empresarios to both encourage and target migration. Sam Houston offered grants to European contractors to recruit European colonists to settle hundreds of families within their granted lands. A significant portion of the land the Republic of Texas granted to European empresarios lay within the Nueces Strip, the land between the Nueces River and Rio Grande. For many of the same reasons Mexico wanted Beales's colony to succeed, as outlined in chapter 2, Texas promoted land in the Rio Grande borderlands to Europeans.[8]

Problematically, Texas had a spurious claim to the lands between the Nueces and Rio Grande Rivers. The administrative territory of Texas since the Spanish era had only reached as far south as the Nueces River. After the Battle of San Jacinto, when Texas forces captured President Santa Anna, the Texas revolutionary government forced the Mexican leader to sign a secret treaty at Velasco recognizing Texas independence with the boundary at the Rio Grande. Mexico never recognized the treaty and continued to claim sovereignty over all of Texas. The Nueces Strip became a no-man's-land, where Texas and Mexico both tried to assert their rights but which neither could physically control. Further, different factions of Mexicans made competing claims to the land.[9]

European-born entrepreneurs and state agents, though, accepted grants in the Nueces Strip, believing that their respective governments would support Texas claims down to the Rio Grande. It was no secret that both the British and French wanted the Texas boundary to be the Rio Grande. Even a British commissioner tasked with suppressing the slave trade wrote matter-of-factly that the southern boundary of Texas was the Rio Grande. "The boundary of Texas as at present defined, is as follows. Beginning at the Mouth of the Rio del Norté, about the 26th degree of North latitude and up that River to its source thence a due North course to the source of the River Arkansas."[10] The French knew that the British wanted the Texas southern boundary to be the Rio Grande based on a supposed British offer to supply a loan to the Republic of Texas for the purchase of the Nueces Strip from Mexico.[11] The French recognized that if they did not accept the Rio Grande boundary, they might lose access to the Texas market. European-born borderlands entrepreneurs took comfort in the knowledge that whatever opportunities they could muster in the Nueces Strip would come with at least tacit approval from their respective governments.

The French legation in Texas, headed by Jean Pierre Isidore Alphonse Dubois de Saligny, saw great potential in the Rio Grande borderlands for France. Based on conversations he had with merchants in Galveston, Dubois de Saligny believed the Rio Grande to be navigable all the way to Santa Fe. He imagined Santa Fe to be the center of a vast New Mexican mining industry primed for French exploitation. French commercial agents had long desired access to Santa Fe, but French loss of territorial claims in North America after the Seven Years' War ended the movement of French merchants to New Mexico. If the French could develop a colony on the Rio Grande, Dubois de Saligny believed he could be the one to give France the full access to Santa Fe it desired. Through his networks within the Republic of Texas and French diplomatic agents, Dubois de Saligny inquired about land grants along the Rio Grande to establish a strong French presence in a place that he viewed to be on the precipice of an economic explosion.[12]

Dubois de Saligny was hard at work attempting to fulfill the interests of the July Monarchy, the French government at the time. The July Monarchy was born out of a highly fragmented French society in July 1830. An entrepreneurial group of French journalists, bankers, businesspeople, and lawyers harnessed the power of newspapers to overthrow the conservative Charles X and install the more liberal Louis-Philippe, Duc d'Orleans, to the throne. The liberal, middle-class government that took power lasted eighteen years. Those in power in Paris generally believed in free trade and state-subsidized infrastructure to support entrepreneurial growth. Leaders also believed themselves to be men of modern thought and sought to make France a modern imperial nation. All these characteristics tended to translate to France's relationship with Texas and its attempts to colonize the Rio Grande borderlands. The July Monarchy produced a rapid, if uneven, industrialization in France and increased competition with Britain for markets and imperial power overseas. This era created a generation of French entrepreneurs looking outward from France, some of whom pushed into the American borderlands.[13]

With its new industrial output and evolving policy to undermine Britain, French foreign ministers looked to Texas as a place to sell its products and establish a new imperial presence in the Americas. The July Monarchy sent diplomats and operatives to Texas to investigate the new republic on the Gulf of Mexico. In 1842 French merchant Alexander Bourgeois d'Orvanne and his partner, Armand Ducos, became key agents for France regarding the Rio Grande borderlands. The former mayor of Clichy-la-Garenne, Bourgeois had networks at the intersections between business and politics in France. In fact the minister of agriculture and commerce sent Bourgeois to the Texas territory to semiofficially pursue reconnaissance and provide his judgement on the economic prospects Texas presented to France. Ducos also had important ties in French political circles, including the minister of finance. Ducos went to Texas to investigate a property claim from a French expatriate. Though he failed in that mission, he attained an empresario contract to gain land grants for his client. Bourgeois and Ducos traveled across the Atlantic to Galveston, where they sought out Texan leaders to extract the most relevant information they desired. While in Texas they pursued their own self-interests and attained empresario contracts.[14]

Dubois de Saligny became quite interested in Bourgeois and Ducos when they informed him that they were seeking empresario grants from the Texas government. He immediately jumped to work to aid them in their quest. If they acquired land grants, he wanted to be involved to ensure France's foreign policy goals. Dubois de Saligny had become a staunch supporter of Sam Houston and his policies, giving him access to a powerful political network in Texas when Houston was president. Through Dubois de Saligny's networks, Bourgeois and Ducos obtained two separate empresario contracts from the Texas executive, one on the Medina River outside San Antonio and the other on the Rio Grande. Excited for the success of his compatriots, the French diplomat rushed a missive to his confidant, the French minister of foreign affairs, François Guizot: "These two concessions cannot fail to expand our interests and influence in Texas."[15] Bourgeois and Ducos used their connections to the French state to both earn profits for themselves and expand French influence in the borderlands.[16]

Before they could realize that profit, Bourgeois had work to do to put together his report for the French minister of commerce. He found his job to be quite difficult because of all the threats that bore upon Texas. Initially, he thought the best route to gain information was through the archives of Texas that the Lamar administration installed in Austin. That proved a dead-end as the people of Austin buried the archives out of fear of a colossal Indian attack. This fear and the responses to it forced Bourgeois to have to travel throughout Texas and the Rio Grande borderlands to assess the commercial viability of the region through oral interviews.[17]

In 1840 the Comanche Empire expanded to one of its largest iterations as raiding threatened areas as far east as Matamoros and south all the way to San Luis Potosí. One Comanche band attacked Linnville on Lavaca Bay, pillaging and burning the town. Anglo-Texans and a group of Tonkawa allies tracked the Comanche raiders and engaged in a day-long running fight of ferocious violence. News of the increase in bloodshed spread fears that transcended ethnicity as Mexican, Anglo-American Texan, and European alike prepared to defend against an attack that may or may never come. The Comanche and other Indigenous groups remained the dominant power in the Rio Grande borderlands, regardless of whatever claims Anglo-American Texans, Mexicans, or Europeans made.[18]

Bourgeois completed his reconnaissance without meeting any Comanche warriors. His report provides considerable insight into how the French viewed the Rio Grande borderlands. One of the overarching themes of Bourgeois's report was that the Nueces Strip could become the place where France would stem the tide of US and British expansion. He believed that American ideas in the Texas population had become a groundswell that threatened to sweep beyond the Rio Grande. To combat it Bourgeois suggested the French subsidize the continued presence of Catholic clergy in the region. In addition to stopping the spread of the United States, the French needed to openly compete with the British in terms of both formal colonization and commercial expansion. In his travels Bourgeois noticed an influx of British immigrants in the Texas territory and worried that their presence would influence the political views of the Texas government. Also, British goods imported to Texas were of a significantly higher quality than what the French were sending across the

Atlantic. Much to his chagrin, Bourgeois noticed that unscrupulous French merchants passed off fermented American grapes as wines from Bordeaux or Burgundy. He worried actions like this injured the national reputation of French industry. Bourgeois's concerns demonstrate how preoccupied the French were with US continental expansion and British global influence.[19]

To reap the benefits that everyone seemed to believe the future of the borderlands offered, Bourgeois provided a list of recom-mendations that the French minister of commerce should consider. Primarily, he wanted France to quickly pursue the creation of firm boundaries between Texas, the United States, and Mexico. He believed the permeable frontiers created constant hostility between Texas and Mexico and opened Texas to annexation by the United States. Both situations were harmful to French interests and commercial hopes.[20]

Bourgeois imagined that established borders would end Indian raiding, which demonstrates his inherited French notions of modernity. For the Frenchman the idea of nation and territory were inextricable. Bourgeois did not recognize the legitimacy of the Comanche in the borderlands because they made no formal boundary claims. The Republic of Texas needed to have an internationally recognized politicized boundary line to be a legitimate nation-state. Anything less would mark Texas as being as backward as Mexico and teetering precariously on the verge of savagery.[21]

To ensure the best outcome for France, Bourgeois suggested that the state should sponsor an emigration program to the Rio Grande borderlands so that French citizens "would carry with them our tastes, our customs, our needs, our principles, and the memory of their native land."[22] Bourgeois looked at the world and noticed European emigration took a rapid uptick in the 1840s. Most French migrants up to 1842 moved to Algeria, which had come under French domain in 1830. Bourgeois hoped to redirect emigrants to the Rio Grande borderlands so that they might modernize the region according to French precepts.[23]

Bourgeois also wanted to ensure French access to the Rio Grande. Like most Europeans in the 1840s, Bourgeois believed the Rio Grande to be an essential waterway for inland shipping. French smugglers like Jean Lafitte and Ramon LaFon made substantial profits moving goods up the Rio Grande during the late Spanish era. Since Mexico's independence, the population of French merchants in Matamoros exploded. One of the most prolific European scientists in the borderlands, Jean-Louis Berlandier, published his calculations about how far various sized boats could travel upriver. He supposed flat-bottomed boats could cruise hundreds of miles inland. Bourgeois, collecting all this information, believed the best route to exploit such a promising new market would be through the concession of Point Isabel to France. At the mouth of the river, Point Isabel acted like a Gibraltar for the Rio Grande. Bourgeois believed that the concession, along with the establishment of a state-supported French company in the region, would divert the Santa Fe trade to France.[24]

When Bourgeois had acquired enough information to file his report, he departed the borderlands to join Ducos in recruiting colonists. In fact he wrote the report on the ship returning to France. The report's focus on the Rio Grande and the issue of French emigration suggests that Bourgeois included his own interests while seeking to acquire the aid of the French government for his colonization scheme. In some ways it worked. While he and Ducos were in eastern France recruiting farmers to colonize their grants, the French minister of interior became concerned about their actions and threatened to shut it down, fearing that the prospective colonists would be exploited. The July Monarchy was always in a tenuous state, and most ministers avoided actions that might spur popular resentment among the poor.[25] However, other members of the French diplomatic community came to Bourgeois's and Ducos's aid. The minister of foreign affairs, François Guizot, wrote the French minister of interior to settle his concerns. He claimed that Bourgeois and Ducos "present no suspicion of improper conduct or fraudulent speculation."[26]

Guizot apparently agreed with Bourgeois's report, recognizing that colonizing the Rio Grande borderlands with French citizens would give the French significant advantages, regardless of what might happen to the emigrants. Additionally, Guizot very much supported expanding European "modern civilization" all over the world. He wrote, "European civilization has entered, if we may so speak, into the eternal truth into the plan of Providence; it progresses according to the intentions of God. This is the rational account of its superiority."[27] Expanding French modern civilization into the Rio Grande borderlands was manifest destiny.

Even with the support of the French government and powerful bureaucrats like Guizot, Bourgeois and Ducos failed to recruit enough French migrants to settle on their grants. News of fighting and unrest in the borderlands encouraged French emigrants to move elsewhere. Ducos essentially gave up on the venture in 1843 as the deadline to settle at least one-third of the total number of colonists came up on December third of that year. Bourgeois, though, pressed forward. He submitted a report to President Sam Houston explaining that he "greatly contributed to the formation of an active intervention, undertaken by France, England and the United States" to bring harmony to the borderlands.[28] He thought a few words would undo almost a decade of tension and warfare. Believing he had helped achieve peace between Texas and Mexico, Bourgeois pressed eastward across the Rhine River to entice German-speaking people to settle in the Rio Grande borderlands. He made positive connections with German princes and became associated with an organization that called itself the Society for the Protection of German Immigrants.[29]

The German principalities sought space for their people overseas in the 1840s as one strategy to offset the economic and social crises that affected agricultural regions throughout Europe. The US Panic of 1837 was part of a larger global economic downturn that gripped Europe for most of the 1840s. Further, industrialization in the Rhineland took a heavy toll on the people in the southwest of the German-speaking territories, particularly Baden and Bavaria. Artisans were hit hard as industrial production displaced their work and contributed to a glut in labor supply. Poverty became a serious problem for the German principalities to deal with. The 1840s witnessed an explosion in the population of the German-speaking territories, creating land and food pressure on top of the rampant pauperism. Rather than risk this volatile mix of poverty and desperation leading to violent revolt, German leaders turned to emigration as a method to ease the pressure.[30]

Bourgeois sought to exploit the Society for the Protection of German Immigrants and the wealth of the twenty-one German noblemen who backed it. Regardless of his report about settling his grant with French citizens to expand French influence, he wanted to meet the terms of his contract to receive his bonus of title to the choicest lands in his grant. He recognized that the society was serious about German emigration and that it was powerful enough to muscle through government officials in Bavaria and Baden who might try to stop it. Often, state policies in Central Europe sought to push so-called undesirable emigrants out, like the Jewish community, while hemming in those they thought to be desirable. The society had the backing of the wealth and power of regional royalty, making any sort of emigration restriction vain. Bourgeois sought to capitalize on the society's vigor.[31]

Bourgeois made two key decisions when he engaged the German society. First, he decided to abandon one of his empresario grants, giving up on the Rio Grande grant to focus on the Medina grant. He likely made this decision because his lands on the Rio Grande were more precarious than the tracts on the Medina. Mexican army personnel crossed the Rio Grande and occupied parts of Bourgeois's grant twice in 1842. Though he claimed to have achieved peace there, Bourgeois knew the grant to be unsettled. Additionally, Mexican landowners had documented title to most of the land in Bourgeois's Rio Grande grant that ran back to the days of Escandón.[32] Finally, the Nueces Strip proved to be an undesirable place for Europeans who saw it. One Swiss traveler wrote of the land north of the Rio Grande, lamenting "the most dreadful monotony seems to augment the ennui which one breathes here."[33] The Medina grant also offered certain benefits. There was already a considerable and growing population of German-speaking immigrants in the area around San Antonio de Béxar, and the Medina grant lay only about sixty miles west of the town. All these conditions likely led Bourgeois to abandon his claim to the Rio Grande grant.

The second key decision he made was to attempt to tie inextricably the Society for the Protection of German Immigrants to the Republic of Texas through financial agreements to keep Texas attached to Europe and to gain an extension for his empresario contracts. In the spring of 1843, he opened and managed negotiations between Ashbel Smith, the ambassador of the Republic of Texas to France, and the society. He convinced the society to offer a loan to the Republic of Texas for $1 million to ensure the republic remained in existence through the society's colonization process. Smith conferred with Bourgeois about the terms of the loan and then submitted it to the Texas secretary of state, Anson Jones. Other than taking issue with a stipulation that gave the society remission of tariffs of up to $200,000 a year for ten years, Smith found it an excellent agreement and encouraged his superiors to consider it.[34]

Unfortunately, the loan and Bourgeois's relationship with the society soon dissolved. The Texas government and the Germans could not agree on the tariff details of the loan and Bourgeois proved an inadequate intermediary to fulfill the needs of both sides. They decided to adjourn discussions until June 1844.[35] That timeframe extended beyond Bourgeois's contract deadline. He desperately needed Texas to renew his contract and kept at the topic. However, by the time Bourgeois could renew discussions between the Germans and Anglo-American Texans, the society removed Bourgeois from its association. Prince Carl of Solms, a key investor in the society, traveled to Texas with Bourgeois to investigate the lands within his Medina grant. Solms found that most of the grant was bad land and hilly country. Solms considered it a positive turn of events for the society that the loan through Bourgeois never came to fruition to allow for the renewal of his grant. Bourgeois called it "an act of treachery."[36] Regardless of perspective, the triangular connections tying Texas, France, and the German nobility crumbled.[37]

The entire project failed before Bourgeois could settle a single colonist on his grants. That should not preclude his colonization venture from study, though. In his entrepreneurial maneuverings to acquire title for Texas lands in the Rio Grande borderlands, Bourgeois encouraged the French government to seriously consider direct colonization of Texas, decided to colonize with German-speaking families instead of French, shrugged the responsibility of colonization onto German nobles, and convinced the Texas foreign office that they could acquire a $1 million loan from the same German nobility in order to extend his contracts with the Texas government. Though he ultimately failed in his speculative scheme, Bourgeois's example provides insight into how European-born borderlands entrepreneurs could utilize states for their own ends and how these speculators imagined their future commercial success. Moving people from Europe to the borderlands, having them impose their culture on the region, and then selling those migrants goods from Europe remained a central pillar of their strategies.

✿ ✿ ✿ ✿ ✿

The British sought many of the same goals as the French, and British entrepreneurs proved just as ready to manipulate states for their own gain. William Kennedy provides one particularly insightful example. In the years between 1840 and 1845, Kennedy wrote a book lauding the Republic of Texas and became an empresario for Texas, then a diplomat representing Texas in London, and finally a consul for Britain in Galveston. In these positions he used the Texas government and the British Foreign Office and, perhaps, encouraged members of Parliament to boost his colonization schemes in the Rio Grande borderlands.

Kennedy, born in Scotland and raised in Ireland, became a journalist interested in how the British Empire functioned. In 1838

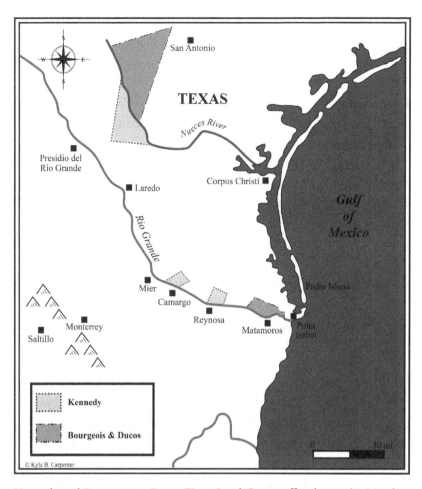

Kennedy and Bourgeois & Ducos Texas Land Grants offered in 1842. Map by Alex Mendoza.

he accompanied the Earl of Durham to Canada as a minor diplomat. Afterward, Kennedy stayed in North America to explore the United States to investigate its state legislatures. He wanted to know how the legislatures worked in order to suggest applications of their functions to local rule in Ireland. When he learned of the new republic formed in Texas, he traveled there and saw opportunity in both land and politics.[38]

To gain access to Texas leaders, Kennedy relied on his journalistic abilities. While in Texas he collected data about Texas history and government. He used that data to publish a book, *Texas: The Rise, Progress, and Prospects of the Republic of Texas*. Kennedy's goal for *Texas* was to help build diplomatic ties between Texas and Britain by highlighting a shared Anglo heritage. He learned through his travels in the United States that Americans tended to hold the British in contempt, and he wanted Anglo-American Texans to feel otherwise about his compatriots. The book became an idealized description of Texas and Anglo-American Texans. It praised the land, climate, and hearty nature of the US-born colonists who migrated there. At the same time, it denigrated Mexico as a "mixed population which, under the general name of Mexican, lay scattered within and adjacent to the Tropic."[39] Kennedy's *Texas* sought to connect the British and Anglo-American Texans by juxtaposing them with Mexicans who were unable to develop the area because of their racial inferiority.

His second goal was to spark greater interest in Europe for Texas. The epigraph he chose for the book, from French diplomat Francois Barbé-Marbois, hints at the strategic thrust to bring Texas and Britain together: "Texas is one of the finest countries in the world; and yet the Europeans, eager as they have been to make conquests in America, have seemed, almost to the present day, ignorant of its existence."[40] The book tried to build connections to the Anglo-American Texans for the British reader and explain how beautiful the land would be for a British emigrant.

Kennedy spent a significant portion of his book discussing the Rio Grande borderlands, in part because he acquired a bundle of documentation from Beales's Rio Grande and Texas Land Company, the failed English colony on the Rio Grande. His two most important documents related to the Rio Grande borderlands were William Egerton's investigative notes and John Beales's journal of the Dolores colony's settlement. Kennedy plucked the most positive details in their writings to highlight all the beneficial aspects of Texas. Early in *Texas* Kennedy describes the land between the Nueces and the

Rio Grande as "well adapted to farming" and "not to be surpassed for the raising of stock."[41] He goes on to compare the Rio Grande to the Mississippi and Orinoco Rivers.[42] Similarly, Kennedy regurgitates Egerton's belief that Matamoros would become the next New Orleans, a vast port city to connect the Rio Grande borderlands with the entire Atlantic World. Whole sections of his book look almost like advertisements for Europeans to choose the Rio Grande borderlands for their future homes.[43]

Texas gave the British writer access to many Texas leaders, including Sam Houston. Houston read Kennedy's book and met him personally. The Texas president found Kennedy quite charming.[44] He also thought Kennedy might further Texas's standing within the British government. Kennedy, for his own part, accepted that role, but strove to make personal gains from his relationship with Texas leadership. In their conversations Kennedy found that Houston and others were particularly interested in promoting European immigration to Texas. Since Kennedy's book was essentially a device designed to do just that, he received empresario contracts near where Beales's contract had been.[45] He also earned an official position as consul general of Texas to Great Britain. Houston gave Kennedy the political means and economic incentive to convince European emigrants to move to the Rio Grande borderlands. Kennedy had the opportunity to succeed where Beales had failed in creating a British-led colony on the Rio Grande.[46]

Like his French counterparts, Kennedy tried to take advantage of every situation to sell the idea of populating his empresario contract with European immigrants to European state agents. By the time he got to Austin in early 1842, the economic situation in Texas had become dire. Kennedy noticed in his travels through New Orleans to Galveston that the financial situation in North America had reached desperate levels as the economic fallout of the Panic of 1837 continued. However, the depression kept the United States and Mexico from taking over Texas, leaving a prime opportunity for Britain. He wrote to George Hamilton-Gordon, Earl of Aberdeen and secretary of state for foreign affairs, that if Texas remained an independent state, a British colony could be developed in Texas. The colony "would render her prosperous and populous supplying to British Emigrants a new field for their industry, and to our Manufacturers a profitable Market for their goods."[47] A colony would be profitable not only for Kennedy but also for all of Britain.

Kennedy did not tarry after he received his appointment as consul and his empresario contracts. In only a few months, he built up several investors for his colonization program, two of whom were Scottish born. James H. Grieve, a lawyer, speculator, and explorer, joined Kennedy because of his interest in lands in southwest Texas. In his travels Grieve built positive relationships with Indian groups and became an important transmitter of information regarding Indian movements and motivations for Kennedy's colony.[48] Kennedy hoped that Grieve would act as diplomat with the Comanche to stem the potential of a Comanche attack that the Beales colony always faced. Additionally, Robert Robson, a Scotsman from Dumfries who became a colonel in the Texas army and gained vast wealth through slave labor, invested in Kennedy. He owned two separate plantations in Texas that produced cotton for export and likely wanted to expand his holdings to the southwest. Robson even housed and supplied the survey crews tasked with plotting the land in the contracted grants.[49] It is likely that Grieve and Robson encouraged Kennedy to recruit Scottish colonists to settle in his grant. By the summer of 1842, Kennedy made straight for Scotland to begin recruiting colonists to make good on his contract.

While only tacitly acting as a consular official between Texas and Britain, Kennedy focused on populating his empresario grant. He claimed to Lord Aberdeen that he was in Scotland to visit "old and kind friends." However, he made a point to mention that he thought organizations like the Engineers Association of Scotland "has some idea of purchasing Texas lands and planting . . . men upon them."[50] If Kennedy had an empresario contract, he could reach out to the Engineers Association for colonists. Kennedy, the savvy journalist, used his writing skills to make subtle suggestions to the British secretary of foreign affairs to benefit his empresario venture.

In addition to powerful government agents like Lord Aberdeen, Kennedy could also count on approval from Parliament to help him recruit emigrants from Scotland. By 1842 Scottish industrialization had taken off and, for the first half of the nineteenth century, Glasgow outpaced Manchester for output of textile products. Scottish success in rapidly industrializing compounded serious demographic displacements. Advances in agricultural production worldwide led to a drop in prices of the grains and oats that Scottish farms produced in the late eighteenth and early nineteenth centuries. Landowners turned to more profitable products like sheep and cattle, displacing tenant farmers who migrated to urban areas to seek work. Additionally, because Scottish industry grew so quickly and efficiently, it drew labor migrants from England, Wales, and Ireland, resulting in a broad and diverse group of extremely poor laborers in Scottish cities. While many members of Parliament agreed that the situation of the poor in Scotland needed to be rectified, few agreed on the means to do it.[51]

One method Parliament considered in rectifying the situation of the poor in Scotland was emigration. Members of the House of Commons became aware in 1842 that the Poor Laws enacted for Scotland had done little to ease conditions there as the number of those living in abject poverty increased daily. Edward Ellice, a Scottish politician and member of the Liberal Party, proposed changes to the Scottish Poor Law to allow for using public funds to assist the poor in Scotland to emigrate out of the country. He believed that publicly supported emigration policies needed to be backed with other funding to ensure that those left behind would not suffer greater destitution than before their relatives left the country. He worried deeply that the situation within the urbanized lowlands may turn "fatal to the health and tranquility of the people." Emigration along with general poor relief remained a serious option.[52]

That Ellice brought the notion of publicly funded Scottish emigration to the floor of Parliament in the summer of 1842 might not have been a coincidence. Ellice and Kennedy knew each other, as both worked on Secretary Lord Durham's diplomatic team for a year in Canada. They clearly interacted in the same social networks that revolved around Lord Durham. Kennedy probably knew that Ellice's family owned large tracts of land in both Scotland and Canada and that Ellice would be attracted to acquiring more landholdings in the Americas. It is quite possible that when Kennedy traveled to Scotland to recruit colonists, he contacted his old colleague, now seated in the House of Commons, to see what he could do to make the movement of Scottish colonists to Texas easier.[53]

Kennedy's hard work to promote his Texas lands in Scotland did not achieve the success he desired. Conflict in the Nueces Strip caused Kennedy and Lord Aberdeen significant vexation. Mexican military forces engaged in strategic raids on San Antonio and the Nueces Strip. In March 1842 General Rafael Vásquez crossed the Rio Grande and drove straight to San Antonio. The surprise attack succeeded, and he quickly took the city. Before Texas could organize a counterattack, Vásquez retreated south of the Rio Grande, taking over a hundred prisoners with him. His attack demonstrated to Texas, and Europeans watching events, that the Rio Grande proved a highly permeable boundary, if a boundary at all.[54]

Six months later Mexico drove home the point that the Rio Grande remained an insecure border. General Adrián Woll, who grew up in France and became an officer in the Mexican army, led a new assault against San Antonio in September 1842. Woll successfully captured the city, marking the second time in a year that Mexican troops occupied San Antonio. Texas volunteers quickly reacted and engaged Woll's troops in a pitched battle at Salado Creek outside the city. The Anglo-American Texans prevailed and Woll retreated back across the Rio Grande. Texas, then, took the initiative and launched an offensive on Mexican towns located south of the Rio Grande. Divided and poorly led, the Texas campaign fizzled at Mier by the end of the year. All the fighting in the Rio Grande borderlands in 1842 showed Europeans the instability of the region.[55]

By the time of Woll's invasion in September 1842, Kennedy understood that he could not introduce settlers due to "the generally disturbed state of the western country."[56] Aberdeen noticed the same and wanted a stronger British voice in both Mexico and Texas to help alleviate the violence. Rather than use Kennedy as a tool to advance British colonization to Texas, Lord Aberdeen appointed Kennedy to be the British consul general to Texas at Galveston. Aberdeen wanted Kennedy to use the influence of his book in Texas to promote a British oriented agenda in Texas. Namely, Kennedy was to boost trade between Texas and Britain and encourage Texas to adopt policies to abolish chattel slavery. Within a year Kennedy shifted positions from journalist to author to empresario to Texas consul in London to British consul in Galveston. Kennedy jumped into his new post with vigor. However, he had to rearrange his affairs as an empresario in Texas.[57]

When he acquired his post as consul at Galveston, Kennedy sold his rights to his empresario contracts but did not surrender his interests in colonizing the Rio Grande borderlands. He helped negotiate a new contract with the Texas government that put his most trusted associate and agent in London, William Pringle, as the primary empresario of record on a new conglomeration of investors interested in settling British colonists in the borderlands. William Pringle was the son of Thomas Pringle, a Scottish poet whom Kennedy admired. After Thomas Pringle's death, Kennedy wrote the epitaph for the elder Pringle's tombstone.[58] Through all the time he spent exploring the Americas, Kennedy relied on William Pringle to handle all his affairs in Britain. The new empresario contract was both a reward for Pringle's service and a way for Kennedy to remain a part of the venture. According to Lord Aberdeen, Kennedy had to contain all his business activities within the Galveston area. Wanting to retain his hold on a potentially lucrative government position, Kennedy told Lord Aberdeen that he sold his interests in lands in the Rio Grande borderlands and would confine himself to act only in the capacity as an agent of the British government.[59] Pringle, on the other hand, could act any way he pleased regarding the lands near the Rio Grande. Pringle's contract, signed November 1, 1843, was almost identical to Kennedy's contract along the Nueces River. Only the names changed. Pringle, James Grieve, and associates agreed to take on the responsibility to introduce six hundred families into the Rio Grande borderlands within three years' time.[60]

The new company executed its contract with a two-pronged strategy. Pringle handled the European operations, trying to recruit colonists to travel across the Atlantic and mobilize political forces in London to make the process as easy as possible. Grieve had the responsibility of surveying and mapping the lands to effectively be able to distribute title to the colonists who arrived. Grieve's survey team included William Bollaert, a British chemist who kept a journal of his explorations of the Kennedy grant that illustratively contrasts the company's expectations for the Rio Grande borderlands with the reality of the region.[61]

Foremost among the company's expectations was that the Rio Grande was navigable. What the survey team found on their travels never challenged their notions. Based entirely on hearsay and legend, Bollaert accepted the fact that an American navigated the river from Santa Fe to the Gulf of Mexico.[62] The survey crew never traveled far enough south to confirm or deny the legend. They remained almost entirely within the granted lands located along the Nueces River. Though Bollaert noted the severe lack of water in the region, as well as descriptions of the ease with which Mexicans forded the Rio Grande, he never once questioned in his journal whether colonists could use the river to ship their goods.[63]

The survey party's notions of the benefits of the Rio Grande played into other expectations the British surveyors had for the colony. Primarily, they believed that the settlements they built would replace San Antonio as the centers of trade in the Rio Grande borderlands. With a flare of haughtiness, Bollaert described San Antonio as a town filled with German and French merchants whom he saw as contaminated by indolence and delay. He could not believe them able to compete with a well-established British colony. He imagined that, upon the land he described as full of "God d—n mean brush"⁶⁴ and "gully after gully and no water,"⁶⁵ a thriving British town would rise to intercept the trade from throughout the Rio Grande borderlands and even draw in more of the market from Chihuahua.⁶⁶ Bollaert willingly ignored much of the hostile environment in favor of British industriousness.

The conclusion of Bollaert and Grieve's investigation of the Kennedy grant coincided with a reinvigoration of popular movements in the United States and Texas for annexation. This news riled British merchants in Texas, who organized a petition to Lord Aberdeen that should the United States annex Texas, Americans would gain a monopoly of trade in North America, cutting out all opportunities for European traders. Kennedy received the petition, had Bollaert and Grieve sign it, and forwarded it to Aberdeen. Annexation would be a total disaster for his goals in Texas. He needed the British Foreign Office to do whatever was in its power to prevent it.⁶⁷

The British project to colonize the Rio Grande borderlands deteriorated shortly after Bollaert and Grieve's investigation. By the fall of 1844, Kennedy recognized the precariousness of his grant in the path of American expansion. The piece of evidence that really spooked him was the Raleigh Letter that Henry Clay had published in the *National Intelligencer* in April 1844. Within it Clay outlined how the American people should temper their stance toward Texas. The United States had made binding international agreements to exclude Texas from its national body and should adhere to those agreements. However, Clay claimed that if any European nation attempted to colonize Texas lands, the United States should swiftly interfere. He advocated for a full call to arms to prevent foreign powers from subjugating Texas.⁶⁸ Clay, who everyone understood to be against Texas annexation, would compromise his stance if it meant keeping Europeans, particularly the British, out of the Americas to forward his American system of building a strong domestic American market.⁶⁹

After reading Clay's speech, Kennedy distanced himself and the British government from the Texas empresario program. As the British consul general to Texas, Kennedy had far more invested in Texas than just his empresario grant. His entire diplomatic career revolved around an open relationship between Texas and Britain. The last thing he wanted to do was be responsible for turning one of the most powerful men in the United States into a proponent for US expansion into Texas. Kennedy turned his attention to the possibility of expanding sugar production in Texas, hoping to encourage Anglo-American Texans to remain independent from the United States with offers of low tariff rates on both cotton and sugar. His political machinations were in vain.[70]

Kennedy's hopes for Texas died when the United States Congress passed the annexation bill on the last day of February of 1845. All Texas empresario contracts were put on notice for termination. The Texas state constitution soon after made it official, suspending all colonization contracts made by the Republic of Texas. Colonists who had settled retained their rights to the land, but contractors had to pursue legal recourse with the state of Texas to receive any indemnity. Texas was to become a part of the United States. There would be no more European state agents attempting to formally colonize north of the Rio Grande.[71]

✺ ✺ ✺ ✺ ✺

Bourgeois, Ducos, and Kennedy failed to fulfill their empresario contracts and attain wealth through vast tracts of Texas land. Bourgeois and Ducos manipulated powerful French and German leaders to support their settlement scheme. Bourgeois particularly became trapped within his own web of misrepresentation. Kennedy's failure proved personally disastrous because he lost his empresario grant and blundered his primary agenda as consul general to Texas. Kennedy gambled on the geopolitics of expanding immigration to the Rio Grande borderlands and lost to American expansionism. However, all their schemes reveal how European borderlands entrepreneurs sought to modernize the Rio Grande into a new European market. Bourgeois and Ducos anticipated how significant Port Isabel would become to Rio Grande shipping. Kennedy utilized his publications to both generate interest in the region and promote modernization through English industriousness. He and his colleagues believed the English culture of hard work would reform the borderlands into a center for Atlantic trade. All the failures of these European borderlands entrepreneurs expose the ways in which they envisioned Europe's place in the future of the American frontier.

From the time of José de Escandón's mixed colonies to William Kennedy's paper colony without colonists, European-born entrepreneurs viewed the Rio Grande borderlands as a space of great potential that needed European settlement to make it into an integral source of natural resources and a market for European products. Problematically for the borderlands entrepreneurs who undertook the risk, formal colonization met with only limited success and resulted in many failures. Indigenous power, limited state influence, and misinformation all contributed to their lack of success. Regardless, their colonization strategies maintained European interest and presence in the region. The failed colonization projects contributed to growing communities of European-born borderlands entrepreneurs in already-established settlements in the region. These communities networked together to reform the borderlands into the commercial utopia Europeans had imagined since 1749.

PART 2

Networks, Modernity, and Economic Expansion

Chapter 4

Constructing Transnational Entrepreneurial Networks

Texas annexation and the subsequent US-Mexico War drove home the point to the entire world that the United States was going to try to control all of the territory down to the Rio Grande. Anglo-Americans wanted to push the US market southwest to the Rio Grande and beyond to sell US-made manufactures in the borderlands. US-born speculators who came to the Rio Grande during the war believed that "the true wealth of these localities, should they ever be made, must be drawn from Mexican coffers, in exchange for domestic manufactures."[1] Anglo-American merchants followed on the heels of US troops to the Rio Grande borderlands. Together, the US Army and a growing US-born merchant elite set about trying to remake the region into an American space and exploit the Mexican population living there.[2]

Across the Rio Grande Mexicans had to pick up the pieces of the US-Mexico War. The United States ripped away half of Mexico's territory. Riots broke out across the country. Guerrilla warfare spread from the Yucatán to Central Mexico. Indigenous raiding reduced several northern Mexican settlements to ashes. Mexican leaders worried they faced a national revolution and the dissolution of their nation. To compound the problems, political factionalism limited pathways toward security. Regional leaders took it in their own hands to bring a semblance of peace and boost their personal power. However, they were often unstable and corrupt. Mexican-born inhabitants on both sides of the river sought some sort of surety in the postwar borderlands.[3]

European-born borderlands entrepreneurs adapted to the changing political economy by focusing on competing commercially with Anglo-Americans by importing European manufactures and providing an alternative for Mexican buyers. European merchants and traders had long been in the Rio Grande borderlands. However, the role of commerce took on new dimensions after the US-Mexico War. European migrants who moved to the region at the time wrote home trying to explain conditions in the borderlands to their peers: "An enormous rudeness is generally prevalent in this country. Nobody cares about enlightenment and education. Nobody lives intellectually. Everybody strives for money and for money only. Money is the idol that is worshipped."[4] The Anglo-American goal to push their manufactures in the region created an atmosphere where success meant seeking trade for profit.[5]

To keep a foothold in the newly US-dominated region, European-born borderlands entrepreneurs created vast interlocking, multiethnic networks that combined family, state, and business connections. Mercantile networks built on trust led to high levels of exchange frequency. European-born entrepreneurs built strong networks among themselves that often included Mexican elites. They also maintained connections with their respective states. In building their networks, European-born borderlands entrepreneurs successfully competed with the Anglo-American merchant elite and contributed significantly to the globalization of the Rio Grande.[6]

Two very different networks established on the Rio Grande enticed global forces to the Lower Rio Grande. The first, centered in Matamoros and Brownsville, became one of the vastest mercantile networks in the entire borderlands. Spanish-born José San Román began by creating transatlantic connections and then tying them into local networks he built on an ad hoc basis. His Atlantic connections provided him with the material for exchange in the local market. Often he sold his inventories through credit mechanisms that drew smaller merchants into his sphere of influence. He globalized business on the Rio Grande by drawing Americans, Mexicans, and Europeans into his systems of credit and material exchange.

Another much smaller network in Laredo highlights the essential contributions of tightly knit multiethnic family connections to constructing a transnational business in the borderlands. The German-speaking John Z. Leyendecker pieced together his mercantile operation through marriage and family connections. He began locally by earning the trust of Mexican elites in Laredo and then sought to tap into broader American and European networks. Both San Román's and Leyendecker's experiences show how European-born entrepreneurs used multilayered, interconnected systems to profitably connect Europeans, Anglo-Americans, and Mexicans together and make the Rio Grande borderlands a center of Atlantic trade.[7]

Through their alliances, European-born borderlands entrepreneurs tied the region together and served as an alternative to the Anglo-American merchant elite. They pushed back against US expansion and enmeshed the Rio Grande borderlands in Atlantic markets. Both San Román and Leyendecker made connections as local as their neighbors and as global as merchant houses in Paris and Amsterdam. They also utilized their connections within American and European states to support their businesses. San Román and Leyendecker pursued and offered opportunities for those disillusioned with the new US commercial order to seek different pathways for exchange.

The US-Mexico War reshaped the Rio Grande borderlands, particularly Laredo and Matamoros, where Leyendecker and San Román began their respective businesses. The US occupation of northern Mexico resulted in the establishment of permanent military garrisons, turned the river itself into a national boundary, and reorganized trade patterns. In Laredo the US Army built Camp Crawford on the western outskirts of the town, which became the permanent site for Fort McIntosh. The camp and subsequent fort gave Laredo ranchers and merchants a ready local market for goods they never had before. Rather than having to ship everything north and south along the former Camino Real, which the US Army rebuilt as the San Antonio Road, Laredoans could produce and sell goods in their own neighborhood. The army brought a considerable boon to the local economy.[8]

Matamoros experienced the US military occupation differently. The army constructed more efficient roads that cut travel times significantly. Soldier-laborers built new paths from Matamoros to San Antonio, Corpus Christi, and Monterrey. Wagon trains could move goods more quickly and safely inland than ever before. Furthermore, Matamoros merchants benefited directly from US military occupation. Not only could they now sell to American military personnel, but also Mexican customs houses closed when US forces captured the city. Goods imported from the United States and Europe entered the Mexican port duty-free for more than an entire year. Merchants fortified trade connections with ports all over the Atlantic at virtually tariff-free rates, making Matamoros a popular entrepôt for goods going into Mexico.[9]

For the Rio Grande borderlands, the most important results of the war came with the Treaty of Guadalupe Hidalgo. In the treaty the United States and Mexico agreed to use the Rio Grande as a boundary between the two nation-states, which meant that Laredo fell into the United States while Matamoros remained in Mexico. However, the river remained a permeable fixture, as goods and people moved back and forth across it regardless of nationality. The boundary was too big and the need for goods and labor too strong. Instead of suppressing trade, the border stimulated a rapid commercial increase because it encouraged construction developments, sparked transnational trade, and promised greater protections against Indigenous raiding.[10]

The imposition of the border set off a construction boom as people along the river began to build sister cities for those across the border. For example, former Mexican leaders in Laredo expanded upon parts of the city built south of the Rio Grande and dubbed the town Nuevo Laredo. North of Matamoros, entrepreneurial Anglo-Americans began constructing the town of Brownsville as an American port to compete with Matamoros. Similar towns popped up all along the Lower Rio Grande in response to the new boundary. Each new town required significant material imports to survive and relied on regional merchants to provide for them.[11]

In addition to establishing the Rio Grande as a boundary, the treaty also encouraged commerce between the United States and Mexico by canceling all Mexican debts to the United States and reinstating the Treaty of Amity, Commerce, and Navigation between the United States and Mexico for eight years. Respect for trade, protections of property, and liberty of mobility between both nations became hallmarks of the peace agreement that proved difficult to change. When the United States or Mexico attempted to impose broad tariffs, merchants turned to smuggling to ensure continued movement of goods. European-born entrepreneurs in both the United States and Mexico took advantage of the permeable border to move their products as the market demanded.[12]

Finally, the treaty established that the United States would restrain and punish Indigenous incursions into Mexico. This article of the treaty ensured a prolonged US military presence along the border. It also promised merchants a feeling of security in opening trading relationships with Indigenous people since both they and Indigenous people knew that any violence would be quickly rebuked. The Comanche, still an extremely powerful society in the borderlands in the 1850s, held tremendous wealth in horses and cattle. European-born entrepreneurs built and maintained trading connections with Plains Indians in the shadows of US Army forts.[13]

The war and subsequent treaty transformed the political economy of the borderlands in significant ways. It established US sovereignty down to the Rio Grande, ensured a presence of US military personnel, and encouraged a broad class of Anglo-American merchants to migrate to the region to capitalize on the nation's postwar expansion. Yet the imposition of the border did not make the region a bordered land. The people who lived there continued to live by the borderland's dynamics of spatial mobility, intercultural exchange, and ambiguous power relations. The Lower Rio Grande was still thoroughly a borderland.[14]

European-born entrepreneurs who migrated to the region had to find the best way to succeed within these new conditions. They had little trouble improvising, as European entrepreneurs all over the world in the mid-nineteenth century worked to gain access to peripheral markets. Some turned to constructing commercial alliances to compete with Anglo-Americans. Others sought marriage and kinship relationships among the Mexican elite to establish themselves. Europeans formed a significant portion of the population who had to find a way to flourish on the Rio Grande.[15]

Spanish entrepreneur José San Román lived most of his life through tumultuous times. Born in Bilbao in 1822, San Román grew up in one of Spain's most important trading centers. Merchants of the city had long participated in the coastal trade with France and developed strong connections with British exporters. In the Basque region of Spain, Bilbao acted as a borderlands transfer center of material and cultural exchange. Marked by constant conflict during San Román's childhood, Bilbao was laid under siege four separate times during the Carlist wars between 1833 and 1839. San Román left the violence of his birthplace to seek opportunity in North America.[16]

The Spaniard moved to New Orleans in the late 1830s to apprentice with an English merchandising firm, Thorn and McGrath. His apprenticeship reached maturation just as the US-Mexico War broke out. Thorn and McGrath wanted an agent of its own on the Rio Grande to capitalize on the conflict. Soldiers carried money and wanted to spend it. The Anglo New Orleans company was more than willing to offer its dry goods stock on consignment to San Román knowing that he was multilingual and had contacts at the Spanish consulate in Matamoros. Fluent in Spanish, English, and French, he could communicate to sell to Mexican and American troops. R. H. Thorn was personally excited to give San Román the opportunity to figure out how best to capitalize on the American war with Mexico to make the company a fine return on its investment.[17]

San Román, who came from a border region in Europe, quickly learned how to be a successful merchant in the American borderlands. He observed that Matamoros was an itinerant town. Soldiers, merchants, journalists, speculators, and adventurers all came through the port during the war years. They needed a place to stay and somewhere to resupply. Within his first year there, he moved his store from near the river, where Thorn and McGrath suggested, to Calle Comercio (modern day Calle González), right across from the Exchange Hotel. The Exchange Hotel was an important meeting place for people from all over the world and was near the municipal center of town. He also became more assertive about the stock his patrons sent him. No more would he receive merino coats or bulky travel trunks. He ordered cotton shirts and pants, cloth caps, parasols, and other products that made sense for northern Mexico's climate and the market to which he catered. Lastly, he learned the value of credit. Completely ignoring an explicit warning from Thorn and McGrath to trade only in hard currency, San Román extended credit to clients who seemed reliable. He quickly found that being a node in the movement of debt around the borderlands proved to be profitable and enlightening. In just his brief few months in town in 1846, he managed to sell $3,524.89 in goods on credit, on which he charged a reasonable 5 percent interest. Through his network of debtors, he learned which markets were growing the fastest in the Rio Grande borderlands. With his extra profits and knowledge of the region, the Spaniard got out from under his first commission in little over a year and looked to expand beyond Matamoros.[18]

Levee Street, Brownsville, Texas, 1865. Louis de Planque, *Levee Street, Brownsville, Texas*, 1864–1866, Lawrence T. Jones III Texas Photography Collection, DeGolyer Library, SMU.

San Román first recognized the new market growing right across the river in Brownsville and moved to capitalize on it. Initially he tried to hire a reliable commission merchant to take his goods on consignment to open shop in Brownsville. This way someone else would do all the work of founding a new store while San Román reaped the profit. However, he found nobody he could trust to complete the expansion for him and decided to open a Brownsville store himself. By January 1850 San Román owned storefronts in both Matamoros and Brownsville.[19]

Having commercial houses in both Matamoros and Brownsville put San Román in direct competition with the most dominant members of the Anglo-American merchant elite in the Rio Grande borderlands. Charles Stillman and Mifflin Kenedy formed the center of a commercial network that sought to monopolize trade on the Lower Rio Grande and cut out all other competitors. Connecticut merchant Charles Stillman founded Brownsville to draw trade away from Matamoros into a US port. He helped fund Mexican entrepreneur Francisco Yturria to open one of the first successful banks in Brownsville to capitalize on the dual-currency nature of the borderlands. Meanwhile, Kenedy earned nearly every US Army transportation contract and purchased majority stakes in all the steamships that plied the Lower Rio Grande until he and his partners controlled the means of travel from the Gulf of Mexico to the ports at Matamoros and Brownsville and beyond. Stillman and his associates developed a trade nexus in the Rio Grande delta that spread throughout the United States and Mexico. San Román had to connect with Europeans and Mexicans to compete.[20]

The Spanish-born entrepreneur realized his advantage lay in his transatlantic connections. San Román pushed himself to look outward from the Rio Grande delta to tap into his family networks and connections through Thorn and McGrath. He first utilized the mobility and expertise of his cousin, Augustin San Román, to integrate his firm more deeply into the Atlantic trade. Augustin San Román had followed José into an apprenticeship in New Orleans with a Spanish merchant house, Caballero and Company. Afterward they partnered to connect the Rio Grande stores with some of the biggest markets in the Western Hemisphere. Augustin traveled to New York, Monterrey, and Paris to find suppliers for the goods most in demand on the Rio Grande—namely, British textiles, Mexican silver, and French wine. Through the connections Augustin built, José San Román was able to market the most popular products at some of the best prices, pulling the region more deeply into the Atlantic market.[21]

José San Román also had a close family friend starting commercial activities in Havana. Simón Celaya traveled from New Orleans to Cuba as a commission merchant for Thorn and McGrath around the same time San Román went to the Rio Grande.[22] Celaya and San Román found that both their ventures became more profitable when they worked together. Celaya sold his stock for as much tobacco as he could get and shipped that across the Gulf of Mexico for San Román to sell at higher margins in Matamoros. They ran their tobacco scheme for several years until San Román's storefronts in Matamoros and Brownsville grew too large for him to manage alone. By the end of the 1850s, Celaya moved to the Rio Grande to manage one of San Román's stores. That did not end his connections with Havana, though. Celaya continued to import Cuban tobacco to sell in San Román's stores at cut-rate prices. The San Román merchant house became a popular supplier of clothing, tobacco, and alcohol. His family and kinship networks paid dividends.[23]

Maintaining his connections to Thorn and McGrath also proved to be a boon to San Román's growing mercantile operation. When he finished paying off his initial commission, he could have gone his own way and cut ties with his former bosses. By remaining in communication and continuing to order supplies from them, San Román benefited when Michael McGrath expanded to New York City. McGrath opened a clothing firm with Scottish entrepreneur Robert Tweed. When their business expanded to New York from New Orleans, San Román gained access to partners he could trust in two of the largest markets in the United States. Both McGrath and Tweed also had connections with firms in London, Liverpool, and Manchester that he could exploit. His family and business connections to the Atlantic market gave him an edge he needed to compete with the Stillman syndicate in the Rio Grande borderlands.[24]

As San Román built the foundations of his Atlantic commercial networks in the years following the US-Mexico War, Anglo-American elites, including the Charles Stillman business group, worked to solidify their political and economic hold locally. They moved into positions of local government, helped impose the US judicial system, and controlled law enforcement. The Stillman syndicate integrated with the new Anglo-American political elite through the practice of lawyers who ensured their land investments and privileged trading status remained intact. The founder of Brownsville sought to make the town he created the seat of a regional commercial empire. Stillman and his allies' local power grew steadily after the war, often crushing outsiders and upstart merchants before they became a threat.[25]

To remain relevant on the Rio Grande, San Román needed to develop his network within the borderlands to build on his customer base and tap into local information flows. His transatlantic connections were meaningless without local allies. He exerted great effort to link with other European-born entrepreneurs he could trust to create an organization to counter Stillman. Utilizing his multilingual skills and ability to manage credit, San Román connected with British, French, and Spanish merchants in the region. In doing so he pushed against the Anglo-American merchant elite. By the end of the 1850s, San Román sat in the center of a web of commercial activity in the Rio Grande borderlands.

The Basque entrepreneur believed the river transportation business to be the best foundation from which to organize Europeans in the borderlands to launch a counter to the Stillman syndicate. San Román initially allied with an American ship captain James B. Armstrong, who won a US Army contract over Kenedy's company. The Armstrong contract provided the sliver of hope for breaking down the Stillman syndicate's transportation monopoly. Armstrong earned the right to pilot boats loaded with goods to provide for the US forts on the Rio Grande. He and San Román put together an investment group of European-born entrepreneurs—including French merchant Theophile Delmas, the Spanish de la Vegas brothers, and the Scottish John Young—to purchase the ships *Swan* and *Guadalupe*. Those two steamships' physical presence on the Rio Grande represented an open challenge to the Anglo-American merchant elite. They also offered an alternative to the American shipping monopoly.[26]

John Young proved to be an important early ally for San Román's steamship scheme. Young moved to the Rio Grande borderlands before the US-Mexico War and bought land north of Matamoros. He built positive relationships with members of the Ballí family. The Ballís had remained one of the most powerful families in the Rio Grande borderlands since the days of Escandón, primarily through their ability to acquire and exploit land. Young ingratiated himself to the Ballí family and married Salomé Ballí. The marriage proved mutually beneficial. Through building kinship ties with a prominent and long-established Mexican family, Young expanded his land acquisitions. Intermarriage with European-born entrepreneurs like Young provided a protection for the Ballís to retain their land and social status in the face of American encroachment. Rather than rest on their already vast landholdings, Salomé and John Young continued to purchase land under US jurisdiction, acquiring land titles sealed by the state of Texas to avoid any American attempts to usurp their land.[27]

In addition to his landholdings, Young ran a small trade route along the Rio Grande and tried to construct a town northwest of Brownsville. The Stillman syndicate's monopoly on Rio Grande steamboat transportation caused him considerable vexation. Kenedy's shipping company charged exorbitant prices to ship to Young's landing on the Rio Grande. Kenedy's and Stillman's interests centered in Brownsville and another nearby town would undermine their plans. By 1855 Young, with the Ballís backing, sought entry into the river transportation market. He engaged San Román and became a primary investor in San Román's fledgling steamship company. Together they offered legitimate competition to the Stillman syndicate for river transport.[28]

With their own steamships plying the river, San Román, John Young, and their network of investors served the demands of the US Army and became key providers of essential goods for the Lower Rio Grande. Armstrong used San Román's boats to supply the quartermasters at Fort Brown and Fort Ringgold outside of Rio Grande City with all the matériel to maintain their troop numbers. They also shipped goods to civilian customers. A key item for their freight business included lumber. The Rio Grande borderlands lacked significant tree sources other than mesquite, driving builders who wanted European-style buildings to import most of their lumber. Demand was such that San Román's boats pulled in about $350 a month just shipping lumber upriver.[29]

Stillman and Kenedy cracked back against San Román's European-owned steamship company. They went directly to the Quartermaster Department of the US Army to get Armstrong's contract transferred to the Kenedy company. Through outright bribes, Kenedy convinced the officers at Fort Brown to draw up orders to have San Román's ships inspected. The inspectors declared the boats to be unsuitable and recommended canceling Armstrong's contract. In response San Román sued both Kenedy's company and the Quartermaster Department. He and his investors earned $17,000 from the US government and, after a settlement, a 12 percent share in the Kenedy shipping company.[30]

San Román's venture into the river transport business demonstrated that European-born entrepreneurs in the Rio Grande could challenge Anglo-Americans' push to dominate the region. Though the company ultimately dissolved, they won recognition from the US government and cut into the Stillman syndicate's profits. San Román and his investors earned a monthly income from Kenedy's ships. The results of the settlement also drew Stillman and San Román into cooperative agreements. Rather than destructive competition and costly court battles, the two sides entered a period of détente that lasted until the end of the US Civil War. Further, San Román's brief stint as a riverboat owner put him in contact with European-born entrepreneurs upriver who became prospective connections to build his local network.

One of San Román's most profitable upriver contacts was French-born John Decker. Decker migrated to the region as a baker but transitioned into a merchant by the mid-1850s. He moved to the newly founded town of Rio Grande City and, like Young, married a Mexican woman. Using his wife's family contacts, Decker deeply integrated himself into the Mexican community around Rio Grande City and Camargo. The Frenchman found a rich market there for textiles and started a business selling cloth and finished clothing. However, he needed additional startup funding to turn a real profit. He turned to San Román to provide goods and credit to get his enterprise off the ground.[31]

Credit became an essential resource in the borderlands in the 1850s. The end of the war and the gold rush in California slowed the movement of currency into the borderlands. The Commercial and Agricultural Bank of Galveston was one of the only US bank branches on the Rio Grande in the 1850s, and it folded in 1858. There were banks in San Antonio and Monterrey, but they tended to refuse to loan to clients on the Rio Grande, fearing their investment would disappear. Thus the control of credit fell into the hands of local merchants like San Román or Charles Stillman. To get a loan, an individual had to be a known entity, someone the merchant-lender could trust. Often, gaining that trust meant finding access to the merchant's network.[32]

San Román had earned the luxury to grow more careful about to whom he lent money. Though he always needed to make positive connections in the borderlands to remain competitive, he wanted every connection to pay off. Decker worked hard to gain the Spaniard's trust and made several maneuvers to enter San Román's network. First, he found a partner in fellow Frenchman Francois Bichotte. Bichotte had experience as a barkeep and grocer. They combined their acumen to open a store in Rio Grande City. The new partners got started through microloans from small merchants in Brownsville, like the German Conrad Bloom and fellow Frenchman Victor Hasslauer. Both Bloom and Hasslauer had larger accounts with San Román. Rather than pay Bloom and Hasslauer back directly, Decker and Bichotte remitted payment to San Román to have him apply the credits to Bloom's and Hasslauer's accounts. Bichotte and Decker's payments demonstrated to San Román their reliability. Further, they showed the success of the business when they sold over $1,700 worth of goods to the Mexican consul in Brownsville, Manuel Treviño, who also had an open account with San Román. The Treviño sale earned Decker and Bichotte a significant line of credit with San Román.[33]

Incorporating Decker into his network of European-born entrepreneurs proved to be extremely profitable for San Román. Decker's small mercantile house struck it rich during the US Civil War by buying and selling cotton at an important crossroads in the Confederate cotton trade. Decker took his cotton profits and invested in expanding his stores and buying land. By 1874 he was considered by one of the leading providers of commercial data in North America as the richest merchant in Rio Grande City. Decker became a lasting and powerful node in San Román's network in the Rio Grande borderlands.[34]

In addition to his British and French associates, San Román made sure to connect with his fellow Spanish expats within the borderlands. Entrepreneurial Spanish set up houses in most of the major cities in northern Mexico. Vicente Lauregue in Montemorelos took a line of credit from San Román of over $1,700.[35] Additionally, Manuel Dosal in Ciudad Victoria and San Román helped each other track individual debtors and their accounts. The Spanish in the borderlands stuck together, shared information, and lent money. Their shared national origin contributed to a foundation for trust in trade.[36]

Most of San Román's Spanish contacts in Mexico were based in Monterrey. The historic crossroads of New Spain's northern road system, Monterrey benefited most from the imposition of the border at the Rio Grande. Primarily, it liberated merchants in the city from the customs duties imposed at Matamoros as more Anglo-American and Mexican smugglers forded goods across the river for trade in Monterrey. A trio of Spaniards—Mariano Hernandez, Valentín Rivero, and Francisco Armendaiz—took advantage of the rampant smuggling market. They found a mutually beneficial relationship with American cotton growers in Texas by founding a textile factory in Monterrey. Planters made a little extra shipping their product tariff free, and the Monterrey merchants saved significantly on both the raw cotton and exporting the finished textiles. The smuggling trade within European networks tied the Rio Grande borderlands together.[37]

Smuggling became big business along the border in the 1850s. Mexico, in dire financial straits after the US-Mexico War, began imposing high tariffs as early as 1849. To ensure merchants paid their duties, the Mexican central government also introduced a permit system that required all freighters to announce the precise route of their shipments and carry a permit that indicated they had done so. The burdensome cost of tariffs and the risk of highway robbery with the permit system encouraged smuggling. As more robberies were reported on the roadways, fewer Europeans applied for permits.[38] Moving goods illegally came at much less cost. The illicit trade became so profitable during the 1850s that it underpinned the successful development of the towns of Roma and Rio Grande City in Texas. Often, European-born entrepreneurs, particularly in Monterrey, facilitated the illegal trade across the Rio Grande as overland routes led to that central city.[39]

Problematically for San Román, the smuggling networks that ran to Monterrey often bypassed Matamoros/Brownsville.[40] San Román remained connected to the Monterrey trade by moving goods upriver, then having them smuggled across the border. In one case Mariano Hernandez was quite specific about how he wanted an order of dry goods shipped. He demanded San Román ship his goods via the carrier Don Fernandez, who would move the shipment up to Roma. From there Hernandez was confident that "in Mier there is a safe person to do the importation."[41] The border and national tariffs gave San Román incentive to inefficiently move goods northwest from Brownsville to cross the Rio Grande at Mier to reach the final destination to the southwest in Monterrey.

The Basque trader from Bilbao probably had few qualms about smuggling and had likely learned tricks for the illicit trade back home. The smuggling of goods had been a part of Basque culture since the establishment of the Spanish-French border in 1512. The Basques developed strategies for continuing the smuggling trade in the face of increased state presence. For the most part, San Román tried to appear to adhere to the letter of the law and pay his taxes. He kept detailed records of the Mexican tariff schedules and went through legal means to petition unfair rates.[42] He also legitimately shipped tobacco, an item that Mexico highly regulated, to Monterrey straight from Matamoros.[43] San Román's penchant for making the illicit trade look legal helped him build a positive reputation among state agents and other merchants.[44]

To stem the contraband trade, the Mexican state of Tamaulipas declared a free-trade zone (*zona libre*) in 1858 along the portion of the south bank of the Rio Grande from Laredo down to the delta. Minus a small municipal tax that importers had to pay to local governments, merchants could move their goods freely into northern Mexico. Many merchants took advantage. San Román moved entire inventories he had stored in Brownsville across to Matamoros. He also imported all his stock straight to the Matamoros store and likely smuggled the merchandise he needed in Brownsville across the river. The free-trade zone shifted the flows of contraband trade from south to north.[45]

By the end of the 1850s, San Román had solidified his commercial position in the region. He constructed a vast network that connected Europeans, Mexicans, and Anglo-Americans in a web of exchange. He began by bringing his Atlantic connections to the borderlands, then branching out locally. His networks helped him harness the powers of credit and lower his transportation costs through direct competition with the Stillman syndicate and smuggling. Though always aware of his position in the relationships he built, San Román slowly included a diverse group of individuals into his systems of credit and exchange. The Spanish-born borderlands entrepreneur prodded the region a little closer toward Atlantic markets.

As another example, John Z. Leyendecker represents how a European-born entrepreneur used marriage and the construction of local kinship networks to build a transnational business in the Rio Grande borderlands in the 1850s. Kinship ties were critical in Laredo because of its relative isolation and characteristic self-sufficiency until the US-Mexico War. Leyendecker worked within the traditional kinship structures and ingratiated himself to the Benavides family and other prominent members of the community. With the family's economic resources, social connections, and political clout behind him, Leyendecker grew his business and connected it firmly to international markets.[46]

Laredo's geographic placement forced it to be self-sufficient and made the town vulnerable to the constant threat of Indian attack. The town originated far from the rest of José de Escandón's original settlements. Tomás Sanchez founded Laredo north of the Rio Grande and far from the Gulf of Mexico. Its isolation bred a tendency among its residents to eschew outside influence, which carried over through the Mexican period and into the 1850s. Consistent Indian raids also increased Laredo's penchant for isolation. Comanche and Apache raiding parties ranged into the settlement, stealing horses and cattle. Sometimes they even captured Laredoans to kill, enslave, or trade. Indian raiding created a demand for trust networks and wariness of strangers. Laredo's history of self-sufficiency and Indian raiding forced its families to remain close to one another.[47]

Even though the US military occupation brought a modicum of economic integration and protection from Indians, Laredo faced new challenges heading into the 1850s. Laredo attracted newcomers willing to take advantage of the economic growth that Fort McIntosh brought, which made the local population nervous. Leaders in the town quickly tried to stem the tide of strangers entering and leaving the town for fear of theft and violence. The board of aldermen passed a resolution in 1850 requiring all strangers in town to register with city officials. By 1854 the push to limit strangers in Laredo turned into full-blown vagrancy laws that led to indefinite incarceration of strangers until town leaders could ascertain their honesty. Unlike Matamoros, which had become a cosmopolitan port city that embraced Atlantic trade, Laredo was generally not a welcoming place to outsiders.[48]

Laredo's isolation and cold embrace of migrants helped prevent a Stillman-like rise of an American merchant monopoly. Many of the Anglo-Americans to settle in Laredo after the US-Mexico War came from the ranks of the army. Few others saw the same opportunities in Laredo as those in Brownsville. Some opened small mercantile operations, but those targeted supplying Fort McIntosh. Most Anglo-Americans in Laredo pursued political rather than economic power. To attain it they had to win over the majority Mexican populace. As one historian of Laredo concluded, "They [Americans] often appeared more Mexicanized than *mexicanos* appeared Americanized."[49] Laredo resisted rapid shifts to the American commercial and political order.[50]

John Z. Leyendecker, born in the Duchy of Nassau in 1827, chose to make Laredo the home of his budding mercantile enterprise.

His family moved to Fredericksburg, Texas, in 1845. At the conclusion of the US-Mexico War, he executed an effective endeavor on the Texas Plains outside of the US Fort Chadbourne at Oak Creek. Built with another European-born entrepreneur, Anton Wulff in San Antonio, the Oak Creek store profited through trade with the US Army and Plains Indians. Though he described them as Chichimecas in his account books, the location of Leyendecker's store likely served Comanche and Kiowa bands. Indians sought out goods like food, bridles, and umbrellas, for which they traded horses and animal hide. When he could get away with it, Leyendecker sold beer and whiskey to his Native American customers. That type of trade, though, could get his store shuttered, as the US Army discouraged Indian drunkenness. Leyendecker received a stern letter from the commander at Fort Chadbourne to cease sale of any alcohol to Indians, stating, "The laws of the United States regulating the intercourse of trade with Indians forbids the selling or trading of whiskey, or any ardent spirits." To keep his business with the personnel at the fort, he did as he was told. For the most part, the Oak Creek store engaged in legitimate exchange with Indians and soldiers on the far west Texas frontier.[51]

Leyendecker had to work through a cost-benefit analysis of moving to Laredo in 1854. The Oak Creek store broke even in 1853 and showed the possibility of profiting the next year. The price for animal skins was on the rise and his customer base already established. However, the store retained a low profit ceiling. Fort Chadbourne sometimes only held as few as fifty men, and the Plains Indians' migration patterns shifted regularly. Fort McIntosh outside Laredo maintained higher troop rolls than Fort Chadbourne, and Leyendecker could still trade with Indigenous people around Laredo. The additional benefits of being nearer settled populations and the Rio Grande proved enticing. Leyendecker could also bring the full benefits of his multilingual upbringing to the Rio Grande. He was fluent in German, English, Spanish, and French. Wulff, who invested in Leyendecker and trusted him after the semisuccessful venture at Oak Creek, encouraged the move south. Together the European-born entrepreneurs would try their luck in the Rio Grande borderlands.[52]

When Leyendecker arrived in Laredo, he realized opening a successful store there would be much more difficult than his Oak Creek venture. Anglo-Americans already cornered the market to supply Fort McIntosh. Other Europeans, too, had carved out a market in Laredo. For example, Raymond Martin was one of the first Euro-American merchants to settle in Laredo after the US-Mexico War. Born in Auzas in Southern France in 1828, Martin immigrated to the United States with his two brothers in the early 1850s. He attempted to settle in Pensacola and New Orleans before he finally found success in Laredo. He opened a small store in Laredo in 1854 and slowly built up a merchant business. At the time, his was one of only three outlets for finished goods in the region. Martin would eventually create a ranching empire that dominated the South Texas market.[53]

The best opportunity Leyendecker saw was trying to enter the local network and marketing to the local populace. To do so he had to ingratiate himself to the local elite. Initially he rented a house from Josefa Treviño, who likely explained to him the politics of the town.[54] The Treviños had been in Laredo since the days of Escandón and carried significant political clout. The family worked to maintain its role in town after the American occupation as Tomás Treviño was mayor and Albino Treviño held the position of justice of the peace through the 1850s.[55]

The Treviños were close to another family, the Benavideses, which likely helped facilitate Leyendecker's relationship with them. Santos Benavides did not particularly like the way other merchants in town did business and sought another outlet to buy the goods he needed. Trust meant as much to Benavides as it did to the rest of the Laredo inhabitants. He thought Leyendecker might be a merchant he could trust in Laredo.[56]

In addition to his connection through Treviño, Leyendecker's Catholicism further aided his character reference. He made his Catholicism a part of his personal record. His family kept documentation of his baptism, first communion, and confirmation. Additionally, in his memorandum book, Leyendecker cataloged these early steps of Catholic ritual by defining which churches, priests, and sponsors were associated with his ascent to full church membership. The German's religious background also helped him make business connections in town outside the Benavides family. Benito García commented that he appreciated Leyendecker's religion as a part of their pleasant trade relationship. Since all the original families who settled Laredo practiced Catholicism, Leyendecker's own religious affiliation contributed to his inclusion.[57]

For Santos and the rest of the Benavides family, kinship cemented trust. Creating kinship ties through marriage became essential to the perseverance of Laredoans because of the town's isolation and the people's fear of outsiders. Santos's grandfather, José Benavides, moved to Laredo as an outsider near the end of the eighteenth century. In order to become a part of the town, he had to become a member of one of the trusted families. The elder Benavides married Tomás Sánchez's granddaughter, Petra Sánchez, creating a permanent kinship network with an elite local family. Leyendecker needed to do more than be Catholic and a good merchant to earn Santos Benavides's trust.[58]

Overall, it made practical sense for Leyendecker to pursue marriage with a Benavides, but it helped that Leyendecker was smitten with Santos's younger sister. Leyendecker began courting María Andrea Benavides in late 1856. They apparently got along rather well. It seems that Leyendecker mentioned her often in his letters to his business partners, who encouraged the German to have a "short court."[59]

María Andrea Benavides, born November 10, 1835, was the first daughter to José and María Tomasa Benavides and was eight years younger than Leyendecker. She received a Catholic education in Galveston under the tutelage of Jean-Marie Odin, the first Catholic bishop in Texas. She was smart, well-cultured, and loyal to her family. She fell deeply in love with Leyendecker as their relationship progressed and wrote him often when he was away on business. She missed him such that "time does not move when you are not with me."⁶⁰ The courting period only lasted about six months, as Leyendecker and María Andrea Benavides wed in June of 1857. The marriage solidified Leyendecker's inclusion into the Benavides family and Laredo networks through kinship.⁶¹

Their marriage declared the union to the entire town and was also meant to tie the Leyendeckers of Fredericksburg with the Benavideses in Laredo. They were wed at three o'clock in the morning on Pentecost Monday in the parish church in Laredo with Santos Benavides and his wife as sponsors and Leyendecker's pastor from Fredericksburg as a witness. Pentecost Sunday, or Whitsunday, is a festival event for the Catholic Church that commemorates the descent of the Holy Ghost on the apostles. Pentecost Sunday marks such an important day that the day after, Whitmonday, is devoted as an Order of Worship. Whitmonday has been especially important for Germans, as that day remains a formal civic holiday in Germany. The wedding day and time shows that the families wanted the union on a particularly holy day and, by holding the ceremony on Whitmonday, recognized the inclusion of the German Catholic heritage into the Benavides's Spanish Catholic tradition.⁶²

After their marriage María Andrea moved into the house Leyendecker leased from Josefa Treviño and helped him with his business. She received and organized his letters and communications and worked as a go-between for her husband and her family when Leyendecker traveled for business. With the help of her younger brother Cristóbal Benavides, who helped keep Leyendecker's books as well as his own mercantile house, María Andrea Leyendecker managed the Leyendecker merchant house's operations. She was particular about the account books and tracked when customers who owed them debt came into town. In addition to raising her new family and keeping it connected to her old one, María Andrea played an essential role in running John Leyendecker's business.⁶³

The importance of family connections to Leyendecker's business went beyond his ties to the Benavideses. When he and Wulff decided to move their business to Laredo, they knew they needed an additional investor to ensure they could get their store established. They brought in a new Anglo-American partner, Bart DeWitt. However, DeWitt was not independently wealthy. His mother held the family's wealth, and she lent the money to Leyendecker on condition that Bart be a partner and Leyendecker pay her back directly. Catherine DeWitt lived in Baltimore and initially mistrusted Leyendecker and her son's venture in Texas. She much preferred the path Bart's brother took in going to Philadelphia and becoming a lawyer. By January of 1857, however, Leyendecker paid off his debt to Catherine DeWitt and her letters to him became far more cordial. Catherine was assured that her son's business partner met his obligations and that their store in Laredo could succeed. In her last letter to Leyendecker, Catherine suggested that the German make the trip to visit her in Baltimore. He was always welcome in her home. They were practically family. The European-born borderlands entrepreneur had established another important kinship connection to his mercantile network, this time through the DeWitt family.[64]

What Catherine DeWitt did not know was that the Laredo store took on a crushing amount of debt during 1857. Leyendecker had spent the hard currency he and Wulff had from Oak Creek and DeWitt's loan on relocating to Laredo. He made good on his rent and impressed the Treviños with timely cash payments. However, they did not have the finances to stock their store. To overcome this Wulff contracted a consignment agreement with Francois Guilbeau's merchant house in San Antonio. Guilbeau sent goods from his merchant house to Laredo for Leyendecker and Wulff to sell. However, Guilbeau set the terms of the consignment, demanding payment within a defined period regardless of whether the goods sold. This placed Wulff and Leyendecker in a subordinate and precarious position.[65]

Francois Guilbeau had moved to San Antonio in 1839 to serve as the French consul for the region, where he leveraged his diplomatic position into a flourishing commercial enterprise. As consul he had the advantage of being privy to international information, close ties to the French and Texas governments, and the ability to import high demand goods cheaply. Guilbeau thrived as an import grocer, bringing in fruits and wines that sold at high margins. He was so successful that by the mid-1850s, he had built one of the most elegant homes in San Antonio, which doubled as the French consulate during the US Civil War.[66]

For Guilbeau the business relationship with Leyendecker and Wulff made sense. He could expand his business from San Antonio 150 miles south into the markets along the Rio Grande. It also allowed him to diversify outside of grocery items, as the Laredo store dealt in general merchandise. If Leyendecker and Wulff succeeded in their venture, he would continually profit as their middleman, providing goods on loan and making gains through interest. If the venture failed, he could take over and convert the Laredo store into a satellite to his San Antonio holdings or simply let the firm die. Together, Leyendecker and Guilbeau established a credit system that sent dry goods to Laredo in exchange for agricultural products shipped to San Antonio. Guilbeau accepted bushels of corn at a price of one dollar a bushel and hides at the market price in New York City. Whatever the French consul fetched for the hides on the New York market, he would apply half of the profit to Leyendecker's account and keep the other half for himself. With their agreement another European network began to develop in the Rio Grande borderlands.[67]

It turned out that 1857 was a bad year for Leyendecker to rely on the hide trade in the United States. The Panic of 1857 hit New York and spread throughout the manufacturing centers in the US Northeast. Banks suspended operations and called in their securities. As a result, factories began to shut their doors, putting laborers out of work and ceasing demand for raw materials, including Rio Grande hides. The price of dried hides going into New York from the Rio Grande dropped to thirty-six cents apiece, which meant that Leyendecker only earned eighteen cents per hide he sent to Guilbeau. Considering the Laredo store owed Guilbeau $2,730 in debt, Leyendecker needed to make swift business in order to avoid falling behind on the interest.[68]

To make up the shortfall, Leyendecker fell back on corn to offset the drop in hide prices. A bushel of corn was worth more than five hides to Leyendecker. A month after he agreed to terms with Guilbeau, the German collected 336 bushels of corn from Nuevo Laredo alone. He shipped hundreds of those up to San Antonio to pay Guilbeau, which left the Frenchman flabbergasted. He had more corn than he could reasonably resell. Guilbeau sent a curt letter to Leyendecker telling him their arrangement had changed: "According to the fall of prices of hides at New York I advice [sic] you I cannot take them at the same price offered to you. Also, I will not buy more corn."[69] In a month the business plan Leyendecker envisioned and enacted fell apart around him. The items of value he could acquire through exchange had lost their value.[70]

Leyendecker was desperate and did what many desperate businesspeople do; he took on more debt. Leyendecker recognized he was geographically removed from all of his creditors. He left Wulff and Bart DeWitt to take the heat from Guilbeau in San Antonio and contracted a new commission agreement with Preau and Couturie Company in New Orleans. Preau and Couturie marked Leyendecker's last shot to make the Laredo store work. Jean Preau, a French Creole born in Louisiana, partnered with the Dutch consul attached to New Orleans, Amedee Couturie, and established a profitable import business in the Crescent City. They made their fortune in much the same way as Guilbeau, cheaply importing wine and liquor from Europe. The difference for Leyendecker was that Couturie could sell his Rio Grande hides in Europe directly, avoiding the tumultuous US market.[71]

Leyendecker commissioned to sell hides to Preau and Couturie for goods and cash. While Guilbeau offered Leyendecker eighteen cents per hide, his new commission paid twenty-three and a half cents. Unlike Guilbeau, Preau and Couturie had no interest expanding their business to Laredo. They just wanted a steady stream of hides to exchange on the market for the cheap booze that made them so much money. Further, Leyendecker's relationship with Preau and Couturie put him in a more enviable position. He personally negotiated their terms of exchange rather than leaving it up to the whims of the markets and merchants around him. By signing on with Preau and Couturie, Leyendecker gave the Benavides family and other suppliers in his network greater access to the European market for their goods.[72]

Leyendecker grew significant connections in Mexico for the goods he sold in San Antonio, New Orleans, and Europe. One of his most important contacts was the governor of Nuevo León, Santiago Vidaurri. Vidaurri trusted the Benavideses and even stayed with them on his travels to the United States. Vidaurri's son-in-law, Irish-born Patricio Milmo, owned one of the largest mercantile houses in Monterrey. Leyendecker transported goods back and forth across the Rio Grande to facilitate transactions with Vidaurri and Milmo. Another Monterrey merchant, Evaristo Madero, built a strong relationship with Leyendecker in the corn and hide trade. The German provided Madero an outlet to sell his goods in Texas and returned horses, mules, and European goods to Monterrey for Madero to resell for more grain and hide. Leyendecker's Mexican connections proved beneficial for all involved.[73]

Throughout 1857 Leyendecker shipped Mexican hides from Laredo to San Antonio and New Orleans through Corpus Christi. He and his brother-in-law Cristóbal Benavides moved at least four hundred hides from Mexico across the Rio Grande and out into the international market.[74] Further, Leyendecker was willing to accept more than just cash for his goods. In one instance customers paid with their surplus of beans and flour, and he in turn shipped nearly three tons of flour and beans to Guilbeau in San Antonio. The French merchant was not happy to be so overwhelmed with food goods but credited Leyendecker several hundred dollars to his account for the effort.[75]

Leyendecker worked constantly in 1857 to get out of debt. He even picked up additional work outside of his commercial enterprise. For example, Leyendecker took advantage of the United States' expansion to the Rio Grande by taking on employment working for the state, where he accepted part-time work as a US customs agent for the port of Laredo. In doing so he was able to make a little extra money. Not only that, but the position also facilitated his ability to import goods more effectively from Nuevo Laredo, since it allowed him to have some control over the duties charged for exporting and importing. In fact there were certainly times he paid no duty at all. As a customs agent, he found an opportunity to merge his commercial interests with those of the state.[76]

Leyendecker also became the postmaster for Laredo in 1858, allowing him access to price news and franking privileges and raising his standing in the community. As explained earlier, Leyendecker's biggest shortcoming as a merchant in Laredo was that he entered agreements with his creditors in which they set the prices. He fell into so much debt with Guilbeau because the French merchant set the prices he would pay for hides and corn. To avoid this trap, Leyendecker needed up-to-the-minute pricing notices so that he would always know the value of the goods he exchanged. Being the postmaster placed him at the center of commercial communications in the Rio Grande borderlands. Additionally, he could send mail without paying postage. He took advantage of the regular mail coach between Laredo and Corpus Christi to ship his inventories at little to no cost. His partner and brother-in-law Santos Benavides obtained a contract in the same year to run the mail coach from Laredo to Corpus Christi, in addition to managing other routes from Laredo. Together their family network dominated the communications of a large swath of the borderlands, making them powerful members of the community.[77]

It was a risky venture for Benavides to take over the mail coach. The US Army had rebuilt the road during the US-Mexico War to bring most of the supplies to Fort McIntosh from New Orleans through the port at Corpus Christi. However, traders avoided using the road in the early 1850s because of the threat of Indian raids and highwaymen. That Santos Benavides and Leyendecker built it into the most important pipeline for Laredo's communications, imports, and exports speaks to the significant impact of their partnership on the Rio Grande borderlands.[78]

By the end of the decade, Leyendecker worked off most of his debts and was becoming a prominent member of the Laredo community. The last invoice Guilbeau sent him recorded a total balance of only thirty-five dollars. The German-speaking entrepreneur also sought to diversify his inventory that same year and placed a large order for textiles with another European-owned mercantile outlet in Roma, Texas. The end of the 1850s brought the promise of profits and success to Leyendecker's business. The local kinship ties he built combined with his network connections in the borderlands and beyond gave him an optimistic projection for the future. Together, Leyendecker and Benavides connected Laredo more deeply into the regional market through kinship and trade and helped globalize Laredo by exporting hides to Europe and strengthening ties with the growing port at Corpus Christi. Their venture also had the impact of nudging Laredo out of its isolation.[79]

José San Román and John Leyendecker built their networks around family, business connections, and the state. Because the social and commercial conditions in Matamoros/Brownsville were unlike those in Nuevo Laredo / Laredo, both merchants utilized different strategies to achieve their goals of creating profitable enterprises on the Rio Grande. Regardless of strategy, they both created systems of exchange that tied the Rio Grande borderlands to Atlantic markets.

Prominent Anglo-Americans recognized the powerful position of European-born merchants by the end of the 1850s. In the spring of 1859, the fiery South Carolina Democrat and US consul in Matamoros, Richard Fitzpatrick, penned a letter to Secretary of State Lewis Cass complaining that few American cargoes entered the port at the Rio Grande and that most goods entering the city came from English manufacturers shipped on foreign vessels. Fitzpatrick went on to note that "the whole of the principal merchants in the trade are foreigners and have no sympathy for American interests."[80] By foreigners the consul meant Europeans—namely, English, French, German, and

Spanish traders who dominated the market in the US-Mexico borderland. He loathed the idea that foreigners controlled the Rio Grande trade. Fitzpatrick believed that Matamoros should be an American port and the Rio Grande borderlands an American market. He was furious not only that European-born entrepreneurs and merchants competed with US dominance in the region but also that they had become successful.

Fitzpatrick's letters reveal that Anglo-American state agents worried that the United States' imperial project in the Rio Grande borderlands might fail. The American consul noted that most cargoes bypassed US settlements on the Rio Grande in favor of transport toward Monterrey. Those goods that did come into the United States were often smuggled to avoid paying American tariffs. As such the United States demonstrated very little control in the borderlands. Fitzpatrick feared that if Europeans continued to dominate the Rio Grande trade, the Texas towns would wither and die out.[81]

Fitzpatrick did not have time to change the commercial conditions of the borderlands. The United States ran headlong toward civil war by the end of 1860, and the consul left his position in support of the Confederacy. The French invasion of Mexico in 1861 brought further conflict and disruption to the region. The mercantile networks that European-born entrepreneurs built in the Rio Grande borderlands became essential to the region because of their stability. They also drove Atlantic commerce in a time of intense violence.

Chapter 5

Walking in Tall Cotton

In 1862 English-born Joseph Morell was anxious all the time. From his store in Monterrey, he worried the French would invade the city and kill him; he believed Tamaulipas would go to war with Nuevo León, leaving northern Mexico in ruin; he fretted his paper currency would become worthless; he suspected his partners were cheating him; he always thought some accident would befall his shipments. Most of all, he feared that the Union army would invade Texas and block the flow of cotton through the Rio Grande borderlands. The cotton trade became his most dependable source of income. He wrote Charles Stillman in Brownsville that he hoped "the Yankees will not stop our little business in Texas the only thing that keeps us alive." All of Morell's livelihood narrowed to one central product, and it was threatened by so many factors beyond his control that he could barely cope.[1]

The US Civil War threatened American cotton exports to Europe. One of the earliest strategies for the Union was to blockade the Confederacy to prevent any cotton shipments leaving or munitions shipments entering the South. However, due to the Treaty of Guadalupe

Hidalgo, the Law of Nations, and northern tolerance, the Union Navy was mostly powerless to stop the movement of cotton out of Mexico on ships flying neutral flags. Further, tons of cotton flowed overland across the Rio Grande to Monterrey and other trading centers in Mexico. The Confederacy desperately needed to export cotton to fund its war effort, and Europe required the fiber to keep the Atlantic textile industry running. These swirling conditions made the Rio Grande borderlands the center of the movement of Confederate cotton to the Atlantic market.[2]

Unfortunately for those involved in the cotton trade, the Rio Grande borderlands remained incredibly unstable in the 1860s. The US Civil War was only one of many conflicts that raged in the region. In Mexico the War of Reform, a civil war between Mexican liberals and conservatives, reached its conclusion, but the conservative losers courted French support to overthrow the liberals and install a European monarch. Regional warlords like Santiago Vidaurri took advantage of the political instability to solidify their power. He extended his power over Nuevo León, Coahuila, and even parts of Tamaulipas. The protracted Mexican civil wars and French Intervention also created power vacuums, like in Tamaulipas, where an election to replace the governor devolved into a protracted battle between two factions that spilled into violence on the streets of Matamoros.[3]

Conditions were not any more stable north of the Rio Grande in Texas. Juan Nepomuceno Cortina proclaimed against American land appropriations and settler encroachment on the Rio Grande. A former Mexican soldier, politician, and rancher, Cortina railed against frauds perpetrated against Mexican landowners. He called on Mexicans on both sides of the river to rally and attack white landowners. Cortina and his men raided Brownsville and wreaked havoc on the countryside up and down the Rio Grande. Moreover, the civil wars in the Rio Grande borderlands reinvigorated Comanche raiders, who targeted ranches on the exposed frontier for horses and cattle. Soldiers, guerillas, brigands, rustlers, and raiders all ranged throughout the region, making it an extremely dangerous place to move one of the most valuable products in the world.[4]

Despite the risks, European-born entrepreneurs in the Rio Grande borderlands took on the dangers to position themselves as essential factors for the continued movement of cotton out of the US South. They mobilized and expanded their networks to profit on the North American crises. San Antonio, Monterrey, and Matamoros became central sites for cotton distribution. Entrepreneurial middlemen received support from European, Mexican, and American states. European consulate agencies encouraged the trade and tried to protect against seizures. Mexican officials tended to favor European-born merchants, particularly after the French invasion and the installation of Maximilian as emperor. Additionally, Confederate and even Union bureaucrats supported European participation in the cotton trade because of their own personal interests in the textile industry. The economic and political conditions in the Rio Grande borderlands offered the possibility for European-born entrepreneurs to rapidly acquire wealth if they were able to take advantage of favorable circumstances and avoid an ever-present catastrophe.[5]

In addition to material profits, merchants in the borderlands hoped the explosion of the cotton trade would help them impose their notions of Western modernity on the region. Across the globe in the nineteenth century, the cotton and textile industry facilitated freedom of commerce and a trend toward uniformity. If those conditions existed in the borderlands, merchants would have a more intelligible market in which they could more easily predict demands. European-born entrepreneurs believed the cotton trade could help them transform the borderlands into a modern global trading center.[6]

To an extent they were right. The European demand for cotton and the political instability in the borderlands brought on by civil and international conflict remade the Rio Grande borderlands into a center of Atlantic trade in which European-born entrepreneurs rose to play an integral role. However, even with the market opportunities and state support, obstacles contributed to many individual failures. Eruptions of violence destroyed lives and inventories, ethnic tensions flared, anti-Semitism ran virtually unchecked, and state policies forced individuals into positions of vulnerability. Even successful merchants knew that the boom could bust at any minute for any reason. Though the conflicts of the US Civil War and the French Intervention in Mexico offered significant opportunities for European-born entrepreneurs to make economic gains, they also turned many lives upside down. Joseph Morell was correct to balance his optimism in the fortuitous cotton trade with the wariness that it could end at any minute.[7]

○ ○ ○ ○ ○

The cotton textile industry had become the most important segment of the global economy as early as 1790. It was at the center of industrial and economic growth on both sides of the Atlantic in the nineteenth century. By 1860 the cotton textile industry became Britain's largest employer and the United States' single biggest industry, and had similar importance in France and Spain. All that industrial production relied on the availability of vast amounts of raw cotton, and most of the cotton for global production came from the US South. Enslaved people underpinned the South's cotton exports. The entire Southern economy was founded on the capacity of the slave system to generate and distribute wealth. Entrepreneurial Southerners utilized slave labor to acquire riches and compete in the market. They also invested in biological innovations to produce superior cotton varieties to increase the efficiency of slave labor. In conjunction with their prosperity, enslavers retained significant political power, which they wielded to push for US territorial expansion and protection of the domestic slave trade. Enslaved people and the Southern elites who mobilized slave labor contributed to the US South, of which Texas was a part, being the leading global cotton producer.[8]

By the end of the 1850s, the free labor North openly challenged slavery's expansion, setting the North and South on a collision course toward civil war. Unified by resentment of Southern power, devotion to the Union, and free labor ideology, Northerners became determined to stop any further expansion of slavery. In the face of mounting northern demands, the Southern aristocracy made the decision to secede. They imagined a partnership with Britain and other European powers that was unbreakably stitched together through the cotton trade. Even with the threat of full-scale war, secessionists remained uncompromising because they believed their importance to the global economy irreplaceable. Cotton weakened the connections between the North and South as Northerners grew to revile slave power and Southerners felt free to divest from the United States.[9]

The European demand for raw cotton in the mid-nineteenth century was insatiable, which made the market for cotton incredibly stable. Between the economically tumultuous years of 1855–1860, prices of cotton exported from Galveston, Texas, varied only $4 per hundred pounds. In contrast, prices for corn and animal hides fluctuated wildly. For example, in 1855 the price of corn dropped 66 percent in the second half of the year from $9 to $4 per bushel. Hide prices saw an even more dramatic change in 1857 when prices dropped from $18 to $6 per hundred pounds. Even with the Panic of 1857 in full swing, cotton prices per hundred pounds only dropped from $13 to $9 and recovered quickly thereafter. The stability of the cotton market seemed to guarantee a return on investment for all involved.[10]

The outbreak of the US Civil War made the future of the cotton market far more insecure. In an attempt to force European nations to recognize its independence, the South banned all cotton exports. However, none of the European powers wanted to recognize the Confederacy and risk war with the United States. By the time Southern leaders realized the folly of their policy, the Union naval blockade was in place. Thousands of bales of Southern cotton sat waiting to rot. Southern growers and European manufacturers needed to find a solution to their supply problems. Both turned to the Rio Grande borderlands as a possible answer.[11]

Northern Mexico proved an enticing place to move cotton out of the Confederacy and place in the hands of European textile manufacturers. Union forces could do little about the transnational cotton trade across the Rio Grande because the Treaty of Guadalupe

Hidalgo declared the river neutral. Cotton traders capitalized on the river's neutrality by flying Mexican or European flags to avoid capture. As a result, Matamoros and Monterrey drew in tons of cotton during the 1860s. Matamoros became the key outlet for cotton exports. Total exports amounted to approximately $4 million a month between 1863 and 1865. Monterrey faired nearly as well, solidifying its position as a Mexican center for textile manufacturing and for exporting necessary military supplies to the Confederate war effort. Furthermore, the mercantile networks that already existed in the Rio Grande borderlands had adopted a smuggling culture that matured for more than a decade before the explosion of the cotton trade. Borderlands entrepreneurs were well prepared to capitalize on the expansion of the illicit commodity exchange.[12]

Those entrepreneurs could rely on the state of Texas for support. Governor Pendleton Murrah's office allocated over $2.5 million to purchase cotton. Drawing mostly from Texas's cache of United States bonds, the governor's office believed they could sell the bonds at 7 percent and still realize a profit on cotton purchases.[13] With those profits, Governor Murrah planned to "invest in cotton factories, importing arms + ammunition in order that our state shall not lag or fall behind others in making herself independent in guarding well her own interests."[14] The state's cotton and money would move through merchants on the Rio Grande.

Since Texas was purchasing its own cotton to sell, the governor moved to protect its shipments. Murrah published a special order to all Texas military personnel that "military authorities will exempt from molestation or impressment the agents, drivers, wagons, and trains, which are necessarily employed in transporting cotton belonging to the State of Texas to Mexico."[15] While Murrah's order may have curbed one potential threat to cotton shipments, threats to the cotton road abounded. Union forces, Comanche, and environmental conditions lurked around the cotton road to upend transportation to Mexico.

Carters who transported the cotton had developed two key roads that coursed from the Deep South, through Texas, and into Mexico.

Elizabeth Street, Brownsville, Texas, 1865. Louis de Planque, *Elizabeth Street, Brownsville, Texas*, 1865, Lawrence T. Jones III Texas Photography Collection, DeGolyer Library, SMU

They ran parallel to one another to avoid capture of a single route. The northern route moved through the Arkansas-Louisiana border, into Central Texas, down to San Antonio, and across the Rio Grande at the ports of Nuevo Laredo or Piedras Negras. From there Mexican carters hauled the cotton downriver along the Mexican river road or shipped it to Monterrey. The southern highway began in Alleyton, Texas, at the terminus of the Buffalo Bayou, Brazos, and Colorado Railway. It tracked southwest, passing through Victoria and angling toward the Lower Rio Grande Valley into Brownsville and Matamoros. Because of the volume of traffic on the two thoroughfares, Alleyton and San Antonio became crammed with bales of cotton waiting for carters to carry it south.[16]

The demand to move all that cotton touched the lives of nearly everyone who lived in Texas and northern Mexico. Enslaved people were forced to plant, pick, and haul cotton. Mexican, European, and American laborers were drawn into packing, shipping, and handling bales. Women took on even more responsibility in labor and finance as they became heads of households with men conscripted to the war effort. Indigenous people also participated in the cotton times in various ways. The Comanche found opportunities to raid trading caravans and ranches. The Choctaw participated directly in the Texas trade. They had their own cotton factory in San Antonio and negotiated prices of Indigenous-grown cotton and organized shipment to Mexico. The transnational cotton trade through Texas and northern Mexico in the 1860s dramatically affected the lives of the borderlanders in various ways.[17]

One of the most dramatic effects came through conscription into the war effort. The Confederacy conscripted Americans, Mexicans, and Europeans living in Texas to operate the carts to haul cotton to Mexico. Henry Baumberger, a brewer and shipping agent from Switzerland, had his life and business completely disrupted by the Confederacy. The government gave him an ultimatum to turn his shipping business to exclusively ship cotton to Mexico or face life as a soldier. Baumberger came to hate his "ruling lords" and wished "this damned war and all those who are to blame for it would go to hell."[18] Baumberger was not alone, as many carters who crossed the desert of the Nueces Strip did so against their will.[19]

To make matters worse, teamsters in the cotton trade lived a dangerous life. Comanche scouts realized the frequency and vulnerability of so much material moving across the open plains into their territory. Comanche attacks on cotton trains grew more frequent on the roads to the Rio Grande. Carters like Baumberger constantly worried they would "fall a prey to the cruelty of the Indians."[20] Other threats included guerrilla Union supporters who ranged throughout South Texas. Juan Cortina, who began his uprising in 1859, continued his raiding into the 1860s. Cortinistas adopted positions against Confederate leaders in Texas and claimed support for the Union. The most successful of these Mexican-born Union guerrillas, Octaviano Zapata, recruited a militia of up to eighty men and attacked Confederate supply wagons near the Rio Grande, killing most of the teamsters.[21] They even hanged a Confederate judge as a public display of their power. Traveling with cotton in the Rio Grande borderlands was dangerous business.[22]

The Cortina troubles were part of increasing political turmoil in northern Mexico that impacted the cotton trade and borderlands economy. In the fall of 1861, the election for governor of Tamaulipas became hotly contested. The liberal candidate, Jesús de la Serna, eked out a victory and received certification from the Juarez administration in Mexico City. His challenger, the conservative candidate, Cipriano Guerrero, issued a pronunciamento against de la Serna and claimed victory for himself. Supporters of both sides clashed in cities throughout Tamaulipas. In one instance a fight in Reynosa in October led to five killed. In another the conservative mayor of Matamoros, with the support the local Mexican military commander, declared martial law within his city. The liberals in Matamoros called for support and received it in the form of General José María Jesús Carvajal and his mix of filibusters from Texas. Carvajal's troops combined with liberal resistance fighters to put Matamoros under siege. From November 1861 to March 1862, Matamoros remained in a state of civil warfare.[23]

Individuals used the conflict in Matamoros to inflict damage on political, economic, and social opponents. Those perceived as foreigners were especially at risk. Carvajal declared that foreigners remained in Matamoros at their own risk and that he and his men "would not be responsible for the lives or properties of foreigners remaining in the town."[24] They backed up their words. French and Jewish merchants became the most frequent targets. In the first few weeks of Carvajal's siege, three French merchants died because of violence from one side or the other.[25]

Additionally, Carvajal and his men robbed and humiliated a prominent Austrian Jewish family. One night near Christmas in 1861, a militia made up of Mexican soldiers and American mercenaries broke into the Schlinger family's dry goods store in Matamoros. With rifles and bayonets, the militia forced the family out of their home, "without permitting them to take sufficient clothing to cover their nakedness," and into the road.[26] The men plundered the store and took all the clothing and goods they could carry. The soldiers verbally harassed the Schlingers, who stood embarrassed and vulnerable in the middle of the commercial district of one of the busiest trade cities in North America. No one came to the Schlingers' aid, and no punishment ever reached the responsible party. The Mexican government and the state of Tamaulipas later tacitly admitted some fault and awarded the family compensation for their injuries and losses, but the family had little recourse for the justice they desired.[27]

The attack on the Schlingers was part of growing anti-Semitism among the borderlands' population, and European-born merchants were no exception. In addition to the fact that nobody came to the aid of the Schlingers during their public humiliation, mercantile correspondence regularly included comments regarding the Jewish community. Swedish-born John Vale explained to Charles Stillman that he did not associate with Sanders and Company in Roma "on account of his mean, Jewish & lying principles."[28] Joseph Morell was just as direct in his opinions about Jewish traders. He believed their mere presence cut into his profits: "All kinds of goods are bound to go down, so many Jews are coming up to spoil trade as usual."[29] Jewish entrepreneurs moved to the borderlands seeking what they hoped to be a pluralistic society. The region had grown a reputation for being a cosmopolitan place where Mexicans and Americans, Indigenous and Europeans, Catholic and Protestant all traded and interacted with each other. The Schlingers found a population deeply divided in political and economic competition where who you knew mattered more than what you did. The Schlingers and others remained outside established networks and vulnerable to attack.[30]

For those who avoided the violence in the Rio Grande borderlands, the focus remained on profiting on cotton. Building broad, overlapping networks became essential to keep up with the cotton trade. Standing outside the trade networks that local power brokers created could be ruinous, as exemplified by the Schlingers. Most entrepreneurs aligned themselves with Confederate Texas to ensure access to cotton supplies. They also supported Mexican leaders who would ensure the flow of cotton across the Rio Grande. Confederate Texas and Santiago Vidaurri became part of the political glue that held together the mercantile networks that drove the cotton trade.

Nassau-born John Leyendecker and his family, including Santos Benavides, were tasked with protecting the cotton roads and ensuring Confederate cotton reached Mexico to be taxed to fund Vidaurri's regional empire. The networks that Benavides and Leyendecker built in the 1850s drew them into defending the cotton trade in the 1860s. By protecting the cotton road and facilitating cotton transport through Laredo, the Leyendecker-Benavides family network solidified into one of the strongest commercial entities in the region.[31]

The Leyendecker-Benavides network became inextricably tied to the Confederate cause for practical and business reasons. Practically, Laredo required a new defense structure. The Texas declaration of secession in February 1861 led to the removal of United States federal troops garrisoned in Texas forts. Major C. C. Sibley hastily moved his troops out of Fort McIntosh, leaving Laredo without its most effective defense against Indians.[32] In less than a month, the Comanches took advantage. A party of over forty raiders attacked the ranches on the outskirts of Laredo, killing at least sixteen men and capturing several women and children. The removal of federal troops offered the Comanche an opportunity to push back against American settlement and to boost their population through captives. Santos Benavides raised a militia of about sixty volunteers from up and down the Rio Grande to launch a counterattack against the raiding Comanche band. They caught half the band at a place called Paraje del Gato, where a breakneck fight on horseback took place. Four Comanche and one of the militia fighters died in the battle. Significantly, newspapers across Texas picked up the story, noting Benavides's success at raising an effective militia so quickly. Texas would continuously call on Santos Benavides, along with his brothers Refugio and Cristóbal, to raise troops for the Confederate cause.[33]

Their motives were anything but selfless, as Santos Benavides and John Leyendecker both protected and profited from the business of civil war. Benavides did most of his work in uniform. He tracked down and snuffed out threats to the cotton trade. He chased Cortinistas and Union guerrillas all over the Rio Grande borderlands, ignoring the national boundary altogether. Union forces captured Brownsville in November 1863 and marched upriver to attempt to block the cotton trade through Texas. With Brownsville captured Laredo quickly became an important port for Confederate cotton, and Benavides was tasked with defending it. The limited Union forces in Texas committed to three attacks on Laredo. Benavides and the militia under his command repelled all three, ensuring the continued movement of cotton across the Rio Grande from his hometown. Benavides's success solidified his command of the Rio Grande during the Civil War era.[34]

Benavides's military achievements coincided with commercial benefits. His family acquired military contracts to handle Confederate supplies at Laredo and elsewhere in Texas. He also assumed control of cotton shipments when he needed to. As the war dragged on and his men ran low on ammunition, Benavides impressed wagon trains of cotton at Laredo that he sold for supplies for his men. While he contributed significantly to the Confederate war effort, Benavides concentrated on using the conflict to build his commercial holdings and local standing.[35]

As Benavides used his military position to grow the family's social currency, Leyendecker utilized the conflict to continue to expand his commercial network. His prewar business partner, Bart DeWitt, joined the war effort to avoid conscription. DeWitt eventually went to work with the Texas Cotton Bureau, an organization designed to manage the cotton trade to snuff out corruption and guide cotton profits toward war matériel. The men who worked for the Cotton Bureau found ways to make themselves wealthy. Namely, the state purchased cotton from planters using Confederate dollars, then exchanged the cotton with Rio Grande merchants for hard currency. The rapidly inflating Confederate currency meant that Cotton Bureau agents could easily skim personal incomes off the top of cotton sales by turning increasingly worthless Confederate paper into pounds and francs, then into gold and silver. One such entrepreneurial agent was Jean B. Lacoste from Gascony, France. DeWitt linked Leyendecker and Lacoste, hoping the two could find a mutually beneficial relationship.³⁶

Carts formed the linchpin of the Leyendecker-Lacoste relationship. As Henry Baumberger could attest, Confederate Texas was at a constant shortage of wagons and carts to ship all the cotton to Mexico and war matériel to Texas. Thanks to his family's connections to Vidaurri and Leyendecker's prewar business of shipping agricultural goods to San Antonio, Leyendecker received regular shipments from Nuevo León by Mexican carters who could not be conscripted into Confederate service.³⁷ Lacoste in Matamoros knew that at least six hundred bales of cotton lay stacked in Alleyton waiting for someone to pick it up and bring it to him. He had English merchants in Matamoros willing to pay almost 100 percent more per pound than the bureau paid the farmers. DeWitt told Leyendecker to "find all the carts you can" and make a trip downriver where he could "make a bargain."³⁸ Leyendecker jumped at the opportunity and mobilized at least forty Mexican carters to ship cotton in Texas. Leyendecker pulled in thousands of dollars in hard currency, the carters earned hundreds of dollars more than they would have in Mexico, and Lacoste became a longtime business partner for the Leyendecker-Benavides commercial network during and after the conflict-ridden 1860s.³⁹

Leyendecker's position as a successful shipping magnate in Laredo drew attention of old acquaintances interested in the booming Rio Grande trade. Charles Lege, a fellow German-speaking Confederate quartermaster, wrote Leyendecker after nearly a decade of silence to tell him that Lege planned on visiting Laredo "to make some money."⁴⁰ Lege openly admitted that he meant to presume on his old friendship to pump Leyendecker for information on how to succeed in business in the Rio Grande borderlands. Lege's imposition turned out to be a boon for Leyendecker as Lege became an agent for Richard King and Mifflin Kenedy and set up shop in Camargo. As the Union continued to threaten shipments from Alleyton to Brownsville from the coast, King and Kenedy redirected their cotton southwest to Laredo and then down to Matamoros through their agents in Camargo. Leyendecker got to charge for his services of inspecting the cotton in Laredo and transferring it across the Rio Grande to his trusted carters in Nuevo Laredo. He was also given leave to draw on Kenedy's account in Matamoros if he needed to. Through Lege Leyendecker gained access to the most prominent American businessmen in the Rio Grande borderlands, which pushed him closer to the American network.[41]

As significant as his networks north of the Rio Grande had become, Leyendecker's connections in Nuevo León proved to be just as profitable. In addition to employing Mexican carters in the cotton trade, he also had mercantile connections that paid dividends. Much of the agricultural products Leyendecker dealt in prior to the war came from Evaristo Madero in Monterrey. Leyendecker kept importing grains from Madero but also worked with him in the cotton trade. Additionally, the Benavides association with Vidaurri put Leyendecker in contact with the largest handler of Mexican cotton in the 1860s, Milmo and Company Irish-born entrepreneur Patricio Milmo, who was Vidaurri's son-in-law, rose to become one of the wealthiest merchants in the Rio Grande borderlands because of the illicit cotton trade. Milmo and Madero combined to supply the Confederacy with Mexican flour, which they exchanged for thousands of bales of cotton. Leyendecker often handled the transfer of those goods across the Rio Grande.[42]

Milmo also partnered with Lacoste to sell and export cotton out of Matamoros. Cotton came into Mexico through Nuevo Laredo or Piedras Negras. A trusted partner like Leyendecker received it and transferred it to Matamoros where Lacoste shipped it to his English partner, Henry Attrill, in exchange for specie, blankets, harnesses, saddles, and gray wool, which Lacoste shipped back to Monterrey through Milmo and up into Texas to supply Confederate soldiers. Near the end of the war, Leyendecker became an assistant quartermaster. From that position he organized purchases from Milmo and Madero for Confederate supplies that he distributed to Fort McIntosh and other military stations on the Rio Grande.[43]

Leyendecker and Benavides played key roles on the cotton road, ensuring Confederate cotton made its way into Mexico and essential supplies came into Confederate Texas. In doing so their network solidified locally and expanded regionally to include some of the most powerful businesspeople of the era. Together, Leyendecker and Benavides made Laredo and its surroundings a key crossroads of the cotton trade between San Antonio, Monterrey, and Matamoros.

Confederate cotton and the increasing significance of Monterrey in the region proved fortuitous for Matamoros. The need to move cotton out of Mexico and the heightened demand for war supplies combined to create an economic explosion on the Rio Grande Delta. Entrepreneurs with already-established mercantile networks were best able to take advantage of the boom time. They harnessed their networks to ensure cotton made it to port and expanded their networks to ship cotton across the Atlantic. Those networks helped offset the losses to the Union blockade that still seized ships regardless of the legal loopholes surrounding the borderland. Unlike Nuevo Laredo / Laredo, merchants in Matamoros and its surroundings aspired to make their city the outlet for goods leaving Monterrey and a new center of Atlantic trade.

Matamoros and the small fishing village of Bagdad, directly downriver from Matamoros on the Mexican side of the mouth of the Rio Grande, burst into boomtowns. Entrepreneurs moved there en masse, making retail space a premium. Rents in Matamoros jumped 1,000 percent between 1858 and 1863. The population of Bagdad exploded from maybe one hundred people up to fifteen thousand. The cotton trade created a space for expansion of other industries in the area, as nearby ranchers had a ready local demand for beef, carpenters and engineers had endless contracts to construct new buildings, and saloon owners did not have enough space to sustain demand. Store owners could barely keep enough beer, wine, and tobacco in stock. The cotton times offered a look into how Matamoros and its surroundings might look like an essential cog in the Atlantic trade machine.[44]

José San Román, who accounted for more than 6 percent of the total amount of cotton exported from Matamoros between 1862 and 1865, built one of the largest mercantile networks in the borderlands at the time. The Basque trader's connections in Monterrey and other parts of Mexico helped facilitate the transformation of the Rio Grande borderlands to a center of global trade.[45] Monterrey became an important transfer post for Mexican cotton. Monterrey's position resulted from Santiago Viduarri's alignment with the Confederacy, the already-established merchant elite in the city, and shifting patterns of violence in northern Mexico. Vidaurri and his son-in-law, Patricio Milmo, benefited from the high tariffs they could place on cotton crossing the Rio Grande and the war matériel and supplies they shipped to Texas. In addition to Milmo, there already existed a powerful group of European-born merchants in Monterrey who could handle the rapid influx of trade and population. While Matamoros remained the most important point of ingress and egress of goods and raw cotton, respectively, internal fighting and foreign invasions disrupted shipping. During the various Cortinista raids, civil violence in Matamoros, the Union invasion of Brownsville, and the French invasion of Matamoros, shipments needed to be stored safely. Monterrey became a key warehousing center. San Román utilized every connection he had in Monterrey to navigate the instability of the Rio Grande borderlands during the cotton times.[46]

Since Monterrey was more stable than Matamoros, San Román tapped his network of Spanish-born contacts in Monterrey to give him access to the city's resources. Mariano Hernández had a head start on the cotton trade through his textile manufacturing investments. He already had direct lines to Texas cotton and the means to store surplus stock. He also expanded to open a Hernández y Hermanos storefront and warehouse in Matamoros that worked closely with San Román.[47] Valentín Rivero played an even larger role in San Román's cotton operation. Not only did he help facilitate the cotton trade, but Rivero also managed important silver shipments to Matamoros, ensuring San Román remained flush with hard currency to pay carters and other cotton brokers. San Román's access to silver also allowed him to turn more of his attention to finance. Credit was his pathway to power. San Román became one of the most prominent lenders in the Rio Grande borderlands during the Civil War era. As smaller merchants turned to him for loans, he solidified his centrality to the cotton trade.[48]

San Román's Spanish contacts also helped him build stronger connections with English-born traders in Monterrey. C. W. Whitis specialized in brokering trade between Confederate Cotton Bureau agents and Liverpool cotton importers. Whitis's business partner, Asa Pullen, worked in Piedras Negras, Mexico, to ensure that shipments made it across the Rio Grande from Eagle Pass, Texas, to be transported to Monterrey. The only missing link in Whitis's chain was a reliable facilitator in Matamoros to ensure his bales of cotton made it from Monterrey to Matamoros and onto ships to cross the Atlantic. Rivero likely suggested that Whitis seek out San Román to fill the gap in his supply chain. Networking paid dividends.[49]

Not only did San Román ensure cotton safely made it aboard ships bound for Liverpool, but he also acted as a banker for Whitis and Pullen. When a client like Whitis shipped his cotton to Matamoros, San Román usually covered the freight costs on delivery, inspected the goods, arranged transport farther downriver to Bagdad, and contracted loading onto transatlantic ships. After he took out his own expenses, he logged the remaining value into Whitis's account in his books. If a client like Whitis needed money right away, he could request a letter of advice that the client could take to a local firm, like Rivero and Compañía, to withdraw sums from their account. The account transfers, of course, garnered their own fees, making men like San Román all the wealthier. They also made the cotton trade work more effectively by ensuring people got paid. No matter where his business took him, if Whitis could get a message to San Román, he could get his money. San Román effectively became a banker in Matamoros, as handling financial accounts quickly became one of his most profitable roles. He was a key mover of both cotton and credit in this era.[50]

Joseph Morell's dealings with San Román brings the interconnectivity of the Rio Grande borderlands and the region's brief period as a center of Atlantic trade into perspective. The English-born merchant, Morell, had been in Monterrey since the US-Mexico War and formed a partnership with Charles Stillman and his company in Brownsville. Morell traded in various goods but primarily bought and sold military supply. He likely supplied Carvajal's troops during the Merchant War and sold shot and powder to all sides during the Mexican Reform War.[51] To stay in business, he paid regular tithes to Santiago Vidaurri and supported the governor throughout the 1850s and 1860s. Though his business often went beyond dubious into the realm of outright malfeasance, his dealings connected northern Mexico to the United States, Britain, and beyond.[52]

Morell was a Stillman man, but the cotton trade was so vast and complex that he needed San Román to ensure his exports. Stillman sold much of the cotton he traded during the war in New York City. Problematically, Stillman's name was tied to the contraband cotton trade. Any cotton he landed in New York under his name risked confiscation. Morell helped fix that problem. He shipped Stillman cotton out of Matamoros under the title José Morell, Monterrey, to avoid suspicion. During times he could not see to the export himself or he felt his identity compromised, he contracted San Román to do it. Though the Spaniard was a longtime Stillman competitor, the cotton trade pushed them all together.[53]

The threat of a Union invasion and the naval blockade also helped draw mercantile networks together. San Román, Morell, Milmo, and other merchants in the cotton trade had to constantly be wary of the Union blockade. The easiest strategy was to make sure to transfer their goods in and out at Bagdad, south of the mouth of the Rio Grande, to avoid Union ships. San Román had a special agent in Bagdad, French-born Joseph Kleiber, to make sure his shipments remained on the Mexican side of the border, safe from capture. Regardless, failure was common as American naval commanders stopped and searched European ships in neutral waters throughout the Gulf of

Mexico and the Caribbean. In 1863 Union sailors boarded five British merchant ships in Mexican waters off the coast of Matamoros. The *Sir William Peel*, *Volant*, *Matamoros*, *Science*, and *Dashing Wave* were all impounded for carrying contraband. All the impounded ships were connected in some way to European-born entrepreneurs in the Rio Grande borderlands.[54]

Milmo and Lacoste relied heavily on the *Sir William Peel* for their cotton exports. Partially owned by Lacoste's partner, Henry Attrill, the *Sir William Peel* had over one thousand bales of cotton aboard when it was seized and sent to New Orleans for investigation. Certainly, John Leyendecker's carters had shipped the cotton to port to be loaded on the *Sir William Peel*. Union naval officers proceeded to impound the ship because they found eleven guns on board and believed them to be contrabands of war. Outraged, the British consul in Matamoros fired off letters of protest to the British foreign office that the cotton, shipped by Milmo and Company, was certified as Mexican cotton by the US consul in Matamoros. It should never have faced seizure. The situation created a firestorm of controversy between the United States and Britain that lasted nearly a decade.[55]

The *Dashing Wave* proved to be a headache for San Román in his shipments from Britain. Even prior to its capture, San Román avoided using the *Dashing Wave* in his transatlantic trade. In August 1862 he had Joseph Railton and Sons of Manchester transfer his shipments of dry goods and other items off the *Dashing Wave* because San Román knew the ship had a reputation for breakage and loss. The *Dashing Wave* lost the commission to ship £30,500 of goods from Liverpool to Matamoros. Instead, San Román chose to pay to have his goods shipped via two separate ships with additional costs rather than on the *Dashing Wave*. Unfortunately, San Román's avoidance of the *Dashing Wave*'s bad luck was short-lived, as he would run afoul of it again within the year.[56]

When San Román learned of the *Dashing Wave's* seizure a year later in 1863, he could probably only shrug and sigh at his bad luck with that ship. This time his business associate was the massive transnational Lizardi company. The Lizardi company had a long history with the transatlantic cotton trade. The merchant family first opened business in Veracruz in the 1750s and quickly grew into one of the largest firms working in the Gulf of Mexico. By the time of Mexico's independence in 1821, Lizardi owned mercantile houses in New Orleans, Paris, and London. Francisco de Lizardi and Company, the London house, worked in tandem with Manuel de Lizardi and Company, the New Orleans house and prominent cotton factor, to export cotton from New Orleans to Liverpool in the 1840s. Problematically for the Lizardi company, the Union blockade concentrated on New Orleans, severing the tie between the two Lizardi firms. F. de Lizardi and Company had to find a replacement cotton factor. The firm sought inroads to the Matamoros trade.[57]

Their search led them to José San Román through one of San Román's business partners, speculator H. N. Caldwell. Caldwell called on F. de Lizardi and Company to jointly purchase cotton in Matamoros. Caldwell had £3,000 in hand with £4,000 on credit with San Román in Matamoros, and he wanted F. de Lizardi and Company to put up another £5,000 so they could get a huge bulk of cotton out of Matamoros in one transaction. Both Caldwell and Lizardi wanted San Román to handle the purchase. They shipped 12,000 gold sovereign coins to San Román via the *Dashing Wave* with detailed instructions on how San Román was to purchase the cotton, inspect it, and ship it to Britain. They gave San Román discretionary power to purchase from £7,000 up to the full £12,000 depending on the market and quality of the product. Caldwell was sent personally to deliver the gold sovereigns and the instructions. When the Union Navy seized the *Dashing Wave*, the gold disappeared. Caldwell fled the ship during its seizure and probably took the gold with him. All F. de Lizardi and Company had to make its case against the United States was a bill of lading. After the incident with the *Dashing Wave*, San Román added a deposit in his cash book from Caldwell's company for £10,000. Though the seizure cost him a ship full of goods, many of the gold coins may have made their way into San Román's hands, based on this mysterious deposit.[58]

The examples of the *Sir William Peel* and the *Dashing Wave* give insight into the growing interconnectedness of the mercantile networks in the Rio Grande borderlands. No matter how large the British firm importing cotton from the Rio Grande, be it Henry Attrill's company or the Lizardis, they needed middlemen who worked locally to ensure shipments. Their money could only go so far without the expertise and local networks of merchants like San Román and Patricio Milmo. Their local connections made it so that they knew when the high and low times would come. They also knew how to boost the value of goods to exchange them at the highest margins. Together, huge European firms and knowledgeable local middlemen made the illicit cotton trade function. Even with the failure and suspicion surrounding the *Dashing Wave*, F. de Lizardi and Company continued to do business with San Román because it was profitable in the long run.[59]

San Román became such an important node in the transatlantic cotton trade because of his network of Europeans in the borderlands who directed cotton shipments down the Rio Grande to his warehouses in Matamoros. John Decker in Rio Grande City and Camargo proved to be another important ally. San Román's budding relationship with Decker in the 1850s blossomed into an incredibly profitable partnership during the US Civil War. Decker's company accepted thousands of pounds of Confederate cotton at Rio Grande City, sorted it, transferred it across the border to Camargo, and shipped the prime cotton downriver to San Román. Decker sold the damaged and subpar cotton to other merchants. In exchange for sending San Román only the premium cotton, Decker asked for small perks in addition to payment, like fine clothing. Their relationship proved mutually beneficial.[60]

Similar to Leyendecker, Decker's connections in Mexico gave him access to Mexican carters. Decker's wife, Antonia Morales, helped boost his standing in Camargo. Though not one of the original families to settle Camargo, the Morales family became important in Camargo politics after Mexico's independence from Spain. Decker opened a store in Camargo, and the family had a home there. When their daughter, Cecilia Decker, wed, they had the wedding in Camargo.

John Decker had standing and connections in Camargo that helped him when he needed to hire Mexican carters to move tons of cotton. He had his best teamsters carry San Román's cotton in shipments that often exceeded four tons.[61]

In Nuevo Laredo another European who married into a Mexican family worked to make sure San Román's cotton made it to Matamoros. English-born Henry Redmond spent the 1850s trying to establish himself as one of the most powerful people on the stretch of the Rio Grande between Laredo and Rio Grande City. He married Refugia Diaz, daughter of Agapita and Teodoro Cuellar Diaz of Ciudad Guerrero, Tamaulipas. The Cuellars were one of the founding families of Guerrero, and they allowed Redmond access to networks of power in the regional Mexican elite.[62] With the help of his new family and others, Redmond aided in the creation of Zapata County in Texas. He consolidated his political power in the county by holding the positions of postmaster, customs collector, justice of the peace, and county judge. He also controlled a virtual mercantile monopoly in the area. Redmond's power grabs made him enemies among Mexican ranchers and laborers in and around Zapata County, however. When the county had to submit its vote for secession, it set off a revolt. The county leadership, including Redmond, announced that anyone who failed to vote in favor of secession would be fined fifty cents. Dissidents who failed to submit a ballot were later ordered arrested, sparking rancher Antonio Ochoa to declare a pronunciamento in favor of Juan Cortina's uprising and the Union cause. Ochoa and over forty Cortinistas took over southeastern Zapata County and attacked Redmond's ranch.[63]

Redmond's time in Zapata County was up. He closed shop and moved in with his wife's family in Ciudad Guerrero. He concluded a letter to Charles Stillman with an ominous statement, "We are living in very serious times."[64] From the relative safety of Guerrero, Redmond had to figure out how to provide for his family. He traveled upriver to Nuevo Laredo, where he had a couple friends and fewer enemies, to start a new mercantile business. One his most prominent contacts in the area was Santos Benavides, who had ridden south to defend Redmond's ranch when the Cortinistas attacked it.[65]

From Nuevo Laredo Redmond initially worked in the hide trade until the cotton market exploded. He utilized his experience with local government and the Mexican elite to his benefit. He paid the alcalde, or mayor, of Nuevo Laredo a percentage of each cotton shipment over the river and openly recorded payments of the municipal and federal tax.[66] He wanted to maintain Mexican support for his business in town. Redmond also gained support from the Brazos Manufacturing Company. Organized by planters in Brazoria County to build a textile mill using Texas state subsidies and cotton sales, the Brazos Manufacturing Company hired Redmond to broker sales of their cotton. He turned to José San Román to buy bulk shipments. In one transaction he sent over 103 bales to San Román in Matamoros.[67] Through the cotton trade in Mexico, Redmond rebuilt his mercantile business in the face of catastrophe. He also made sure that San Román received the cotton he needed from Texas.

During the cotton times in the Rio Grande borderlands, mercantile networks expanded, intersected, and melded together. As the cases of Leyendecker and San Román demonstrate, regional networks were essential to the movement of cotton out of Texas and into the Atlantic market. Individuals who had already crafted relationships of trade and trust took most advantage of the economic explosion that came with the political and social disruptions of civil war and foreign invasion. Because of the sheer volume of trade, former competitors had to work alongside one another to keep up. The violent factors that constantly threatened the trade forced them to work in tandem. Global forces came together to make the borderlands one of the most important regions for economic exchange between 1861 and 1867, and the people who lived there took advantage of the opportunity. Those who did hoped to retain the significance of the region in the decade that followed.

Chapter 6

Railroaded in the Rio Grande Borderlands

Mifflin Kenedy stormed into José San Román's office on a Sunday in May 1872. Agitated and angry, the Anglo-American steamship company owner accosted the Spanish merchant. San Román had just invested in a railroad project that would finally bring the iron horse to the Rio Grande borderlands; however, back in 1860 San Román had won a lawsuit against King, Kenedy, and Company and earned a 12 percent stake in Kenedy's steamship company. Kenedy worried that San Román would leverage his shares in the steamship company to hamstring it in favor of the new railroad company. Kenedy threatened, "to make war to the knife, Steamboat vs. R.R." Kenedy went on to explain that he would have taken his profits and "withdrawn in good grace but now he left [*sic*] like seeing it out to the bitter end." Though this last statement was probably a falsehood, Kenedy's declarations reveal that by 1872 competition between Anglo-American business interests and European-born entrepreneurs had heated up. The race to build the railroad fractured both factions into a ruinous competition that would lead both sides to lie, cheat, and bribe their way to victory. Kenedy and his partners triumphed and drove a powerful group of European-born entrepreneurs from the borderlands.[1]

Like in the 1850s, the fight between factions revolved around transportation.[2] Immediately after the Civil War, King, Kenedy, and Company quashed a European-led movement to build a railroad from the mouth of the Rio Grande to Brownsville. The company owned the steamship monopoly in which the most powerful merchants in the region had invested. A rail line would have complicated and challenged their monopoly, especially since the proliferation of carting companies had proved to be challenging enough. A competing railroad could be catastrophic. Chicago's recent meteoric rise at the expense of St. Louis certainly vexed the steamship captain, as railroad networks put the steamship landing at St. Louis at a disadvantage to Chicago. Shipping through St. Louis declined precipitously, destroying steamship companies that plied their trade on the Mississippi River. As a result, Kenedy and his partners anxiously worked to undermine any further competition from overland transport.[3]

Environmental conditions compounded overland shipping competition. Steamboating became more limited every year. Decreased rainfall, increased agriculture, and damming projects lowered the volume of water in the Rio Grande. Boats just could not go as far upriver as they could in previous centuries. Merchants demanded more effective transport. Additionally, European-born borderlands entrepreneurs thought of the steamboat as an antebellum technology. It was dated and used up. The future lay in the railroad. Modernity came with the railroad. In secret, an increasing number of entrepreneurs, most of whom were European born, worked to build a rail line parallel to the Rio Grande on the north bank. They made political maneuvers within the Reconstruction government in Austin and raised money in Europe to fund construction. Eventually, this group of mostly European borderlands entrepreneurs openly challenged King, Kenedy, and Company.[4]

The schism erupted on that Sunday afternoon in May when Kenedy accosted San Román. Kenedy and his closest business partner, Richard

King, saw the writing on the wall for their steamboat monopoly. Rather than fight, "Steamboat vs. R.R." like Kenedy had threatened, Kenedy pursued the fight railroad versus railroad. He and King teamed up with a boastful promoter from Albany, New York, Uriah Lott. Lott, who had just opened a shipping company to transport borderlands wool and hides from Corpus Christi to New York City, tried to raise money to build a narrow-gauge rail line from Corpus Christi to Laredo. Lott provided Kenedy and King with an opportunity. They both invested heavily in Lott's project to have a railroad line that connected the Rio Grande to Corpus Christi rather than the European line that would run upriver through Brownsville. The competition was on.[5]

The timing of the break between Anglo-American and European rail-building factions favored the American group. Southern Democrats returned to power in Texas by the mid-1870s and moved to destroy most Republican policies of the Reconstruction era. Concurrently, Porfirio Díaz rose to power in Mexico and sought to expand Mexico's economy by inviting foreign investors to help him do it. American railroad magnates turned south, hoping to exploit the Mexican market. Kenedy and King's northeast-to-southwest rail line put it in the direct pathway of significant American and Mexican investment. The European faction faltered and never recovered. Kenedy had declared war on San Román in 1872. It took a little over a decade, but he successfully destroyed his European competitors on the Rio Grande.[6]

More effective roads and competitive overland shipping rates began to divide Anglo-American and European borderlands entrepreneurs in the wake of the Civil War in the early 1870s. Overland shipping offered European and Mexican entrepreneurs opportunities to undermine the Anglo-American monopoly on river shipping. Road conditions improved as military engineers and private projects worked on troubled roads to make them passable. The cotton times also encouraged young Mexican men throughout the borderlands to take up carting.[7] The increase in experienced carters lowered shipping rates. Goods could be moved faster and cheaper overland rather than up and down the Rio Grande. Joseph Kleiber from Strasbourg wrote "there was very little private freight to go. Most of that now goes by carte."[8]

Hanoverian-born August Santleben took advantage of the overland trade opportunities after 1867. He ran a profitable stage line between San Antonio and Monterrey. His network, predominantly European and Mexican-born businesspeople, guaranteed his line protections and privileges. German-speaking merchants in Monterrey, Eagle Pass, and San Antonio all relied on the line. Of these powerful merchants, some of the biggest names were Ulrich and Weber in Monterrey and F. Groos and Company in San Antonio. Even Evaristo Madero, the powerful textile manufacturer, trusted Santleben to import merino sheep from Texas to Monterrey.[9]

Carters like Santleben benefited from improved roads in the Rio Grande borderlands, but the overland trade was as dangerous as it was profitable. The United States repaired the road between San Antonio and Eagle Pass to ensure regular mail deliveries. According to Santleben, "The road was good in dry weather."[10] This was a ringing endorsement compared to some of the descriptions during the early cotton times. However, dangers persisted. Indigenous raiders and highwaymen took advantage of the increasing traffic of wealth between Texas and Mexico. Santleben noted that he "often saw the trails of marauding parties of Indians where they crossed the road and have found the mutilated bodies of many men lying where they had been murdered."[11]

Overland transport was already cutting into King, Kenedy, and Company's profits even before the railroad came. After the war carting companies like Santleben's had to compete for fewer transportation contracts, lowering the cost of overland transport. Since the end of the wartime cotton boom, shipping demand decreased. Cart teams could be purchased on the cheap to bypass high steamship rates. King, Kenedy, and Company tried to counter. They began offering no commission freight charges for advancing from the port at Brazos de Santiago to Brownsville and other points upriver.[12]

Additionally, natural and manmade changes had significant effect on the steamship business on the Lower Rio Grande. In October 1867 a major hurricane whipped through the Gulf of Mexico, skirting the Yucatán Peninsula and following the Gulf Stream to make landfall at the mouth of the Rio Grande. The storm destroyed Bagdad and caused considerable damage in Brownsville and Matamoros, ripping off the roof of the building that housed Kenedy and King's headquarters. They were lucky that was the extent of the damage as hundreds of homes and buildings in Brownsville and Matamoros were destroyed. One of Kenedy's agents wrote about the storm, "Words cannot describe the terrible and unexpected calamity which has come over Brownsville."[13] The company also lost four ships in the tempest. *The Daily Ranchero* newspaper went so far as to declare, "The Rio Grande steamboat interest lost enough in the late tornado to build the railroad from Brownsville to the Gulf connection."[14] King and Kenedy may have faced up to $200,000 in property damage losses because of the storm.[15]

What ships remained had less and less water in which to ply their trade. Steamers had always had trouble making it any farther upriver than Laredo. After the Civil War, that was nearly impossible. From 1850 to 1870, the number of acreages using the Rio Grande for irrigation more than doubled. With each acre of cultivated land requiring approximately 900,000 gallons of water, the amount of water flowing through northern Mexico and southern Texas decreased considerably. By the mid-1870s the situation became dire. A Brownsville steamboat captain wrote Kenedy in 1877, "The River is lower than I ever seen it this time of year . . . if the River does not rise any more this Season Boats will not be able to run more than one or two months."[16] New shoals appeared near Roma and Mier that blocked passage upriver. Natural conditions were limiting the value of steamboat transport on the Rio Grande at an alarming rate.[17]

In addition to declining steamboat traffic, Kenedy and King had lost their most aggressive partner. Charles Stillman suffered a stroke in 1866 that affected the entire left side of his body and weakened his competitive spirit. Stillman withdrew from the partnership and returned to New England, leaving the management of most of his Texas businesses to his brother, Cornelius. Charles and his son, James Stillman, reinvested most of their fortune in the National City Bank of New York. Charles Stillman never returned to the Rio Grande. He died in New York in 1875. Kenedy had lost an incredibly important partnership.[18]

With their cotton profits made during wartime and a weakened Anglo-American syndicate, European borderlands entrepreneurs saw that the time was ripe to solidify the Rio Grande borderlands as a center of Atlantic trade from which they would reap the gains. The keystone of the plan was to build a rail line along the Rio Grande. Investors like Spanish-born M. J. Gomila, José San Román, Simon Celaya, and Simon Mussina, had both the "desire as well as [the] interest to have the road built."[19] A main railroad trunk line that ran along the river with spurs that ranged north to connect with the transcontinental lines and south to incorporate Mexican trade centers would make the towns along the river essential hubs. This was especially true for Brownsville and Matamoros since those towns would handle the imports and exports via the Atlantic trade. By being the first to claim a rail line to replace steamboats, European-born borderlands entrepreneurs could seize a monopoly on transportation and leverage it to force their competition out of business. It took time, patience, and political manipulation, but the predominately European-born network used railroads to try to take control of the Rio Grande borderlands.

The railroad epitomized progress and modernity in the transatlantic. In the United States, nearly every major rail line was built by networks of friends who pooled finances, sold bonds, fought over congressional support, and manipulated newspapers. They lobbied to gain allies through promises of profit and outright bribes. The notion of friendship masked their corruption. It also enabled them to compete with the corruption of their opponents. Anglo-American railroad men transported their modern mentality to Mexico. They petitioned the Mexican government for land concessions with promises of massive economic rewards. With their Mexican allies, Anglo-Americans sold Mexico on the idea of a modern North American railroad network.[20]

In Europe railroad development was much more of a state-run process. While the US federal government invested significant land resources into railroad development, large private investments supported rail building. That deep-pocketed investment capital just did not exist in Europe outside of Britain. State coffers invested huge sums into national rail lines. According to historian Richard Evans, by midcentury France had invested 13 percent of its GDP in railways while Prussia allocated almost a third of its national budget every year. European states competed to create modern internal transportation networks and spent great sums of money to do so.[21]

European-born borderland entrepreneurs brought both American and European ideas of rail building to their project on the Rio Grande. They recognized the need for private funds but wanted as much support from the state as they could get. These ideas went hand in glove. The more money they could raise, or at least appear to have raised, the more support they could garner in the state capitol in Austin. One of the leading facilitators of the European group, Joseph Kleiber, pulled strings for the Rio Grande Railroad Company. He built a network of investors, lobbied congress, tried to manipulate the executive branch, and pondered a run for congress himself, making him one of many European-born entrepreneurs who combined American and European notions of railroad building in the borderlands.

Kleiber and his associates did not have to start their rail building projects from scratch. The skeleton for a rail line already existed along the river. During the Union occupation of Brownsville in 1865, soldiers hastily put down track from the town down to the Gulf to ensure their supply line, since Union steamships could take days to navigate the winding pathway of the Rio Grande just to cover the twenty-five miles from Fort Brown to the coast.[22] The federal government put the rinky-dink line up for sale after the war. Kenedy and King tried to make the purchase but were outbid by a silent owner. The bidder's identity became moot after the hurricane in 1867 washed away most of the track.[23]

With the old line rendered derelict by the storm, Kenedy and King pushed the state of Texas to grant them the charter to construct a permanent railroad from the coast to Brownsville. They won the charter and did nothing. They were not motivated to actually lay any track. Merchants in Brownsville and Matamoros knew the moment that King, Kenedy, and Company got the charter that they never intended to build the railroad. Joseph Kleiber wrote that "the parties who obtained the charter never intended nor ever will build the road."[24] People along the Rio Grande still had to pay King, Kenedy, and Company's steamship company or individual carters to ensure their supplies. Kleiber and his associates were fed up. "<u>This road will be built</u> & break up the steamboat monopoly." They created the Rio Grande Railroad Company (RGRRC) to do so.[25]

An entire movement to transfer the charter to an organization that would build a rail line developed in secret. Any businessperson who wanted to support the transfer of the rail charter had to do so quietly to avoid financial ruin. For example, Anglo-American H. E. Woodhouse, a partner in King, Kenedy, and Company since 1854, wanted the convenience and speed that a railroad would provide to the Rio Grande trade. Woodhouse was even willing to finance a part of its construction. He quietly collaborated with Kleiber to raise funds and political support. In exchange Kleiber tried to keep Woodhouse's name from being tied to the railroad. He wrote Simon Mussina, "If you undertake to carry out this project in connection with Mr. W. you must bear in mind that it is absolutely necessary that his name shall not appear in the matter nor be heard of in connection with it untill [sic] the charter is obtained and <u>work</u> is undertaken in earnest."[26] Working against Kenedy and King threatened all of Woodhouse's investments in the Rio Grande borderlands, but a rail line offered seemingly endless possibility. It was worth the risk.[27]

Woodhouse was not the only prominent member of the old Stillman syndicate to break ranks with King, Kenedy, and Company. Francisco Yturria, the group's banker, also supported the new rail line. He even tried to convince Charles Stillman's son, James Stillman, to invest in the project. Additionally, Irish-born Jeremiah Galvan, who worked with the Stillman syndicate as a front to ship Confederate cotton to New York, supported the RGRRC construction despite Kenedy and King's endorsement for Galvan's run as state representative. One of Kenedy's agents was surprised to find out Galvan joined the RGRRC: "Galvan surrendered, the man that would not be tied up by any Spanish lay out, but he is I think as well tied now as we are."[28] A cohort of powerful business owners on the Lower Rio Grande challenged Kenedy and King in favor of actually constructing the railroad.[29]

Though the organization of investors Kleiber recruited had the funds to ensure the railroad would be built, they still had to earn the official charter from the state of Texas. The RGRRC began engaging politicians from the governor's office to the state House of Representatives. Republican Edmund J. Davis spent time during the Civil War in Matamoros conspiring to bring down the Confederacy and returned to Texas to win election to governor in 1869. He worked to bring law and order and economic development to Texas. In terms of law and order, Davis was particularly concerned with the Rio Grande borderlands. He encouraged stock laws to limit cattle rustling. Rustling grew exponentially in the postbellum period, causing significant strains between Anglo-Texans and Mexicans. Both Anglos and Mexicans participated in cattle raids. However, Anglo ranchers regularly blamed Mexicans for the increase in theft, calling for state support to expel Mexicans from South Texas. Further, Davis wanted to eliminate the presence of Indigenous people from the borderlands. He believed that "peace seems absolutely hopeless as long as one of them [Indians] lives or roams at large."[30] In a clearly contradictory policy, Davis believed that the path to ending frontier violence was to condone violence against Mexican and Indigenous people.[31]

Davis's law-and-order policy played into his larger goal of creating economic growth through railroad building. Overall, he wanted to integrate Texas more deeply into markets in the United States. Additionally, Davis believed railroads promoted internal improvements. He pushed for a policy that encouraged liberal charters and granting right-of-way. Often giving significant power over the land to railroad companies, the charters and right-of-way helped the RGRRC to build its line from Point Isabel to Brownsville. Kleiber made that clear in his letters to Davis. He wrote, "We intend to build a railroad in fact and not on paper and that we have not trifled with the State Govt . . . the intention is to cut the line as straight as possible from point to point."[32] Without having to fret over property rights and rights-of-way, the RGRRC benefited from the Davis administration.[33]

The legislative representative for Cameron County in the state House of Representatives was Ferdinand Schlickum, a bookseller from Bergen. With Kleiber's encouragement, Schlickum introduced a bill to revoke the charter from Kenedy and King and reissue it to another ownership group. Helped along by Republican lawmakers like Ira Evans, the legislature passed the new charter for the RGRRC in May 1871. Kenedy's agent in Austin, observing the charter's passing wrote, "I repeat all I have ever said in favor of this charter—it is the best charter ever granted by any public authority In the U. States if not in the world."[34] Schlickum personally benefited from his efforts. Kleiber assured Schlickum "that he would be remembered" by his friends in Cameron County.[35] The RGRRC took advantage of the era of Reconstruction and Republican rule to gain the political upper hand over the Kenedy and King transportation monopoly.[36]

Though its members changed over time, the positions of directors of the RGRRC were dominated by Europeans. Spanish-born Simon Celaya, Francisco Armendaiz, and M. J. Gomila had the most money invested in the project. San Román, a silent partner like Woodhouse, also sunk considerable money into the railroad. Other directors, such as Alexander Werbiski, R. Deffendorfer, and Joseph Kleiber, all hailed from Europe and built a European-born core to the company. In addition to calling the company "the opposition," Mifflin Kenedy's Anglo-American agents in South Texas referred to the RGRRC as "the Spaniards."[37] The fight over the railroad on the Rio Grande largely reoriented the competition among borderlands entrepreneurs between American-born and European-born factions.

The RGRRC made powerful friends in the oceangoing shipping business as well. The shipping magnate Charles Morgan built a massive transportation system based in New Orleans that integrated most of the Gulf of Mexico and expanded into Mexico and Central America. Morgan spent significant sums integrating his ocean vessels with overland rail systems. Kenedy and his agents believed that the RGRRC was Morgan's next acquisition. "This is I suppose the entering wedge to Morgan getting the Road, I would sooner see it in any other hands than his, but this they have worked for since the first Rail was laid."[38] Connecting the RGRRC to the Morgan Line would have ensured the railroad's long-term success. Having a partner that large guaranteed continued intra-Gulf trade in addition to the directors' transatlantic trading network.[39]

Since it consisted of primarily European-born entrepreneurs, the RGRRC sought material and financial assistance in Europe. Simon Celaya and H. E. Woodhouse traveled abroad to purchase iron, engines, rolling stock, and other necessities. They bought most of their iron for rails from Railton and Sons in Manchester, England. The British iron industry experienced a massive boom in 1870, producing 5,960 tons for the global market. British-made iron and locomotives supplied the railroad building boom in both the United States and continental Europe. Additionally, the RGRRC marketed in Europe for investors. When they tapped out all their resources in the Rio Grande borderlands, the company's directors planned "to borrow the money in Europe."[40] Essentially, Celeya wanted to imitate American railroad tycoons by creating bond certificates and selling them abroad. If they could spread the RGRRC's debt across Europe, it would bring a massive cash infusion into the project and make the directors of the company a tidy profit. It would also give the railroad a huge advantage over their steamboating competitors.[41]

With the hurricane damages, decreasing river volume, and the increasing success of the RGRRC, Kenedy and King made the difficult decision to dissolve the steamship operations of King, Kenedy, and Company. They essentially sold the company to the RGRRC since they lost the transportation monopoly and saw no profits in competition. The exact thing Kenedy was worried about when he confronted San Román had happened. His partners leveraged their power to bring the railroad to the Rio Grande. To add insult to injury, one of the directors of the RGRRC wrote Kenedy on King, Kenedy, and Company letterhead that "by our agreement with you neither of these boats can run in the Brazos, or mouth of the Rio Grande, nor in the River in opposition to us without violating our contract."[42] Even the last couple of steamships they had left on the Rio Grande could not haul goods. Kenedy felt betrayed and furious. He plotted his strategy to destroy his new opposition.[43]

Kenedy tried to use the courts as his first means to destroy the RGRRC. He filed a lawsuit against the company, which essentially stated that since the RGRRC was chartered as a railroad company, it should not legally be able to run steamships on the Rio Grande. The suit went on to argue that the RGRRC secured a monopoly contrary to the public good and should thus return the steamships they purchased from King, Kenedy, and Company to Kenedy.[44] Coming from a man who held a transportation monopoly on the Lower Rio Grande for nearly two decades, this argument stretched the boundaries of hypocrisy. If Kenedy won, the RGRRC would own the King, Kenedy, and Company name but not be able to function as a steamship company. The court ruled in favor of the RGRRC.

By the end of 1874, the RGRRC weathered the first storm of Kenedy's challenge. The network of predominantly European-born entrepreneurs took control of the Rio Grande market and focused on making it a center of Atlantic trade. They integrated into the Morgan Line and planned on sending agents to Europe. It appeared European-born entrepreneurs and their networks in the Rio Grande borderlands controlled the future of the political economy of the region. They held vast wealth and a dominant hold on regional transportation and had sympathetic politicians working to ensure their interests. They were

Rio Grande Railroad Locomotive. Floyd Elton and Jewel Griffith Reese Collection, South Texas Archives and Special Collections, Texas A&M University–Kingsville.

bringing modernity to the Rio Grande. Kleiber, Celaya, San Román, and their partners also understood that they stood to lose it all with one misstep. They knew Kenedy would persist in coming after them. "Kenedy will cry & beg & make any appeal."[45] These borderlands entrepreneurs girded themselves for the future.[46]

Kenedy did not cry, beg, or make appeals. He fought dirty. Though his and King's footing in Brownsville and Matamoros slipped, they repositioned themselves farther north in Corpus Christi. They consolidated their landholdings at the peak of a major cattle boom, King on the Santa Gertrudis ranch and Kenedy on his Laureles ranch. From Laureles Kenedy licked his wounds and plotted his revenge. His plan revolved around strangling the RGRRC in the courts and tarnishing its reputation while he built a competing rail line from Corpus Christi to Laredo. He marketed the Corpus Christi line throughout the United States to attract the attention of the biggest railroad investors in the country. He also negotiated with the Porfirio Díaz administration for rights to extend the line into Mexico. If any of the major rail lines in the United States dropped down to connect with his line, it would essentially cut off the RGRRC from the continental trade. Rail traffic would follow the major trunk lines, and that is what Kenedy wanted to integrate his rail line into. If he did so, oceangoing vessels would have no choice but to turn to Corpus Christi as its primary South Texas port of entry. Kenedy utilized geography and politics to recapture power and cut out his European "opposition" once and for all.

While on the Laureles ranch, Kenedy wanted to maintain a clear picture of everything going on with the RGRRC. He dispatched agents across Texas to keep an eye on the company's directors. Ed Downey and Robert Dalzell wrote to Kenedy with regular updates. Downey traveled all over the Gulf of Mexico, from Galveston to New Orleans, following the company's directors. Dalzell remained fixed in Brownsville. Folks in the RGRRC suspected Kenedy had spies on them. Kleiber wrote, "Lovenskiold is here—he is Kenedy's bower in Corpus—I expect his visit here is for some machinations probably to fix up some new trick on us—He is the man for the work. We will see."[47] Kleiber's suspicions proved correct. One of Kenedy's lawyers, Lovenskiold, sent Kenedy telegraph updates about the RGRRC lawyer, Nestor Maxan, and railroad business from Austin.[48]

Kenedy also may have hired outside help to disrupt his opposition's business. P. M. Spinelli wrote Kenedy from San Diego to "beg to inform you that if there was any possible chance to worry and harass the RGRRC I am willing to use my best energies to that effect."[49] Even if he did not hire Spinelli, Kenedy still used nefarious tactics in his surveillance campaign. He bought off the postmaster of Corpus Christi to gather information and sway political opinion.[50] Kenedy relied on a vast network of agents to gather information for him.

In addition to building a system of spies, Kenedy and his friends wrote letters to the RGRRC's creditors and business partners implying that the company acted inappropriately. Someone from King, Kenedy, and Company wrote to Joseph Railton and Sons, San Román's associates in Manchester, England, implying that the RGRRC would not be able to pay its invoice on a large order of iron rails. When Joseph Kleiber learned that Railton worried about the company's debts, he was shocked. Kleiber wrote, "I fear you have been led to feel uneasy by misrepresentations made by some of your own and my enemies as I am already in formed [*sic*] by some of my best friends and also yours."[51] Kenedy kept at it. He wrote one of Railton's lawyers in New York explaining that he sued H. E. Woodhouse because of his financial problems. Kenedy wrote, "In a suit between Woodhouse & myself pending in Brownsville, in which is involved the question of damage to his commercial credit..."[52] Kleiber tried to figure out who was saying what to Railton. He wrote Woodhouse, stating, "I have also heard from several of our friends severe complaints about the Railtons—Letters have been written to Europe to find out who did write and what was really written."[53] Kenedy attempted to snap an important transatlantic connection for the RGRRC.

Until Kenedy's machinations, Railton and Sons had maintained a profitable relationship with the directors and investors of the RGRRC. José San Román and Joseph Kleiber shipped tons of cotton to the Railtons during the cotton boom of the 1860s. This gave the Railton firm an upper hand on its competition in the Manchester textile industry in a time when cotton supplies constricted. Their success ensured Railton and Sons a high rating on the Manchester Commercial List. They could take on significant credit from any lender in England and extend that credit on investments like the RGRRC. However, at the same time Kenedy maneuvered to torpedo the railroad's relationship with Railton and Sons, the patriarch, Joseph Railton, had just retired and left the company's operations to his sons. Kenedy's letters left the Railton sons questioning their company's investments in a railroad project across the Atlantic in the Rio Grande borderlands.[54]

Kenedy also attempted to disrupt the RGRRC's ability to lay track. While King and Kenedy held the charter to build the Rio Grande line, Kenedy acquired land in the Espiritu Santo grant northeast of Brownsville. The RGRRC had to lay track through the Espiritu Santo to get from Port Isabel to Brownsville. Kenedy tried to make that impossible. By the terms of their charter, the company could condemn lands in their right-of-way in order lay track. When the RGRRC did that, Kenedy filed another lawsuit demanding a $2,000 annual rental fee, $5,000 in damages to the Resaca, and $25,000 in overall damages to the land.[55] The RGRRC tried to settle with Kenedy. The company's director, Gomila, even offered to pay $10,000 for the land to make the suits go away.[56] Out of either vindictiveness or as a means to posture, Kenedy continued to tie up the company in the courts through 1879 over the issue of the right-of-way.

The directors of the RGRRC and the Kenedy business network also competed for political favor in state and local politics. For the RGRRC state politics turned against them when Democrats retook the legislature and governor's office in Austin. In January of 1874, the Democratic legislature assembled and forced Governor Davis from his post. Davis technically had until April as acting governor under the state constitution, but fearing Davis's opposition, the legislature immediately inaugurated Richard Coke. Davis appealed to the Grant administration to no avail. Reconstruction Republicans lost Texas.[57]

One key economic platform from the Davis era that Democrats held on to was to continue railroad expansion in Texas. They just shifted the power center from Austin to local politics. The Texas Constitution of 1876 severely restricted the powers of the state and limited the ability of the legislature to finance large projects. County government became a center for power. The RGRRC refocused its energies on county elections. Democrats were the only party that could win a state election after 1876, but the party split locally between Reds and Blues. The powerful Anglo-American merchants, including Kenedy, tended to support the Reds, while the Blues gained support from smaller business owners and a hodgepodge of other groups. The RGRRC backed the Blues and threw significant resources at the 1878 county election. One of Kenedy's agents wrote him, "The Rail Road and Galvan are doing everything in their power to ellect [sic] Russell, the Ellection [sic] will I think be close in this county."[58] It was close, but the Blues pulled out the victory by motivating voters to get to the polls. The same agent stated, "The whole county now is in the hands of the Rail Road and Galvan they spent a great deal of money in this Ellection [*sic*], and they made about Eight hundred new voters a grate [*sic*] many of whom do not live on this side."[59] The RGRRC consolidated its hold in Cameron County.[60]

Kenedy spent a few thousand dollars combating the RGRRC in Cameron County politics but redistributed most of his investments in a competing rail line. He engaged the partnership of New York–born entrepreneur Uriah Lott. Lott was a man on the make. He first traveled to Illinois to work on the Chicago and Alton Railroad. Finding little opportunity for advancement there, he looked to the Rio Grande borderlands as his place for opportunity. Lott boarded a train in Alton and rode the Illinois Central down to the city of New Orleans, where he bought passage on a Morgan steamship to Brownsville. Another Anglo-American borderlands entrepreneur sought wealth and power on the Rio Grande.[61]

Lott got his start in the borderlands as a correspondent for *Le Courrier du Rio Grande*, a French, Spanish, and English newspaper in Brownsville. He started his job right in the middle of a newspaper war in Brownsville. The *Ranchero*, *Courrier*, and *Republican* all competed for readers. In 1868 the *Ranchero* bought out its competitors, leaving Lott without a paper for which to correspond. He had to pivot. Lott decided, likely based on a recommendation from Richard King, to move to Corpus Christi, where he founded a forwarding company, U. Lott and Company. Transportation to and from Corpus Christi became central to his business.[62]

Unfortunately for Lott, Corpus Christi was falling behind in transportation. The Galveston, Houston, and San Antonio Railroad had facilitated deeper connections between San Antonio and the port at Galveston. The RGRRC drew more shipping to Brownsville from the Morgan Lines in New Orleans and dominated the Atlantic trade. Corpus Christi was being left behind and in between. Lott believed he needed a rail line to Corpus Christi to ensure his business. Thus, he became the primary booster for building a Corpus Christi railroad.[63]

When Kenedy and King learned of Lott's plans, they invested heavily and became primary shareholders in the company. Kenedy was particularly intrigued at the route Lott had chosen, from Corpus Christi to Laredo. That pathway would cut off the Rio Grande Railroad. He put $10,000 into the project and likely encouraged King to kick in an additional $20,000. King saw value in building a rail line through his cattle lands. It offered fast, cheap transport that was more efficient than driving the cattle long distances. Texas also offered massive land subsidies to railroads that extended farther than twenty-five miles. King understood he could incorporate many of the acres the railroad gained into his growing ranching empire. Both Anglo-American borderlands entrepreneurs invested in the Corpus Christi, San Diego, and Rio Grande Narrow Gauge Railroad Company (CCRR) to ensure its completion.[64]

In the process of building the Corpus Christi to Laredo railway, Lott, Kenedy, and King had assistance in the Texas state legislature. Kenedy made sure to have state senators in his pocket. He extended Senator William H. Russell thousands of dollars in credit and forwarded Russell a barrel of whiskey from New Orleans. In return, Russell ensured Lott's railroad charters made it through Congress.[65]

The CCRR also needed additional funding. Initially the company pursued a bond plan in 1874 that included an attempt to extract $300,000 from Duval and Nueces Counties. Voters in Corpus Christi interpreted it as another railroad scam and the bond election failed. The public had just learned in 1873 of the levels of corruption railroad owners were willing to go to after the publication of the Crédit Mobilier scandal. The Crédit Mobilier construction company had used its position in the Union Pacific Railroad company to steer fraudulent contracts to their company, bilking millions in taxpayer dollars. It was a national embarrassment. Duval and Nueces Counties did not want to be the next victims of men in octopus suits. Not to be deterred, the Corpus Christi railroad group found another way to gain public support. Once a railroad line in Texas reached a distance of twenty-five miles of completed track, it qualified for state land bonuses. Kenedy and King lent the financial support for Lott to get to the twenty-five-mile threshold, then petitioned Austin for land grants. In total Texas granted 855,680 acres to the CCRR. Much of the excess land ended up becoming a part of the King Ranch.[66]

The CCRR project took on more significance to Kenedy after 1876. Major railroad promoters in the United States turned their sights on Texas and Mexico. Jay Gould looked south to build a massive system that would interconnect all North America. He saw Texas as the best place to extend his Missouri Pacific system and acquired the Texas and Pacific Railroad from Tom Scott. Gould seemed to make money appear everywhere he went, regardless of actual economic conditions. One of the investors in the CCRR, J. J. Dull of Harrisburg, Pennsylvania, wrote Kenedy, urging him to speed completion of the line to Laredo. Dull had an idea that "Gould is trying to gobble his [Scott's] Mexican part."[67] What eventually materialized was the Missouri Pacific Railroad to Laredo. Kenedy wanted to make sure the CCRR connected with the north-south trunk lines coming from the east-west transcontinentals. It would be a dagger to his European opposition in Brownsville.[68]

By 1880 New York financiers and Mexican politicians looked to the Rio Grande borderlands as the next place for significant railroad development. In addition to railroad moguls like Jay Gould, financial goliaths in New York City like J. P. Morgan, William Rockefeller, and James Stillman sought access to Mexican land and expanding trade with Mexico. Building railroads into Mexico provided the means to those ends. Porfirio Díaz, a Mexican general who ascended to the presidency in 1876 by overthrowing a constitutional government, encouraged American investment in Mexico. He went so far as to cancel a concession to a British railroad group, Barron-Forbes, and fined the London group $150,000 for breach of contract. Then Díaz offered new concessions for the Mexican Central Railroad and Mexican National Railroad to American firms. Díaz opened the door to American investment, and that New York money was going to flow through the Rio Grande borderlands into Mexico.[69]

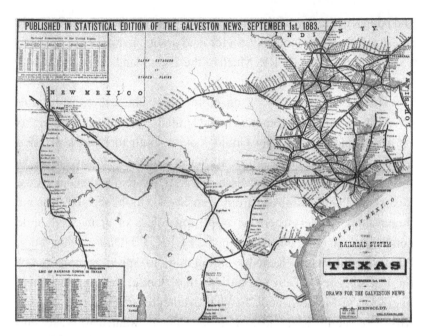

Map of the Railroad System of Texas on September 1, 1883. E. A. Hensoldt and Rand McNally and Company, *The Railroad System of Texas on September 1st* (Chicago: Rand McNally, 1883), Library of Congress, https://www.loc.gov/item/2001622093/.

Mifflin Kenedy and his network, including Richard King and Charles Stillman's sons, developed significant interest in the prospect of the Mexican National Railway. For Kenedy, if the Mexican National took its intended route from Mexico City through San Luis Potosí and Monterrey and terminated at Nuevo Laredo, it would essentially make the Rio Grande Railroad irrelevant. He could connect his Corpus Christi, San Diego, and Rio Grande Railroad to the Mexican National, making it a part of a vast transnational network. King, who had investments in the CCRR, expected the Mexican National to bring a fat return on those investments and would open an unimpeded market for his beef cattle in Mexico. James Stillman had financial and nationalistic motives. He believed the rail line would open Mexico's mineral wealth to the United States. It would also slowly transfer territory from Mexicans to Americans. Since his father's former partners had already begun a rail line to Laredo, it made sense for James Stillman to encourage the point of ingress into Mexico at Laredo.[70]

Kenedy and Uriah Lott went full steam to ensure their rail line reached Laredo by the time the quiet river town transformed into "the great international gateway" local boosters claimed Laredo would be. In 1878 Lott had only completed twenty-five miles of the CCRR, enough to get the Texas state land subsidies. By mid-1880 the track ran to Realitos, nearly two-thirds of the way to Laredo. Lott and Kenedy also conspired to keep the international focus on Laredo. Lott collaborated with Thomas Pearsall, the president of the International and Great Northern Railroad Company, to lobby Congress to subsidize the San Antonio and Border Railroad Company. Lott couched his plea in terms of border security. "By granting us the aid in the manner named, the military headquarters at San Antonio are provided with an additional competitive rail outlet to the gulf, via Corpus Christi, which would be a very great advantage to the government, besides being placed in rail communication with Fort Duncan, Fort McIntosh, Ringold Barracks, and San Diego, directly from San Antonio."[71] Lott simultaneously promoted Corpus Christi as the Gulf entrepôt for South Texas and the idea that his rail projects were essential to US national security.[72]

While Uriah Lott publicly promoted the CCRR, Kenedy worked behind the scenes to make sure his railroad connected with the transnational trunk lines and the RGRRC did not. He negotiated a charter with the Mexican secretary of state for a Rio Grande railroad south of the border. The charter, created in 1880, called for a railroad and telegraph to run from Matamoros through Reynosa, Camargo, Mier, and Cerralvo, terminating at Monterrey. With this charter in hand, Kenedy prevented the RGRRC from becoming a fully transnational line. He would do nothing with it. Anglo-American investors valued the CCRR over the RGRRC after 1880.[73]

When news spread that the Mexican National would be built to Laredo, Kenedy and King's railroad became one of the most valuable projects in the United States. One of Jay Gould's system building projects, the Missouri Pacific Railroad, planned to connect San Antonio to Laredo in 1881. Those two railroads would transform Laredo from a sleepy river town to a central hub of transnational shipping. The CCRR was scheduled to terminate at Laredo, connecting it to both transnational railroad lines and one of the largest transcontinental systems in the United States. When the Palmer-Sullivan Group, owners of the Denver and Rio Grande Railway and the concession to the Mexican National Railway, inquired to purchase the CCRR, Kenedy, King, and Lott could not sell fast enough. Kenedy and King managed to earn $5 million for their unfinished narrow-gauge line from Corpus Christi to Laredo and essentially had a guarantee that somebody else would do the work to complete it for them. The CCRR became the Texas Mexican Railroad. Kenedy made a bundle of money and ensured the RGRRC remained isolated from the rest of the North American trade.[74]

Through all this, Simón Celaya, Gomila, and other members of the RGRRC worked to avoid being cut out of the North American trade between Mexico and the United States. They also sought new partners for investment and state assistance. Francisco Yturria, the former banker for King, Kenedy, and Company, contacted James Stillman to probe the notion of Stillman financing the expansion of the RGRRC. Stillman, with his goals wrapped up in the Mexican National Railway, declined to invest. In fact he wrote Yturria that he did not want to contribute to a rail line that would put Brownsville in "the hands of Woodhouse and the Spaniards."[75] Further, Simón Celaya, the general manager of the RGRRC, used his position as the Spanish vice consul in Brownsville to encourage more European investment, and he expanded trade through Brownsville and Matamoros. It all amounted to very little. The RGRRC was dying.[76]

From 1881 the RGRRC began a steep decline in carriage. A decade later it was wrecked and robbed of nearly $60,000 worth of silver. The company eventually defaulted and entered receivership under American ownership in 1910. Kenedy had declared war on "the Spaniards" and the RGRRC in 1872. It took years, but he successfully destroyed his European competitors on the Rio Grande.[77]

On reflection of the era of brief European dominance of the Lower Rio Grande, Mifflin Kenedy glossed over his failures and the nearness he came to ruin. In an interview he gave about his life, Kenedy claimed "he gave up his steamboat business" because "he became interested in railroads."[78] In his memory Mifflin Kenedy's decision to sink his wealth in railroad building came from personal curiosity and an entrepreneurial spirit, not the fury he had at having his steamboat company ripped from him. Some of his friends thought that Kenedy's investments in rail building were a mistake because railroading was a young man's game. In the 1880s Kenedy was in his 60s. J. H. Stephens wrote Kenedy, "Glad to know of your success in R Roading, especially as it is rather a departure from your regular line of business and one in which a man of your age should I think a 'leedle [sic] out.'"[79] Though it shocked his friends at the time, in Kenedy's hindsight the 1870s merely marked a time of transition from steamships to locomotives. His selective memory helped obscure his European competitors from history.

Ironically, had the European entrepreneurial group not constructed the Rio Grande Railroad, Kenedy might not have invested in railroad building and likely would have maintained his steamboat monopoly. It was the European-born borderlands entrepreneurs who made the effort to bring modern transportation networks to the Rio Grande. They pushed back against Anglo-American business hegemony in the borderlands and briefly succeeded in capturing the market. Though they ultimately failed to hold on to it, this period reveals that Europeans continued to challenge Americans on the fringes of their empire well into the Gilded Age.

And the battle was fierce. The European-born borderlands entrepreneurs and their allies wanted to break Kenedy's steamship monopoly for the opportunity to expand trade. When they did, Kenedy operated with a personal vendetta to destroy the European group. He dragged the RGRRC through the court system, bribed the company's political allies, and sent spies to find ways to undermine the railroad's operations. He even went so far as to invest in his own railroad development. Eventually, the path to victory lay through Mexico. Reconstruction politics in the United States and Texas mattered for getting charters, rights-of-way, and land grants. For the most part, the European group won that battle. However, Porfirio Díaz clinched Kenedy's victory when he opened Mexico for American railway moguls. Transnational jockeying and a fair bit of luck led to Kenedy's success and the European group's downfall.

Epilogue

The transnational space between San Antonio, Texas, and Monterrey, Nuevo León, looks very different today than it did when Mexican laborers laid the last rails of the Mexican National Railway. Irrigation projects and scientific agriculture transformed the desert of the Nueces Strip into a national producer of crops. Soybeans, melons, corn, citrus, and cotton farms stretch across the landscape. The once-dominant cattle industry now only makes up about 25 percent of the region's agricultural production. The Mexican border cities are also a hub of economic activity. Maquiladoras, tourism, and the smuggling trade, among other industries, drive commerce in northern Mexico. San Antonio remains a key location for trade and has swelled to be the seventh largest city in the United States. Monterrey is the second largest metropolitan area in Mexico in terms of both population and GDP. European-born borderlands entrepreneurs certainly stimulated some of that economic growth and transformation.[1]

José de Escandón spearheaded many significant changes in the Rio Grande borderlands. He embraced prevailing shifts within the Spanish imperial program to combine commerce with expanding Spanish settlement. Bourbon policy changes opened opportunities for Escandón to offer peaceful trade with Indigenous borderlanders, recruit entrepreneurial colonists from central New Spain, and challenge outmoded strategies for expansion. Though he was not successful in entirely reforming New Spain's northern frontier, Escandón set an example for borderlands entrepreneurialism. The Rio Grande borderlands had the potential to become one of the commercial utopias that Europeans began to seek across the globe.

John C. Beales provides another example of the European drive to develop the American borderlands. As an empresario Beales blended his family connections in Mexico with his professional connections in the British imperial apparatus to try to enrich himself with thousands of acres of land on the Rio Grande. He recruited other European entrepreneurs to join him in the settlement venture. Merchants, artisans, and their families moved into the heart of the vast Rio Grande borderlands. They brought with them modern European notions of impersonal exchange and expectations of state support. However, they failed to impose their world on the borderlands. When the colony they built collapsed, its physical remnants quickly decayed.[2]

Taken on its own, the Beales example fits neatly into the Turnerian thesis of the frontier. Europeans moved into the frontier line and attempted to re-create a Europeanized settlement far from population centers but failed to develop local connections with Mexican and Indigenous groups. Additionally, they tried to impose their will on the environment. It is almost as if Frederick Jackson Turner was speaking about Beales when he wrote, "In short, at the frontier the environment is at first too strong for the man. He must accept the conditions which it furnishes, or perish."[3] Beales and his colonists did not accept local conditions, so their project failed. If the story ended there, the subtitle of this book might be *European Entrepreneurial Failures on the Frontier*. However, Europeans continued to try to remake the Rio Grande borderlands into a modern European space.

The idea of building borderlands settlements full of modern-thinking European entrepreneurs persisted, and the Rio Grande borderlands' potential sustained European attention. British consul general William Kennedy became interested in the same lands Beales failed to settle, and he set out to make himself wealthy by extending the presence of the British state to the Rio Grande. His book, *Texas*, made a lasting impact on readers' imaginations of the Rio Grande borderlands and his diplomatic work nudged the British Foreign Office to consider having a stronger physical presence in the region. Though Kennedy never built the settlements he dreamed of and instead returned to England, his plans to modernize and reform the borderlands seeped into the minds of other European borderlands entrepreneurs. Europeans continued to invest time, money, and other resources. Future migrants to the Rio Grande applied new strategies that wholly transformed the region.[4]

Perhaps one of the most successful European borderlands entrepreneurs, José San Román, both challenged Anglo-American expansion and used it to his benefit based on prevailing conditions. He saw profits in tying vast networks together, bringing massive transatlantic exchange to the borderlands. To do so San Román variously Americanized, Mexicanized, and remained staunchly European. To some Anglo-American allies, he was Joseph San Roman, European immigrant to the USA. To others he was a successful Mexican merchant. In the end, to himself, he was Spanish, for when his business career ended in the borderlands, he returned home to Bilbao. His experience demonstrates the fluidity of the borderlands.[5]

San Román and his partners harnessed this fluidity and instigated the most significant transformation of the Rio Grande borderlands. The cotton boom, brought on because of the unique conditions of the borderlands, produced a massive influx of wealth that borderlands entrepreneurs wanted to reinvest. Feeling confident after the era of civil wars on the Rio Grande, San Román and other European-born entrepreneurs openly challenged the most powerful Anglo-Americans in the region by investing in a European-owned rail development project on the Rio Grande. For a moment it seemed all the potential that began when Escandón founded commerce and capitalism on the Rio Grande was unleashed in favor of European-born entrepreneurs. The Rio Grande Railroad would allow the transportation inland that the river promised but never permitted. It failed when King and Kenedy outmaneuvered the European syndicate.

After the collapse of the RGRRC, European borderlands entrepreneurialism changed in the region. Many of the most prominent Europeans left. San Román returned to Bilbao. Joseph Kleiber also left the borderlands after the RGRRC began its decline. He left the mercantile life altogether, moving north of Austin to try his hand in land and cattle. Those who stayed had to work within a new framework. The borderlands had begun to lose its fluidity. Anglo-American control became more certain with the coming of the Mexican National Railway. Though European borderlands entrepreneurs left significant archives of documents behind them, their stories became subsumed in the narrative of American domination.[6]

Instead of leaving, Laredoan John Leyendecker went a completely different direction. Rather than bail on the borderlands after the establishment of Anglo-American commercial dominance, he joined them. With the new railroads running through Laredo, Leyendecker capitalized on his connections to Corpus Christi with King and Kenedy to support Laredo becoming a crossroads of North American trade. He and the Benavides family committed to the Texas Democratic Party and worked toward Americanizing Laredo. They maintained business and political connections with Americans in Corpus Christi seeking to promote the interests of American trade with local power politics. In consequence, Leyendecker is less remembered for his contribution in tying Laredo to Atlantic trade and more for Americanizing the town. His descendants know him for his positions as postmaster general of Webb County and acting as both secretary and treasurer of Laredo. Indeed, Laredo opened the John Z. Leyendecker elementary school in 1953, an institution designed to turn Laredo children into productive American citizens. Leyendecker is not remembered as a European borderlands entrepreneur who tried to modernize the Rio Grande borderlands and connect it to the Atlantic World. Instead, he was a German immigrant who achieved the American dream.[7]

After King and Kenedy's triumph, European-born entrepreneurs continued to move to the Rio Grande borderlands. However, instead of trying to reorient the region toward Europe, the immigrants of the late nineteenth century embraced the idea of the American dream and engaged in reforming notions of American identity in the borderlands. Though they failed to globalize and modernize the Rio Grande in the ways they imagined, European-born borderlands entrepreneurs added to the diversity and complexity of borderlands society, transforming the region in tangible ways.[8]

In addition to the case studies discussed herein, other significant European entrepreneurial enterprises in the borderlands similarly have been forgotten. French entrepreneurs made several attempts to establish mining companies and colonies in Northern Sonora. For example, in 1852 Lepine de Sigondis led up to eighty miner/colonists into the Santa Cruz Valley in modern-day Arizona. The venture disbanded rather quickly, but Sigondis was provided French state support and resources through the French consulate in California.[9]

Meanwhile, a group of English and Canadian entrepreneurs tried a similar venture north of Austin, Texas. The United States Land Company, an organization of English investors, promoted their lands in Texas with the prospects of mining gold and copper. The company even hired George Catlin, the famous painter of the American West, to write a pamphlet to promote the colony of New Britain. The venture ended in absolute disaster and Catlin lost his entire gallery to creditors. These failures mark other attempts by Europeans to leave their footprint in the borderlands and show how persistent they were in establishing a European presence on the American frontier.[10]

Even through their failures and the imposition of Anglo-American mercantile domination of the borderlands, European-born entrepreneurs did leave a significant mark on the region. José de Escandón's original settlements persist along the Rio Grande. John Beales's legacy of mismanagement informed William Kennedy and formed the basis of Kennedy's book about the borderlands. Kennedy, who actively sought to push against American expansion, may have helped expedite American intervention in the Rio Grande borderlands through his politicking in Texas. Alexander Bourgeois spurred the most powerful German-speaking emigration network to focus on settling in Texas. The networks that Leyendecker and San Román built affected the entire transportation infrastructure between northern Mexico and South Texas. Laredo would likely not have been the northern terminus of the Mexican National Railway had San Román and his partners not succeeded in building the Rio Grande Railroad or had Leyendecker not facilitated connections between Laredo and Corpus Christi. They all affected the historical trajectory of the Rio Grande borderlands, collectively globalizing the Lower Rio Grande.

Endnotes

Notes for Introduction

1. Joseph Crawford report to the British Foreign Office, April 1837, FO 50/109, the National Archives of the United Kingdom (hereafter cited as TNA).
2. A note on terms: when I use the term *European*, I mean individuals born in Europe. I often default to *European-born* to make that fact explicit. I use *Mexican* to define individuals born in Mexico. This extends past the US-Mexico War to those who may have been born in Mexican Texas but found themselves in the United States after the war. Finally, I utilize *Anglo-American* to denote individuals born in the United States. I understand the complications of this phrasing. When Herbert Bolton used Anglo-American in *The Spanish Borderlands*, he did so with the notion that American conquerors of the Southwest succeeded because of the traits of industriousness they inherited from the English. I am explicitly attempting to unhook that association and merely denote that they were English-speaking individuals born in the United States.
3. The Spanish dealt with various Mexican attempts to expel the Spanish from Mexico. See: Harold Sims, *The Expulsion of Mexico's Spaniards, 1821–1836*, Pitt Latin American Series (Pittsburgh: University of Pittsburgh Press, 1990), 3–7.
4. Armando C. Alonzo, *Tejano Legacy: Rancheros and Settlers in South Texas, 1734–1900*, 1st ed. (Albuquerque: University of New Mexico Press, 1998), 27–36; Lawrence Francis Hill, *José de Escandón and the Founding of Nuevo Santander, a Study in Spanish Colonization* (Columbus: Ohio State University Press, 1926); Patricia Osante, *Orígenes Del Nuevo Santander (1748–1772)*, 1st ed., Serie Historia Novohispana 59 (Ciudad Victoria, México: Universidad Nacional Autónoma de México, Instituto de Investigaciones Históricas, Universidad Autónoma de Tamaulipas, 1997); Graham Davis, *Land! Irish Pioneers in Mexican and Revolutionary Texas*, 1st ed., Centennial Series of the Association of Former Students, Texas A&M University 92 (College Station: Texas A&M University Press, 2002); Leroy P. Graf, "Colonizing Projects in Texas South of the Nueces, 1820–1845," *Southwestern Historical Quarterly* 50, no. 4 (April 1947): 431–48; Mary Virginia Henderson, "Minor Empresario Contracts for the Colonization of Texas, 1825–1834," part 1, *Southwestern Historical Quarterly* 31, no. 4 (April 1928): 295–324; Louis E. Brister, "Eduard Ludecus's Journey to the Texas Frontier: A Critical Account of Beales's

Rio Grande Colony," *Southwestern Historical Quarterly* 108, no. 3 (January 2005): 368–85.
5. "1860 United States Federal Census," Ancestry.com, accessed November 22, 2016, https://www.ancestry.com/imageviewer/collections/7667; Arnoldo DeLeon and Kenneth L. Stewart, *Tejanos and the Numbers Game: A Socio-Historical Interpretation from the Federal Censuses, 1850–1900* (Albuquerque: University of New Mexico Press, 1989). For my census data, I aggregated the totals for Webb, Cameron, and Starr Counties.
6. David J. Weber, *The Mexican Frontier, 1821–1846: The American Southwest under Mexico*, 1st ed., Histories of the American Frontier (Albuquerque: University of New Mexico Press, 1982); Brian DeLay, *War of a Thousand Deserts: Indian Raids and the U.S.-Mexican War* (New Haven, CT: Yale University Press, 2008); Pekka Hämäläinen, *The Comanche Empire* (New Haven, CT: Yale University Press, 2008); Sam W. Haynes, *Unfinished Revolution: The Early American Republic in a British World* (Charlottesville: University of Virginia Press, 2011); Andrew J. Torget, *Seeds of Empire: Cotton, Slavery, and the Transformation of the Texas Borderlands, 1800-1850* (Chapel Hill: University of North Carolina Press, 2015).
7. Alfred D. Chandler, *The Visible Hand: The Managerial Revolution in American Business* (Cambridge: Belknap Press, 1977), 51, 54, 298; Shino Konishi, "J. C. Byrne, Entrepreneurial Imperialism and the Question of Indigenous Rights," *Journal of Imperial and Commonwealth History* 48, no. 6 (2020): 983; Mary Poovey, "Risk, Uncertainty, and Data: Managing Risk in Twentieth-Century America," in *American Capitalism: New Histories*, ed. Sven Beckert and Christine Desan (New York: Columbia University Press, 2018), 222.
8. C. A. Bayly, *The Birth of the Modern World, 1780–1914: Global Connections and Comparisons*, Blackwell History of the World (Malden, MA: Blackwell, 2004), 2–3.
9. Bayly, *Birth of the Modern World*, 9–10; Davis, *Land!*, 6, 238–39.
10. Andrés Reséndez, *Changing National Identities at the Frontier: Texas and New Mexico, 1800–1850* (New York: Cambridge University Press, 2004), 1–5; Janet Tai Landa, *Trust, Ethnicity, and Identity: Beyond the New Institutional Economics of Ethnic Trading Networks, Contract Law, and Gift-Exchange*, Economics, Cognition, and Society (Ann Arbor: University of Michigan Press, 1994), 3–6.
11. David Montejano, *Anglos and Mexicans in the Making of Texas, 1836–1986*, 1st ed. (Austin: University of Texas Press, 1987), 24–75; Rodolfo F. Acuna, *Occupied America: The Chicano's Struggle toward Liberation* (San Francisco: Harper & Row, 1972); Carey McWilliams,

North from Mexico: The Spanish Speaking People of the United States (New York: Monthly Review Press, 1948); Arnoldo De León, *They Called Them Greasers: Anglo Attitudes Toward Mexicans in Texas, 1821–1900* (Austin: University of Texas Press, 1983); Alonzo, *Tejano Legacy*; Timothy Paul Bowman, *Blood Oranges: Colonialism and Agriculture in the South Texas Borderlands*, 1st ed., Connecting the Greater West Series (College Station: Texas A&M University Press, 2016); DeLay, *War of a Thousand Deserts*; Hämäläinen, *Comanche Empire*.
12. Leroy P. Graf, "The Economic History of the Lower Rio Grande Valley, 1820–1875" (PhD diss., Harvard University, 1942).
13. Miguel A. González-Quiroga, *War and Peace on the Rio Grande Frontier, 1830–1880*, New Directions in Tejano History 1 (Norman: University of Oklahoma Press, 2020), 1–4; Omar S. Valerio-Jiménez, *River of Hope: Forging Identity and Nation in the Rio Grande Borderlands* (Durham, NC: Duke University Press, 2013), 2–5.
14. Bruno Latour, *Reassembling the Social: An Introduction to Actor-Network-Theory* (Oxford: Oxford University Press, 2007), 11–12.
15. Bayly, *Birth of the Modern World*, 6.
16. Sven Beckert, *Empire of Cotton: A Global History* (New York: Vintage Books, 2014), xvi–xxi; Beckert and Desan, *American Capitalism*, 14–17.
17. Some of the key collections to my research include: José San Román Papers, 1823–1934, Dolph Briscoe Center for American History, University of Texas at Austin (hereafter cited as JSR Papers); John Charles Beales Papers, 1832–1855, Dolph Briscoe Center for American History, University of Texas at Austin (hereafter cited as JCB Papers); Bustillo Family Papers, 1772–1936, Col 879, Daughters of the Republic of Texas Library, San Antonio, Texas; Charles Stillman Business Papers, 1847–1884 (MS Am 800.27), Houghton Library, Harvard University (hereafter cited as CSBP).
18. The most important government document collections include: Archivo General de Mexico, 1538–1849, Dolph Briscoe Center for American History, University of Texas at Austin (hereafter cited as AGM); Despatches from United States Consuls in Matamoros, Mexico, 1826–1906, Microfilm Mf79.01, DeGolyer Library, Southern Methodist University (hereafter cited as Despatches; Ephraim Douglas Adams, *British Diplomatic Correspondence Concerning the Republic of Texas, 1838–1846* (Austin: Texas State Historical Association, 1918); Nancy Nichols Barker and A. Dubois de Saligny, *The French Legation in Texas* (Austin: Texas State Historical Association, 1971); Texas Secretary of State colonization records, Archives and Information Services Division, Texas State Library and Archives Commission;

Foreign Office: General Correspondence before 1906, the National Archives, Kew-Foreign Office.
19. The ability to read and write, purchase paper, and engage in mercantile activity was reserved to the wealthier families in the borderlands. Therefore, their voices take prominence in the narrative. However, they did employ a significant number of laborers, whose lives these entrepreneurs attempted to change.
20. Mario Cerutti, *Burguesía, capitales e industria en el norte de México: Monterrey y su ámbito regional (1850–1910)* (México, DF: Alianza Ed, 1992), 51–61; Miguel Ángel González-Quiroga, "Conflict and Cooperation in the Making of Texas-Mexico Border Society, 1840–1880," in *Bridging National Borders in North America: Transnational and Comparative Histories*, ed. Benjamin Heber Johnson and Andrew R. Graybill (Durham, NC: Duke University Press, 2010), 33–52.
21. Contemporaries conceived of the regional market within similar geographic terms. An advertisement for a new transportation line in 1849 makes the market boundaries clear. Three American investors sought to establish routes connecting Corpus Christi to San Antonio and Mier. From Mier the new company assured traders would have access to the "Mexican market," which basically meant Monterrey. Other advertisers on the very same page privilege Matamoros or Laredo, but all seem to have the same basic understanding of the region in which they worked. See: *Corpus Christi Star*, vol. 1, no. 51, ed. 1, Saturday, September 8, 1849.
22. Jeremy Adelman and Stephen Aron, "From Borderlands to Borders: Empires, Nation-States, and the Peoples in between in North American History," *American Historical Review* 104, no. 3 (June 1999): 816; P. Hämäläinen and S. Truett, "On Borderlands," *Journal of American History* 98, no. 2 (September 2011), 345–54; Sabri Ateş, *The Ottoman-Iranian Borderlands: Making a Boundary, 1843–1914* (New York: Cambridge University Press, 2013), 1–4; Peter Sahlins, *Boundaries: The Making of France and Spain in the Pyrenees* (Berkeley: University of California Press, 1991), 4–7.

Notes for Chapter 1

1. *Indios bárbaros* was a term the Spanish in the Americas often used to describe Indigenous people who they perceived as wild, ignorant, heathen, or savage. David J. Weber, *Bárbaros: Spaniards and Their Savages in the Age of Enlightenment* (New Haven, CT: Yale University Press, 2005), 14–15.

2. Weber, *Bárbaros*, 5–8; Donald E. Chipman and Harriett Denise Joseph, *Notable Men and Women of Spanish Texas*, 1st ed. (Austin: University of Texas Press, 1999), 124–29.
3. Allan J. Kuethe and Kenneth J. Andrien, *The Spanish Atlantic World in the Eighteenth Century: War and the Bourbon Reforms, 1713–1796* (Cambridge: Cambridge University Press, 2014), 271–304; David J. Weber, *The Spanish Frontier in North America* (New Haven, CT: Yale University Press, 1992), 194.
4. Kuethe and Andrien, *Spanish Atlantic World in the Eighteenth Century*, 17, 335–36; Brian R. Hamnett, "Mercantile Rivalry and Peninsular Division: The Consulados of New Spain and the Impact of the Bourbon Reforms, 1789–1824," *Ibero-Amerikanisches Archiv* 2, no. 4 (1976): 273–305.
5. Kuethe and Andrien, *Spanish Atlantic World in the Eighteenth Century*, 1–28.
6. Peter Gerhard, *The North Frontier of New Spain* (Princeton, NJ: Princeton University Press, 1982), 358–68.
7. Juanita Elizondo Garza, "Indian and Spanish-Mexican Cultural Influence in the Lower Rio Grande Valley," (MA thesis, Pan American University, Edinburg, 1984), 29–32.
8. Robert S. Weddle, *San Juan Bautista: Gateway to Spanish Texas* (Austin: University of Texas Press, 1968), 3–28; Hämäläinen, *Comanche Empire*, 32–40, 129; W. W. Newcomb Jr., *The Indians of Texas from Prehistoric to Modern Times* (Austin: University of Texas Press, 1961), 102–9.
9. Max L. Moorehead, *The Presidio: Bastion of the Spanish Borderlands* (Norman: University of Oklahoma Press, 1975).
10. Report of the Junta de Guerra y Hacienda to the Viceroy, December 2, 1716, AGM, box 2Q213, vol. 180, 4–25; Weber, *Spanish Frontier*, 160–62.
11. David La Vere, "The Caddo Chiefdoms of Texas," in Sam W. Haynes & Cary D. Wintz, *Major Problems in Texas History: Documents and Essays*, 2nd ed. (Boston: Cengage Learning, 2017), 41–46; Weber, *Spanish Frontier*, 172–86.
12. John Huxtable Elliott, *Empires of the Atlantic World: Britain and Spain in America, 1492–1830* (New Haven, CT: Yale University Press, 2007), 229–34.
13. Osante, *Orígenes del Nuevo Santander*, 102–7; John Tutino, *Making a New World: Founding Capitalism in the Bajío and Spanish North America* (Durham, NC: Duke University Press, 2011), 7; Chipman and Joseph, *Notable Men and Women*, 127–33.

14. Report of El Marquess de Altamira, AGM, box 2Q213, vol. 179, part II, 531.
15. Reséndez, *Other Slavery*, 238; Weber, *Bárbaros*, 105–7; Weber, *Spanish Frontier*, 229–30.
16. Osante, *Orígenes del Nuevo Santander*, 107–8.
17. Sean F. McEnroe, *From Colony to Nationhood in Mexico: Laying the Foundations, 1560–1840* (Cambridge; New York: Cambridge University Press, 2014), 21–56, 123–25.
18. Florence Johnson Scott, *Historical Heritage of the Lower Rio Grande: A Historical Record of Spanish Exploration, Subjugation and Colonization of the Lower Rio Grande Valley and the Activities of José Escandón, Count of Sierra Gorda together with the Development of Towns and Ranches Under Spanish, Mexican and Texas Sovereignties 1747–1848* (Rio Grande City, TX: La Retama Press, 1965), 18–30.
19. Debbie S. Cunningham, "The Exploration and Preliminary Colonization the *Seno Mexicano* under Don José de Escandón," (PhD diss., Texas A&M University, 2010), 72–74, 90.
20. Mark Kurlansky, *Salt: A World History* (New York: Penguin Books, 2002), 6–8; John J. Terrell, *Biennial Report of the Commissioner of the General Land Office of the State of Texas* (Austin: Gammel-Statesman, 1905), 31; "La Sal del Rey," *Ancient Landscapes of South Texas*, University of Texas Rio Grande Valley, accessed September 25, 2023, https://www.utrgv.edu/ancient-landscapes-southtexas/landscapes/la-sal-del-rey/index.htm.
21. Cunningham, "Exploration and Preliminary Colonization," 77.
22. Kurlansky, *Salt*, 10–12.
23. Kurlansky, *Salt*, 206–7; Carlos Marichal, *Bankruptcy of Empire: Mexican Silver and the Wars between Spain, Britain, and France, 1760–1810* Cambridge Latin American Studies 91 (New York: Cambridge University Press, 2007); Anne Staples, "Mexican Mining and Independence: The Saga of Enticing Opportunities," in Christon I. Archer, ed., *The Birth of Modern Mexico, 1780–1824* (Wilmington: Scholarly Resources Inc, 2003), 151–53.
24. Hill, *José de Escandón*, 75; Osante, *Orígenes del Nuevo Santander*, 194–96; P. Koujianou Goldberg and R. Hellerstein, "A Structural Approach to Identifying the Sources of Local Currency Price Stability," *Review of Economic Studies* 80, no. 1 (January 1, 2013): 175–210, https://academic.oup.com/restud/article-lookup/doi/10.1093/restud/rds015.
25. Cunningham, "Exploration and Preliminary Colonization," 52, 95–96, 189, 199; Osante, *Orígenes del Nuevo Santander*, 194–95; John Hazelton, "Nuestra Senora de los Dolores Hacienda," *Handbook of Texas Online*,

accessed June 03, 2019, http://www.tshaonline.org/handbook/online/articles/uen02.
26. Cunningham, "Exploration and Preliminary Colonization," 51; Jack E. Davis, *The Gulf: The Making of an American Sea* (New York: W. W. Norton, 2018), ebook; Osante, *Orígenes Del Nuevo Santander*, 191–94; Hill, *José de Escandón*, 111.
27. James C. Scott, *The Art of Not Being Governed: An Anarchist History of Upland Southeast Asia* (New Haven, CT: Yale University Press, 2009), 43–45; George W. White et. al., *Essentials of World Regional Geography*, 3rd edition, (New York: McGraw Hill, 2014), 6.
28. Chipman and Joseph, *Notable Men and Women*, 142–49.
29. Hill, *José de Escandón*, 106–39.
30. Provincias Internas, AGM, box 2Q213, vol. 180, 4–25.
31. Sección de Historia, Villa de Camargo, AGM, box 2Q180, vol. 56, 297–341.
32. Hill, *José de Escandón*, 97–99.
33. Hämäläinen, *Comanche Empire*, 104–6.
34. Gilberto Miguel Hinojosa, *A Borderlands Town in Transition: Laredo, 1755–1870* (College Station: Texas A&M University Press, 1983), 3–17; Hill, *José de Escandón*, 99–100; Osante, *Orígenes del Nuevo Santander*, 143; Weber, *Bárbaros*, 105–7.
35. Hill, *José de Escandón*, 110–11.
36. Hill, *José de Escandón*, 110–11.
37. A fanega was a measure of volume that is roughly equivalent to fifty-six liters.
38. Osante, *Orígenes del Nuevo Santander*, 197–98.
39. Hill, *José de Escandón*, 128–39; Hazelton, "Nuestra Señora de los Dolores Hacienda"; Herbert Eugene Bolton, "Tienda de Cuervo's Ynspeccion of Laredo, 1757," *Quarterly of the Texas State Historical Association* 6, no. 3 (January 1903): 194, 198–203.
40. Chipman and Joseph, *Notable Men and Women*, 142–43.
41. Patricia Osante, "Un Proyecto de Antonio Ladrón de Guevara para las poblaciones de Nuevo Santander, 1767," *Estudios de Historia Novohispana* 49, no. 1 (2013): 170–91.
42. David M. Vigness, ed., trans., "Nuevo Santander in 1795: A Provincial Inspection by Félix Calleja," *Southwestern Historical Quarterly* 75, no. 4 (April 1972): 462.
43. Scott, *Historical Heritage of the Lower Rio Grande*, 60–64; Chipman and Joseph, *Notable Men and Women*, 142–43.
44. One league was about 4,428 acres; one *caballería* was approximately 108 acres.
45. Scott, *Historical Heritage of the Lower Rio Grande*, 64.

46. That is an extra 164,000 acres.
47. Chipman and Joseph, *Notable Men and Women*, 142–43; Scott, *Historical Heritage of the Lower Rio Grande*, 101–9.
48. Omar S. Valerio-Jiménez, "Neglected Citizens and Willing Traders: The Villas Del Norte (Tamaulipas) in Mexico's Northern Borderlands, 1749–1846," *Mexican Studies/Estudios Mexicanos* 18, no. 2 (August 2002): 255; Scott, *Historical Heritage of the Lower Rio Grande*, 101–9.
49. Colegio Apostólico de Propaganda Fide de San Fernando, "Informe a el Rey nro. sr. en su el consejo de indias, cerca de las misnes del seno mexicano," December 3, 1749, DeGolyer Library, Southern Methodist University.
50. Martin Salinas, *Indians of the Rio Grande Delta: Their Role in the History of Southern Texas and Northeastern Mexico*, 1st ed., Texas Archaeology and Ethnohistory Series (Austin: University of Texas Press, 1990), 5; Chipman and Joseph, *Notable Men and Women*, 143–44.
51. Minnie Gilbert, "The Valley's Earliest Pioneers," in *Roots by the River* (Canyon, TX: Staked Plains Press, 1978), 9–14.
52. Hämäläinen, *Comanche Empire*, 137–38; Osante, *Orígenes del Nuevo Santander*, 273–75; Weber, *Spanish Frontier*, 227–35.
53. Hämäläinen, *Comanche Empire*, 79; Vigness, "Nuevo Santander in 1795," 466.
54. Vigness, "Nuevo Santander in 1795," 461–67.
55. Vigness, "Nuevo Santander in 1795," 494–95.
56. Vigness, "Nuevo Santander in 1795," 479.
57. Vigness, "Nuevo Santander in 1795," 480.
58. Jean Louis Berlandier, *Journey to Mexico during the Years 1826–1834*, vol. 2 (Austin: Texas State Historical Association and Center for Studies in Texas History, 1980), 460.
59. Hinojosa, *Borderlands Town in Transition*, 18–20.
60. James Brooks, *Captives & Cousins: Slavery, Kinship, and Community in the Southwest Borderlands* (Chapel Hill: University of North Carolina Press, 2002), 180–93; DeLay, *War of a Thousand Deserts*, 48–59; Hämäläinen, *Comanche Empire*, 186–89.

Notes for Chapter 2

1. Eduard Ludecus, *John Charles Beales's Rio Grande Colony: Letters by Eduard Ludecus, a German Colonist, to Friends in Germany in 1833–1834, Recounting his Journey, Trials, and Observations in Early Texas*, trans. Louis E. Brister (Austin: Texas State Historical Association, 2008), 46.

2. John Woodward, *An Abstract of the Constitutions, Laws, and Other Documents Having Reference to and Including the Empresario Grants and Contracts Made by the State of Coahuila y Texas to and with John Charles Beales; Also Deeds of the Same from Him to John Woodward; to which is Appended and Argument Sustaining the Rights and Titles of John Woodward* (New York: Narine and Co., 1842), "Deeds," 28–31.
3. Carl Coke Rister, *Comanche Bondage: Dr. John Charles Beales's Settlement of La Villa de Dolores on Las Moras Creek in Southern Texas of the 1830's* (Glendale, CA: A. H. Clark, 1955), 26–30.
4. E. House, *A Narrative of the Captivity of Mrs. Horn, and her Two Children, with Mrs. Harris, by the Camanche Indians, after they had Murdered their Husbands and Traveling Companions* (St. Louis: C. Keemle, 1839), 6–8.
5. Ludecus, *John Charles Beales's Rio Grande Colony*, ix–xvii; Mary Virginia Henderson, "Minor Empresario Contracts for the Colonization of Texas, 1825–1834," part 2, *Southwestern Historical Quarterly* 32, no. 1 (July 1928): 1–28; Lucy Lee Dickson, "Speculation of John Charles Beales in Texas Lands" (MA thesis, University of Texas, 1941).
6. Reséndez, *Changing National Identities at the Frontier*, 93–96; Valerio-Jiménez, *River of Hope*, 111–28; Davis, *Land!*, 72–96.
7. Some works that highlight other empresarios in northern Mexico include Gregg Cantrell, *Stephen F. Austin, Empresario of Texas* (New Haven, CT: Yale University Press, 1999); Davis, *Land!*; A. B. J. Hammett, *The Empresario, Don Martin DeLeon: The Richest Man in Texas* (Kerrville, TX: Braswell, 1971).
8. Pat Kelley, *River of Lost Dreams: Navigation on the Rio Grande* (Lincoln: University of Nebraska Press, 1986).
9. Bayly, *Birth of the Modern World*, 1–12.
10. Hämäläinen, *Comanche Empire*, 181–82; DeLay, *War of a Thousand Deserts*, 16–30.
11. H. P. N. Gammel, *The Laws of Texas, 1822–1897*, 10 vols. (Austin: Gammel, 1898), 1:95–107.
12. Travel accounts of Texas became quite popular in Europe. One of the Beales colonists carried a copy of Mary Austin Holley's book with him. There also existed accounts from German travelers about Texas: Mary Austin Holley, *Texas: Observations, Historical, Geographical and Descriptive, in a Series of Letters* (Baltimore: Armstong & Plaskitt, 1833); J. Valentin Hecke, *Reise Durch Die Vereinigten Staaten von Nord-Amerika in Den Jahren 1818 Und 1819: Nebst Einer Kurzen Uebersicht der Neuesten Ereignisse Auf Dem. Und West-Indien* (Berlin: H. Ph. Petri, 1821). For more on Austin's colony see: Eugene C. Barker, *The Life of Stephen F. Austin, Founder of Texas, 1793–1836:*

A Chapter in the Westward Movement of the Anglo-American People (Nashville: Cokesbury Press, 1925); Cantrell, *Stephen F. Austin*; Sarah K. M. Rodriguez, "'The Greatest Nation on Earth': The Politics and Patriotism of the First Anglo American Immigrants to Mexican Texas, 1820–1824," *Pacific Historical Review* 86, no. 1 (February 2017): 50–83.

13. Barker Eugene C., *Mexico and Texas, 1821–1835* (Dallas: P. L. Turner, 1928), 49–51; Cantrell, *Stephen F. Austin*, 179–88.
14. Manuel de Mier y Terán to the Governor of Coahuila y Texas, June 24, 1828, in *Texas by Terán: The Diary Kept by General Manuel de Mier y Terán on His 1828 Inspection of Texas*, ed. Jack Jackson, trans. John Wheat, with botanical notes by Scooter Cheatham and Lynn Marshall, 1st ed., Jack and Doris Smothers Series in Texas History, Life, and Culture 2 (Austin: University of Texas Press, 2000), 96.
15. Mier y Terán to the president of Mexico, June 30, 1828; Mier y Terán to the secretary of foreign relations, July 7, 1828, in *Texas by Terán*, 96–101, 104–5.
16. Decreto de 6 de Abril de 1830, April 6, 1830, Broadside Collection, Dolph Briscoe Center for American History, University of Texas at Austin; Barker, *Life of Stephen F. Austin*, 256–84. Randolph B. Campbell, *An Empire for Slavery: The Peculiar Institution in Texas, 1821–1865* (Baton Rouge: Louisiana State University Press, 1989), 35–37.
17. Davis, *Land!*, 3-9; 72-106; Mier y Terán, *Texas by Terán*, 2.
18. The Soto y Saldaña family name carried a modicum of weight in the region, as just a generation earlier José Antonio Soto y Saldaña, a prominent licenciado, held an important position in the Valladolid Conspiracy in Michoacán in 1809, making the family publicly known as trustworthy patriots in independent Mexico. That trust allowed María Dolores Soto y Saldaña to retain her first husband's contract after his death and transfer it to her second husband after their marriage. For more on the Valladolid Conspiracy see: Margaret Chowning, *Wealth and Power in Provincial Mexico: Michoacán from the Late Colony to the Revolution* (Stanford, CA: Stanford University Press, 1999), 76–81; Jaime E. Rodríguez O., *"We Are Now the True Spaniards": Sovereignty, Revolution, Independence, and the Emergence of the Federal Republic of Mexico, 1808–1824* (Stanford, CA: Stanford University Press, 2012), 91–96.
19. Raymond Estep, "Exter, Richard," *Handbook of Texas Online*, accessed September 07, 2018, http://www.tshaonline.org/handbook/online/articles/fex03.
20. Woodward, *Abstract of the Constitutions, Laws, and Other Documents*, "Deeds," 14–15.

21. James Grant and John Charles Beales Petition for Empresario Contract, October 9, 1832, JCB Papers, box 2E95; Rio Grande and Texas Land Company Scrip, August 21, 1834, JCB Papers, box BC OB 1830–1835.
22. Stuart Reid, *The Secret War for Texas*, 1st ed., Elma Dill Russell Spencer Series in the West and Southwest 28 (College Station: Texas A&M University Press, 2007), 24–25.
23. Michael P. Costeloe, *Bonds and Bondholders: British Investors and Mexico's Foreign Debt, 1824–1888* (Westport, CT: Praeger, 2003).
24. Grant from government of Coahuila and Texas to John C. Beales with Grant to him in fee of several leagues; Also grant from Mr. Beales to Thomas E. Davis Es., November 3, 1833, JCB Papers, box 2E95.
25. Woodward, *Abstract of the Constitutions, Laws, and Other Documents*, 28–31; Rister, *Comanche Bondage*, 26–27.
26. William Kennedy, *Texas: The Rise, Progress and Prospects of the Republic of Texas*, 2nd ed., 2 vols. (London: R. Hastings, 1841), 1:18. Kennedy copied entire sections from Egerton's report and Beales's journal for his history of Texas. He eventually became an empresario for the Republic of Texas and earned a contract for the area of land that basically encircled the same grant as Beales, which I analyze in chap. 3.
27. Kennedy, *Texas*, 1:176.
28. Kennedy, *Texas*, 1:175–77.
29. Edward E. Baptist, *The Half Has Never Been Told: Slavery and the Making of American Capitalism* (New York: Basic Books, 2014), 257–59; Beckert, *Empire of Cotton*, 103–14; Torget, *Seeds of Empire*, 157–61; Eugene C. Barker, "Land Speculation as a Cause of the Texas Revolution," *Quarterly of the Texas State Historical Association* 10, no. 1 (1906): 76–95.
30. Terms of indenture, John C. Beales to Thomas E. Davis, October 26, 1833, JCB Papers, box 2E95; Joseph Alfred Scoville, *The Old Merchants of New York City*, 5 vols. (New York: Thomas R. Knox, 1885), 4:251–57; George Brown Tindall and David E. Shi, *America: A Narrative History*, 5th ed. (New York: Norton, 1999), 385–87; James E. Lewis Jr., *The Burr Conspiracy: Uncovering the Story of an Early American Crisis* (Princeton, NJ: Princeton University Press, 2017), 185–90, 443.
31. Helen I. Cowan, "Charles Williamson and the Southern Entrance to the Genesee Country," *New York History* 23, no. 3 (July 1942): 260–74; Charles E Brooks, *Frontier Settlement and Market Revolution: The Holland Land Purchase* (Ithaca, NY: Fall Creek Books, 2012), 18–20, 107.
32. Terms of indenture, John C. Beales to Thomas E. Davis, October 26, 1833, JCB Papers, box 2E95.

33. Historians of US capitalism have argued that Eastern elites turned to making investments in the West after the Civil War to supplement their portfolios dominated by investments in manufacturing. Beales's example, among others that include the Galveston Bay and Texas Land Company, reveal that the Eastern monied elite continuously invested in the American West throughout the nineteenth century. See: Sven Beckert, *The Monied Metropolis: New York City and the Consolidation of the American Bourgeoisie, 1850–1896* (New York: Cambridge University Press, 2001); Noam Maggor, *Brahmin Capitalism: Frontiers of Wealth and Populism in America's First Gilded Age* (Cambridge, MA: Harvard University Press, 2017).
34. Charles Edwards, "Colony of the Rio Grande and Texas Land Company," *New York Commercial Advertiser*, October 24, 1834; Charles Edwards, "Colony of the Rio Grande and Texas Land Company, To Emigrants and Others," *Charleston Courier*, October 25, 1834.
35. Rister, *Comanche Bondage*, 26–30.
36. Eduard Ludecus, *Reise durch di Mexikanischen Provinzen Tumalipas, Cohahuila und Texas im Jahre 1834* (Leipzig: Johan Friedrich Hartknoch, 1837). Louis Brister has translated this work into English: Ludecus, *John Charles Beales's Rio Grande Colony*.
37. House, *Narrative of the Captivity of Mrs. Horn*.
38. Ludecus, *John Charles Beales's Rio Grande Colony*, 42.
39. Beales Empresario Contract with Mexico, 1833, JCB Papers, box 2S165.
40. Ludecus, *John Charles Beales's Rio Grande Colony*, 46–47; House, *Narrative of the Captivity of Mrs. Horn*, 6–8.
41. Ludecus, *John Charles Beales's Rio Grande Colony*, 46. The approximate value of $50,000 in 1833 relative to today would come out to about $1.5 million. For more on historical relative values, see: Samuel H. Williamson, "Seven Ways to Compute the Relative Value of a US Dollar Amount, 1774 to present," MeasuringWorth.com, accessed March 08, 2019, http://www.measuringworth.com/uscompare/.
42. House, *Narrative of the Captivity of Mrs. Horn*, 6.
43. Brister, "Eduard Ludecus's Journey to the Texas Frontier," 371–72; Ludecus, *John Charles Beales's Rio Grande Colony*, 57.
44. House, *Narrative of the Captivity of Mrs. Horn*, 6–8.
45. House, *Narrative of the Captivity of Mrs. Horn*, 6–8.
46. Ludecus, *John Charles Beales's Rio Grande Colony*, 100; House, *Narrative of the Captivity of Mrs. Horn*, 9–10.
47. DeLay, *War of a Thousand Deserts*, 54–56; House, *Narrative of the Captivity of Mrs. Horn*, 9–10.
48. Ludecus, *John Charles Beales's Rio Grande Colony*, 118.

49. Kennedy, *Texas*, 2:46–51; Ludecus, *John Charles Beales's Rio Grande Colony*, 122–23, 126. It was unusual for the Shawnee to have migrated so far south as the Rio Grande, but not unlikely. Both Beales and Ludecus described their short-term allies as Shawnee.
50. Rister, *Comanche Bondage*, 44–46; Ludecus, *John Charles Beales's Rio Grande Colony*, 127.
51. Ludecus, *John Charles Beales's Rio Grande Colony*, 147–54; House, *Narrative of the Captivity of Mrs. Horn*, 12.
52. Ludecus, *John Charles Beales's Rio Grande Colony*, 131.
53. Ludecus, *John Charles Beales's Rio Grande Colony*, 134–36.
54. Brister, "Eduard Ludecus's Journey to the Texas Frontier," 378; Ludecus, *John Charles Beales's Rio Grande Colony*, 102.
55. Kennedy, *Texas*, 2:51–56.
56. Cantrell, *Stephen F. Austin*, 135.
57. Quoted in Brister, "Eduard Ludecus's Journey to the Texas Frontier," 378–79.
58. Ludecus, *John Charles Beales's Rio Grande Colony*, 155–74.
59. House, *Narrative of the Captivity of Mrs. Horn*, 14–19.
60. DeLay, *War of a Thousand Deserts*, 62–70.
61. Deposition of Thomas Herbert O'Sullivan Addicks, Nov. 18, 1839, JCB Papers, box 2E95; Davis, *Land!*, 5–6.

Notes for Chapter 3

1. The Texas rebellion was quite popular in New York newspapers. See the Texas Revolution Newspaper Collection, Southwest Collection/Special Collections Library, Texas Tech University, http://collections2.swco.ttu.edu/.
2. "Contract between the Government of the Republic of Texas and the late French Aid de Camp A. Rullmann from New York," May 21, 1838, Box 2-9/27, Folder 5, Texas Secretary of State Colonization Records, Archives and Information Services Division, Texas State Library and Archives Commission (hereafter cited as TSLAC).
3. Rullmann to Secretary of State, May 21, 1838, box 2-9/27, folder 5, TSLAC.
4. Bobby D. Weaver, *Castro's Colony: Empresario Development in Texas, 1842–1865*, 1st ed. (College Station: Texas A&M University Press, 1985), xi–xiv, 109–11.
5. The French did have a successful empresario under the Republic of Texas, Henri Castro. His example has been written about extensively. See: Weaver, *Castro's Colony*; Cornelia E. Crook, *Henry Castro* (San Antonio: St. Mary's University Press, 1988); Julia Nott Waugh,

Castro-Ville and Henry Castro, Empresario (San Antonio: Standard Press, 1934).
6. Eugene C. Barker, "The Annexation of Texas," *Southwestern Historical Quarterly* 50, no. 1 (1946): 49–74. Alasdair Roberts, *America's First Great Depression: Economic Crisis and Political Disorder after the Panic of 1837* (Ithaca, NY: Cornell University Press, 2012), 176–79; Torget, *Seeds of Empire*, 179–91.
7. Michael P. Costeloe, "William Bullock and the Mexican Connection," *Mexican Studies/Estudios Mexicanos* 22, no. 2 (August 2006): 275–309; Torget, *Seeds of Empire*, 202–210; Campbell, *An Empire for Slavery*, 35–50.
8. Barker, "Land Speculation," 76–95. George J. Morgenthaler, *Promised Land: Solms, Castro, and Sam Houston's Colonization Contracts*, 1st ed., Sam Rayburn Series on Rural Life 19 (College Station: Texas A&M University Press, 2009); Jesús F. de la Teja, Paula Mitchell Marks, and Ronnie C. Tyler, *Texas: Crossroads of North America* (Boston: Houghton Mifflin Co, 2004), 227–33; Weaver, *Castro's Colony*. For more on German colonization in Texas see: Julia Akinyi Brookins, "Immigrant Settlers and Frontier Citizens: German Texas in the American Empire, 1835–1890" (PhD diss., Unviersity of Chicago, 2013).
9. Randolph B. Campbell, *Sam Houston: And the American Southwest*, 3rd ed, Library of American Biography (New York: Pearson Longman, 2007), 89–90; 123; Weber, *Mexican Frontier*, 251.
10. James Hook to Lord Viscount Palmerston, April 30, 1841, in Adams, *British Diplomatic Correspondence*, 31.
11. Dubois de Saligny to Thiers, October 30, 1840, in Barker and Dubois de Saligny, *French Legation in Texas*, 167.
12. Barker and Dubois de Saligny, *French Legation in Texas*, 27–28; Weber, *Spanish Frontier*, 196–98.
13. For an overview of the July Monarchy, see: H. A. C. Collingham and R. S. Alexander, *The July Monarchy: A Political History of France, 1830–1848* (New York: Longman, 1988).
14. Dubois de Saligny to Guizot, June 1, 1842, June 8, 1842, and June 15, 1842, in Barker and Dubois de Saligny, *French Legation in Texas*, 334–38.
15. Dubois de Saligny to Guizot, June 15, 1842, in Barker and Dubois de Saligny, *French Legation in Texas*, 337–38.
16. Nancy N. Barker, "Dubois De Saligny," *Handbook of Texas Online*, accessed May 30, 2019, http://www.tshaonline.org/handbook/online/articles/fdu02.
17. Bourgeois d'Orvanne to the minister of commerce, May 26, 1842, in Barker and Dubois de Saligny, *French Legation in Texas*, 332–33.

18. DeLay, *War of a Thousand Deserts*, 80–85; Hämäläinen, *Comanche Empire*, 221–23; Sam W. Haynes, *Unsettled Land: From Revolution to Republic, the Struggle for Texas*, 1st ed. (New York: Basic Books, 2022), 293–94; Cruger & Moore, *Telegraph and Texas Register* (Houston, TX), vol. 6, no. 15, ed. 1, Wednesday, March 3, 1841, accessed April 26, 2019, https://texashistory.unt.edu/ark:/67531/metapth48124/, University of North Texas Libraries, Portal to Texas History, https://texashistory.unt.edu; crediting the Dolph Briscoe Center for American History.
19. Bourgeois D'Orvanne to the minister of commerce, July 4, 1842, in Barker and Dubois de Saligny, *French Legation in Texas*, 344–48.
20. Bourgeois D'Orvanne to the minister of commerce, July 4, 1842, in Barker and Dubois de Saligny, *French Legation in Texas*, 344–48.
21. Thongchai Winichakul, *Siam Mapped: A History of the Geo-Body of the Nation* (Honolulu: University of Hawaii Press, 1997), 16; Sahlins, *Boundaries*, 7.
22. Bourgeois D'Orvanne to the minister of commerce, July 4, 1842, in Barker and Dubois de Saligny, *French Legation in Texas*, 348.
23. Bayly, *Birth of the Modern World*, 112–34.
24. Bourgeois D'Orvanne to the minister of commerce, July 4, 1842, in Barker and Dubois de Saligny, *French Legation in Texas*, 348; Kelley, *River of Lost Dreams*, 24–25.
25. Collingham, *July Monarchy*, 19–21.
26. Guizot to the minister of interior, February 16, 1843, in Barker and Dubois de Saligny, *French Legation in Texas*, 413.
27. François Guizot, William Hazlitt, and Larry Siedentop, *The History of Civilization in Europe* (Indianapolis: Liberty Fund, 2013), 35.
28. Second Report to President Sam Houston, July 8, 1844, box 2-9/27, folder 11, TSLAC.
29. Rudolph Leopold Biesele, *The History of the German Settlements in Texas, 1831–1861* (Austin: Von Boeckmann-Jones, 1930), 71–76. In German the society was called Verein zum Schutze Deutscher Einwanderer.
30. David E. Barclay, "Political Trends and Movements, 1830–1850: The *Vormärz* and the Revolutions of 1848–1849," in *Germany 1800–1870*, ed. Jonathan Sperber (Oxford: Oxford University Press, 2004), 46–68; Bayly, *Birth of the Modern World*, 158–60.
31. Biesele, *History of the German Settlements in Texas*, 1–6; Tara Zahra, *The Great Departure: Mass Migration from Eastern Europe and the Making of the Free World* (New York: W. W. Norton, 2016), 3–42.
32. Scott, *Historical Heritage of the Lower Rio Grande*.
33. Berlandier, *Journey to Mexico*, 2:422.

34. Smith to Jones, October 14, 1843, in George P. Garrison, ed., *Diplomatic Correspondence of the Republic of Texas*, vol. 2, part 3, (Washington, DC: Government Printing Press, 1911), 1467–68.
35. Bourgeois to Anson Jones, April 20, 1844, in Garrison, *Diplomatic Correspondence of the Republic of,* 1561–62.
36. Bourgeois to secretary of state, Aug. 08, 1844, box 2-9/27, folder 11, TSLAC.
37. Biesele, *History of the German Settlements in Texas*, 75–76.
38. Adams, *British Diplomatic Correspondence*, 43fn.
39. Kennedy, *Texas*, xix.
40. Kennedy, *Texas*. The quote was placed on the title page of the second edition of the book.
41. Kennedy, *Texas*, 17–18. The passages Kennedy used to describe the Rio Grande early in the book were cribbed directly from Egerton's report on the region.
42. Both rivers were the most recognizable rivers in the Americas. They remain two of the longest rivers in the Americas and both are navigable for most of their lengths. The Rio Grande was definitely not navigable for its entire length. In fact steamships rarely made it farther upriver than Laredo, and even then only in times of very high water. Egerton, however, promoted the navigability of the Rio Grande in his report. See: Kennedy, *Texas*, 53–60.
43. Kennedy, *Texas*, 53–60.
44. Sam Houston to William Kennedy, January 28, 1842, in Sam Houston, *The Writings of Sam Houston, 1813–1963*, ed. Eugene C. Barker, vol. 2 (Austin: University of Texas Press, 1939), 450.
45. Copy of contract between the president of the Republic of Texas and William Kennedy and another, February 15, 1842, box 2-9/27, folder 1, TSLAC.
46. Weaver, *Castro's Colony*, 14–16.
47. Kennedy to Aberdeen, Jan. 10, 1842, in Adams, *British Diplomatic Correspondence*, 56.
48. Carl Solms-Braunfels, *Voyage to North America, 1844–45: Prince Carl of Solms's Texas Diary of People, Places, and Events*, translation and notes by W. M. Von-Maszewski (Denton: German-Texan Heritage Society and University of North Texas Press, 2000), 35; William Bollaert, *William Bollaert's Texas*, ed. W. Eugene Hollon and Ruth Lapham Butler (Norman: University of Oklahoma Press, 1956), 331.
49. Bollaert, *William Bollaert's Texas*, 242–43.
50. Kennedy to Aberdeen, August 01, 1842, in Adams, *British Diplomatic Correspondence*, 93.

51. Sir George Nicholls, *A History of the Scotch Poor Law, in Connexion with the Condition of the People* (London: Knight & Co., 1856), 205; I. G. C. Hutchison, "Workshop of Empire: The Nineteenth Century," in *Scotland: A History*, ed. Jenny Wormald (New York: Oxford University Press, 2005), 207–40.
52. *Hansard Parliamentary Debates*, "Poor Law (Scottish)," HC June 17, 1842, v. 64, accessed December 3, 2018, http://hansard.parliament.uk.
53. Jonathan Spain, "Ellice, Edward (1810–1880)," *Oxford Dictionary of National Biography* (Oxford: Oxford University Press, 2013), accessed December 06, 2018, http://www.oxforddnb.com/view/10.1093/ref:odnb/9780198614128.001.0001/odnb-9780198614128-e-8651.
54. Campbell, *Sam Houston*, 120–21.
55. Sam W. Haynes, *Soldiers of Misfortune: The Somervell and Mier Expeditions* (Austin: University of Texas Press, 1997); Campbell, *Sam Houston*, 122–24.
56. Kennedy to Jones, Nov. 01, 1843, box 2-9/27, folder 10, TSLAC.
57. Kennedy to Aberdeen, May 22, 1843, in Adams, *British Diplomatic Correspondence*, 195–96; Torget, *Seeds of Empire*, 239–42.
58. Sidney Lee, ed., *Dictionary of National Biography*, vol. 46 (New York: MacMillan, 1896), 389–90.
59. Kennedy to Aberdeen, October 24, 1842, in Adams, *British Diplomatic Correspondence*, 120.
60. "Colonization Contract Between the Republic of Texas and William Pringle, James Grieve, and Associates," copy, November 1, 1843, reprinted in Bollaert, *William Bollaert's Texas*, 380–84.
61. Bollaert still called it the Kennedy grant even after Kennedy withdrew for the Galveston consulship.
62. Bollaert, *William Bollaert's Texas*, 334.
63. Bollaert, *William Bollaert's Texas*, 361.
64. Bollaert, *William Bollaert's Texas*, 357.
65. Bollaert, *William Bollaert's Texas*, 372.
66. Bollaert, *William Bollaert's Texas*, 350.
67. Ephraim Douglass Adams, "British Correspondence concerning Texas, XV," *Southwestern Historical Quarterly* 19, no. 1 (July 1915): 91–93.
68. Henry Clay, *The Works of Henry Clay Comprising his Life, Correspondence and Speeches*, ed. Calvin Colton, vol. 3 (New York: G. P. Putnam's Sons, 1904), 25–30.
69. Daniel Walker Howe, *What Hath God Wrought: The Transformation of America, 1815–1848*, Oxford History of the United States (New York: Oxford University Press, 2007), 270–75.
70. Kennedy to Aberdeen, February 26, 1845, in Adams, *British Diplomatic Correspondence*, 451–53.

71. William F. Weeks, *Debates of the Texas Convention* (Houston: J. W. Cruger, 1846), 35.

Notes for Chapter 4

1. Bryant Parrot Tilden, *Notes on the Upper Rio Grande, explored in the months of October and November 1846 on board the U.S. Steamer Major Brown, Commanded by Capt. Mark Sterling of Pittsburgh* (Philadelphia: Lindsay & Blakiston, 1847), 30
2. Amy S. Greenberg, *Manifest Destiny and American Territorial Expansion: A Brief History with Documents* (Boston: Bedford/St. Martin's, 2012), 23–26; Montejano, *Anglos and Mexicans in the Making of Texas*, 41–48; Lindsay Schakenbach Regele, *Manufacturing Advantage: War, the State, and the Origins of American Industry, 1776–1848* (Baltimore: Johns Hopkins University Press, 2019), 135–37.
3. DeLay, *War of a Thousand Deserts*, 274–77; Will Fowler, *Santa Anna of Mexico* (Lincoln: University of Nebraska Press, 2007), 291–309; T. R. Fehrenbach, *Fire and Blood: A History of Mexico*, 1st Da Capo Press ed., updated ed. (New York: Da Capo Press, 1995), 400–405; Amy S. Greenberg, *A Wicked War: Polk, Clay, Lincoln, and the 1846 U.S. Invasion of Mexico*, 1st ed. (New York: Alfred A. Knopf, 2012), 258–60.
4. Henry Baumberger, San Antonio, Texas, to Father, beloved brothers and sisters, brothers-in-law, and friends, October 13, 1856, Henry Baumberger Letters, 1856–1867, Doc 5171, Daughters of the Republic of Texas Library, San Antonio, Texas (hereafter cited as HB Letters).
5. Montejano, *Anglos and Mexicans in the Making of Texas*, 24–75; Valerio-Jiménez, *River of Hope*, 139–51, 238; González-Quiroga, "Conflict and Cooperation," 33–52; Alicia M. Dewey, *Pesos and Dollars: Entrepreneurs in the Texas-Mexico Borderlands, 1880–1940* (College Station: Texas A&M University Press, 2014), 36–37; John M. Hart, *Empire and Revolution: The Americans in Mexico since the Civil War* (Berkeley: University of California Press, 2002), 1–5, 21–31.
6. David R. Schaefer, "Resource Characteristics in Social Exchange Networks: Implications for Positional Advantage," *Social Networks* 33, no. 2 (May 2011): 143–51.
7. I chose to focus on San Román and Leyendecker in this chapter for several reasons. Primarily, there is a degree of separation between the two. They created their own networks without influence from one another. Also, they are geographically removed from each other but also within the same regional market, allowing for a more effective compare and contrast analysis. Finally, they are both European born but

from very different backgrounds. Their examples show that, regardless of many other factors, European-born entrepreneurs utilized forms of human networking to develop their businesses on the Rio Grande and connect to larger markets after the US-Mexico War.

8. John A. Adams, *Conflict and Commerce on the Rio Grande: Laredo, 1755–1955* (College Station: Texas A&M University Press, 2008), 82–85
9. Milo Kearney and Anthony K. Knopp, *Boom and Bust: The Historical Cycles of Matamoros and Brownsville*, (Austin: Eakin Press, 1991), 64–66; Adams, *Conflict and Commerce on the Rio Grande*, 82–83; *Testimony taken by the Special Committee on Texas Frontier Troubles*, Resolution of the House of Representatives, report no. 343 (Washington, DC: Government Printing Office, 1876), 38–39.
10. Consul Peter Seuzeneau to Secretary of State Lewis Cass, April 04, 1858, Despatches, reel 4; Graf, "Economic History of the Lower Rio Grande Valley," 235–36.
11. Daniel D. Arreola and James R. Curtis, *The Mexican Border Cities: Landscape Anatomy and Place Personality* (Tucson: University of Arizona Press, 1993), 13–20. Other important sister cities to develop in this era besides Nuevo Laredo and Brownsville were Roma across from Mier and Rio Grande City north from Camargo.
12. Hamilton Fish, *Treaties and Conventions Concluded between the United States of America and Other Powers since 1776* (Washington, DC: Government Printing Office, 1871), 544–56; Adams, *Conflict and Commerce on the Rio Grande*, 74; George T. Diaz, *Border Contraband: A History of Smuggling across the Rio Grande* (Austin: University of Texas Press, 2015), 13–36
13. DeLay, *War of a Thousand Deserts*, xiii–xv.
14. Adelman and Aron, "From Borderlands to Borders," 816–17; Hämäläinen and Truett, "On Borderlands," 338, 358–59.
15. John Darwin, *Unfinished Empire: The Global Expansion of Britain* (New York: Bloomsbury Press, 2013), xi–xiii, 150–57; González-Quiroga, "Conflict and Cooperation," 44–48; Valerio-Jiménez, *River of Hope*, 3–4.
16. Raymond Carr, ed., *Spain: A History* (New York: Oxford University Press, 2000), 203–9; Roberto Mario Salmón, "San Roman, Jose," *Handbook of Texas Online*, accessed March 12, 2020, http://www.tshaonline.org/handbook/online/articles/fsa16; William A. Douglass and Jon Bilbao, *Amerikanuak: Basques in the New World*, Basque Series (Reno: University of Nevada Press, 1975), 9–20.
17. Thorn & McGrath to San Román, December 14, 1846, box 2G41, JSR Papers; advertisement, *Daily Picayune*, (New Orleans), January 13, 1852.

18. Fleeson & Palmer, *American Flag* (Matamoros, Tamaulipas, Mexico), vol. 2, no. 110, ed. 1 Saturday, June 26, 1847, University of North Texas Libraries, Portal to Texas History, accessed October 20, 2017, texashistory.unt.edu, crediting Abilene Library Consortium; invoice of goods shipped by Thorn & McGrath, January 22, 1847, box 2G41, JSR Papers; ledgers, November 1846–January 1849, box 2G129, JSR Papers; E. Rouger-Laroche, "Plano del Puerto de Matamoros," 1874, accessed September 26, 2023, http://mediateca.inah.gob.mx/repositorio/islandora/object/mapa percent3A404.
19. Montejano, *Anglos and Mexicans in the Making of Texas*, 42–43; *American Flag*, Cameron County and Matamoros Advertiser (Brownsville, TX), vol. 3, no. 235, ed. 1, Wednesday, November 22, 1848, University of North Texas Libraries, Portal to Texas History, accessed October 24, 2017, texashistory.unt.edu, crediting Abilene Library Consortium; *Centinela del Rio Grande* (Brownsville, TX), vol. 1, no. 11, ed. 1, Wednesday, March 13, 1850, University of North Texas Libraries, Portal to Texas History, accessed October 24, 2017, texashistory.unt.edu, crediting San Jacinto Museum of History.
20. Hart, *Empire and Revolution*, 22–26; Kearny and Knopp, *Boom and Bust*, 70–84; Graf, "Economic History of the Lower Rio Grande Valley," 227–41.
21. Augustin San Román to José San Román, May 16, 1855, box 2G47, JSR Papers.
22. Simón Celaya to José San Román, November 29, 1847, box 2G41, JSR Papers.
23. Simón Celaya Account, July 14, 1855, box 2G48, JSR Papers; Jorgé Romano to Simón Celaya, June 6, 1858, box 2G54, JSR Papers. They were paying about 2.5¢ for each Cuban cigar they imported. That worked out to be about 30 percent cheaper than the average price of a cigar in the United States. See: Carroll D. Wright, *Comparative Wages, Prices, and Cost of Living* (Boston: Wright & Potter, 1889), 149.
24. McGrath, Tweed, & Co. to José San Román, May 30, 1855, box 2G47, JSR Papers; H. Wilson, *Trow's New York City Directory* (New York: John F. Trow, 1859), 512.
25. Montejano, *Anglos and Mexicans in the Making of Texas*, 34–47; Hart, *Empire and Revolution*, 22–31.
26. Kelley, *River of Lost Dreams*, 55–71; Jane Clements Monday and Frances Brannen Vick, *Petra's Legacy: The South Texas Ranching Empire of Petra Vela and Mifflin Kenedy* (College Station: Texas A&M University Press, 2007), 55. James Grogan, an important partner in the group, has no identifiable birthplace on record. He may have been American or Irish. I cannot confirm. For a full list of investors,

see: *Joseph San Romons and William Armstrong, Administrators of James B. Armstrong vs. The United States*, December 18, 1860, in Congressional Series of United States Public Documents, United States Congressional Serial Set, vol. 1109 (Washington, DC: US Government Printing Office, 1861).
27. Mary Margaret McAllen Amberson, James A. McAllen, and Margaret H. McAllen, *I Would Rather Sleep in Texas: A History of the Lower Rio Grande Valley and the People of the Santa Anita Land Grant* (Austin: Texas State Historical Association, 2003), 126–27; Florence Johnson Scott, *Royal Land Grants North of the Río Grande, 1777–1821: Early History of Large Grants Made by Spain to Families in Jurisdiction of Reynosa Which Became a Part of Texas After the Treaty of Guadalupe Hidalgo, 1848* (Rio Grande City, TX: La Retama Press, 1969), 64.

For more on Americans dispossessing Mexican-owned land, see: Alonzo, *Tejano Legacy*, 146–78; Valerio-Jiménez, *River of Hope*, 180; Montejano, *Anglos and Mexicans in the Making of Texas*, 59–74.
28. Amberson, J. McAllen, and M. McAllen, *I Would Rather Sleep in Texas*, 7, 66–67, 155–58; Scott, *Royal Land Grants North of the Río Grande*, 64.
29. *Wood Book of the* Swan, 1857, box 2G131, JSR Papers; *Armstrong vs. United States*.
30. Amberson, J. McAllen, and M. McAllen, *I Would Rather Sleep in Texas*, 158–59; Kelly, *River of Lost Dreams*, 65–71.
31. "1860 United States Federal Census"; Montejano, *Anglos and Mexicans in the Making of Texas*, 37; John Decker to José San Román, June 6, 1858, box 2G54, JSR Papers.
32. Dewey, *Pesos and Dollars*, 33; John M. Hart, *Revolutionary Mexico: The Coming and Process of the Mexican Revolution* (Berkeley: University of California Press, 1987), 111.
33. Francois Bichotte to José San Román, January 16, 1858, box 2G54, JSR Papers; John Decker to José San Román, September 21, 1858, box 2G54, JSR Papers; José San Román Cash Book Journal, May 1858–May 1865, box 2G131, JSR Papers; "1860 United States Federal Census."
34. Dewey, *Pesos and Dollars*, 31.
35. Vicente Lauregue to San Román, April 27, 1858, box 2G54, JSR Papers.
36. Manuel Dosal to San Román, April 27, 1858, box 2G54, JSR Papers; Landa, *Trust, Ethnicity, and Identity*, 3–6.
37. Juan Mora-Torres, *The Making of the Mexican Border* (Austin: University of Texas Press, 2001), 29–36; Alex M Saragoza, *The Monterrey Elite and the Mexican State, 1880–1940* (Austin: University of Texas Press, 1988), 42–51.

38. C. Broyda y Cia. en Matamoros, un manifestor de efectos robados, December 08, 1851; C. Solis en Matamoros, un relación de prendas robadas por asaltantes, December 08, 1851; Pedro Hale en Matamoros, una relación de perdidas sufridas, December 06, 1851, Spanish Material from Various Sources, Matamoros Archives, vol. LXII, box 2Q281, Dolph Briscoe Center for American History, University of Texas at Austin.
39. Graf, "Economic History of the Lower Rio Grande Valley," 286–90; Valerio-Jiménez, *River of Hope*, 144–47.
40. Plenty of smuggling occurred around the area of Matamoros/Brownsville. However, Mexican and American officials made more successful efforts to clamp down on the illicit trade in the delta region than upriver. The success of Mexican authorities to exact tariffs at Matamoros led to an outbreak of violence called the Merchant's War, in which the American merchants of Matamoros/Brownsville funded a Mexican federalist revolt against the Mexican army stationed in northern Mexico. See: Graf, "Economic History of the Lower Rio Grande Valley," 320–32; Kearney and Knopp, *Boom and Bust*, 82–83; Amberson, J. McAllen, and M. McAllen, *I Would Rather Sleep in Texas*, 133–41.
41. Mariano Hernandez to José San Román, August 11, 1855, box 2G48, JSR Papers.
42. Joseph San Roman, et al. to F. Gauties, Consul of France in Matamoros, September 20, 1850, Despatches; "Protest of the Merchants and Residents of the City of Matamoros, Mexico against the acts of the Government of the United States and its representatives," January 16, 1866, box 2.325/C113c, JSR Papers; Tarifa General de la Republica Mexicana, box 2G41, JSR Papers.
43. Bill of lading to Valentin Romero, November 16, 1855, box 2G48, JSR Papers; Valentín Rivero to San Román, July 26, 1858, box 2G54, JSR Papers.
44. Douglass and Bilbao, *Amerikanuak*, 13.
45. Adams, *Conflict and Commerce*, 85–88; Graf, "Economic History of the Lower Rio Grande Valley," 656–80; Cerutti, *Burguesía, capitales e industria*, 47–51.
46. Hinojosa, *Borderlands Town in Transition*; Alexander Mendoza, "'For Our Own Best Interests': Nineteenth-Century Laredo Tejanos, Military Service, and the Development of American Nationalism," *Southwestern Historical Quarterly* 115, no. 2 (October 2011): 125–52; Jerry D. Thompson, *Warm Weather & Bad Whiskey: The 1886 Laredo Election Riot* (El Paso: Texas Western Press, 1991); Jerry D. Thompson, *Tejano Tiger: José de Los Santos Benavides*

and the Texas-Mexico Borderlands, 1823–1891 (Fort Worth: TCU Press, 2017).

47. Bolton, "Tienda de Cuervo's Ynspeccion," 194, 198–203; Hämäläinen, *Comanche Empire*, 220–21; Hinojosa, *Borderlands Town in Transition*, 14.
48. Hinojosa, *Borderlands Town in Transition*, 70.
49. Hinojosa, *Borderlands Town in Transition*, 71.
50. Adams, *Conflict and Commerce*, 76–79.
51. Felix Garcia, *The Children of John Z. Leyendecker: A Brief Genealogical Sketch* (Laredo: Felix Garcia, 1984), 17–20; Francis Paul Prucha, *American Indian Policy in Crisis: Christian Reformers and the Indian, 1865–1900* (Norman: University of Oklahoma Press, 1976), 217–21; Indian Account Book, 1854, Oak Creek Store, box 2M316, John Zirvas Leyendecker Papers, 1842–1979, Dolph Briscoe Center for American History, University of Texas at Austin (hereafter cited as JZL Papers); Lt. Alfred Pleasonton to Leyendecker, October 20, 1854, General Correspondence, box 2M315, JZL Papers.
52. Account for Oak Creek, 1853, Oak Creek Store, box 2M316, JZL Papers; Charles G. Davis, "Fort Chadbourne," *Handbook of Texas Online*, accessed June 21, 2019, http://www.tshaonline.org/handbook/online/articles/qbf08.
53. Stan Green, *Border Biographies*, 2nd ed., vol. 1 (Laredo: Texas A&M International University Press, 1993), 93–94.
54. Leyendecker rented his room and store from the Treviños for twenty pesos a month, which he usually paid out three months at a time. Leyendecker always made sure to pay his rent on time or early to make a good impression on the prominent Laredo family. See: Rent Receipts, 1855–1859, J. Z. Miscellaneous Receipts, box 2M317, JZL Papers.
55. Thompson, *Tejano Tiger*, 191; Hinojosa, *Borderlands Town in Transition*, 73.
56. S. Benavides to Leyendecker, March 26, 1857, Benavides Letters, box 2M314, JZL Papers.
57. Leyendecker Memorandum Book, November 11, 1886, Genealogy, box 2M317, JZL Papers; Benito García to Leyendecker, April 4, 1858, General Correspondence, box 2M315, JZL Papers; Carlos E. Castañeda, *Our Catholic Heritage in Texas, 1519–1936* (Austin: Von Boeckmann-Jones Company, 1936).
58. Benavides Family Tree, Genealogy, box 2M317, JZL Papers. Tomás Sánchez was the founder of Laredo.
59. Bart J. DeWitt to Leyendecker, January 8, 1857, box 2M314, JZL Papers.
60. María Andrea Leyendecker to John Leyendecker, October 23, 1859, box 2M314, JZL Papers.

61. Leyendecker Memorandum Book, November 11, 1886, box 2M317, JZL Papers; María Andrea Leyendecker to John Leyendecker, October 16, 1859, box 2M314, JZL Papers.
62. Leyendecker Memorandum Book, November 11, 1886, box 2M317, JZL Papers; T., "The Church Calendar," *Messenger*, May 31, 1876, p. 5; "Whit Monday. (News)," *Christian Century* 21, no. 13, (2003): 17.
63. María Andrea Leyendecker to John Leyendecker, October 23, 1859, box 2M314, JZL Papers.
64. Catherine DeWitt to Leyendecker, February 7, 1856, B.J. DeWitt Letters, box 2M314, JZL Papers; Catherine DeWitt to Leyendecker, January 9, 1857, B.J. DeWitt Letters, box 2M314, JZL Papers.
65. John Z. Leyendecker Account with Francois Guilbeau, 1857, Business Records, box 2M316, JZL Papers.
66. Jonathan Beecher, *Victor Considerant and the Rise and Fall of French Romantic Socialism* (Berkeley: University of California Press, 2001), 366; Barker and Dubois de Saligny, *French Legation in Texas*, 339.
67. Guilbeau to Leyendecker, January 4, 1857, General Correspondence, box 2M315, JZL Papers.
68. Charles W. Calomiris and Larry Schweikart, "The Panic of 1857: Origins, Transmission, and Containment," *Journal of Economic History* 51, no. 4 (December 1991): 807–34; Eric Foner, *Free Soil, Free Labor, Free Men: The Ideology of the Republican Party before the Civil War* (Oxford; New York: Oxford University Press, 1995), 24–25; "Market Report: Markets," *New York Daily Times*, March 24, 1857, *Proquest Historical Newspapers: The New York Times*, 2.
69. Guilbeau to Leyendecker, February 14, 1857, General Correspondence, box 2M315, JZL Papers.
70. US Department of the Treasury, Impost Books, Laredo, 1851–1914, vol. 1, United States National Archives, Fort Worth, Texas, 2791232 (hereafter cited as US Dept. of Treasury, Impost Books).
71. Martin Ruef, *Between Slavery and Capitalism: The Legacy of Emancipation in the American South* (Princeton, NJ: Princeton University Press, 2014), 144; Baptist, *Half Has Never Been Told*, 381; Tindall and Shi, *America*, 707–8.
72. Preau & Couturie to Leyendecker, February 21, 1857, General Correspondence, box 2M315, JZL Papers.
73. Thompson, *Tejano Tiger*, 66–78; González-Quiroga, "Conflict and Cooperation," 44–48.
74. US Dept. of Treasury, Impost Books.
75. John Leyendecker account with Francois Guilbeau, 1857, box 2M316, JZL Papers.
76. US Dept. of Treasury, Impost Books; Diaz, *Border Contraband*, 18–22, 178; Gautham Rao, *National Duties: Custom Houses and the Making*

of the American State (Chicago: University of Chicago Press, 2016), 1–14.

77. D. D. T. Leech, *List of the Post-Offices in the United States: With the Names of the Postmasters on the 1st of April, 1859 ; Also, the Laws and Regulations of the Post Office Department with an Appendix Containing the Names of the Post Offices Arranged by States and Counties* (Washington, DC: John C. Rives, 1859), 83; David M. Henkin, *The Postal Age: The Emergence of Modern Communications in Nineteenth-Century America* (Chicago: University Of Chicago Press, 2006), 19–20; Richard R John, *Spreading the News: The American Postal System from Franklin to Morse* (Cambridge, MA: Harvard University Press, 1998), 115–24; Thompson, *Tejano Tiger*, 63–64.
78. Adams, *Conflict and Commerce*, 80–82; Thompson, *Tejano Tiger*, 63–64.
79. Guilbeau Invoice, 1858, Business Records, box 2M316, JZL Papers; Stadeker, Mecklenburger, y Cox Invoice, Nov. 19, 1858, Business Records, box 2M316, JZL Papers.
80. Richard Fitzpatrick to Lewis Cass, April 4, 1859, Despatches, reel 4.
81. Fitzpatrick to Cass, October 01, 1859, Despatches, reel 4.

Notes for Chapter 5

1. Joseph Morell to Charles Stillman, Nov. 18, 1861, Letters from various others to Charles Stillman, November 1861, CSBP, MS Am 800.27, (25) CSBP; Morell to Stillman, July 29, 1861, Letters from various others to Charles Stillman, July 1861, CSBP; Morell to Stillman, Feb. 25, 1862, Letters from various others to Charles Stillman, February 1862, CSBP; Morell to Stillman, July 27, 1862, Letters from various others to Charles Stillman, July 1862, CSBP; Morell to Stillman, Feb. 16, 1862, Letters from various others to Charles Stillman, February 1862, CSBP; Morell to Stillman, Nov. 27, 1862, Letters from various others to Charles Stillman, November 1862, CSBP.
2. Robert M. Browning Jr., *Lincoln's Trident: The West Gulf Blockading Squadron during the Civil War* (Tuscaloosa: University of Alabama Press, 2014), 163–64; James W. Daddysman, *The Matamoros Trade: Confederate Commerce, Diplomacy, and Intrigue* (Newark: University of Delaware Press, 1984); James A. Irby, *Backdoor at Bagdad: The Civil War on the Rio Grande* (El Paso: Texas Western Press, 1977); William Diamond, "Imports of the Confederate Government from Europe and Mexico," *Journal of Southern History* 6, no. 4 (November 1940): 470–503; Mitchell Smith, "The 'Neutral' Matamoros Trade, 1861–1865," *Southwest Review* 37, no. 4 (Autumn 1952): 319–24;

Walter E. Wilson, *Civil War Scoundrels and the Texas Cotton Trade* (Jefferson, NC: McFarland, 2020), 1–31.

3. Mark Wasserman, *Everyday Life and Politics in Nineteenth Century Mexico: Men, Women, and War*, 1st ed. Diálogos (Albuquerque: University of New Mexico Press, 2000), 106–35; Mora-Torres, *Making of the Mexican Border*, 41–51; Kearney and Knopp, *Boom and Bust*, 122–25; Ronnie C. Tyler, *Santiago Vidaurri and the Southern Confederacy* (Austin: Texas State Historical Association, 1973), 13–41.
4. Jerry Thompson, *Cortina: Defending the Mexican Name in Texas* (College Station: Texas A&M University Press, 2013), 7–32; Hämäläinen, *Comanche Empire*, 313–19.
5. Matamoros Seizures (1863–1869), vols. 1–5, FO 5/1181–1185, National Archives of the UK; Compañía Anónima de Navegación del Lago de Chapala y Río Grande documents, 1866–1867, BANC MSS M-M 1809, University of California Berkeley, Bancroft Library; Wasserman, *Everyday Life and Politics in Nineteenth Century Mexico*, 112–32; Philip Leigh, *Trading with the Enemy: The Covert Economy during the American Civil War* (Yardley, PA: Westholme, 2014), ix–xvii.
6. Bayly, *Birth of the Modern World*, 1-3; Peter Wagner, *Modernity: Understanding the Present* (Malden, MA: Polity, 2012), 4–6.
7. Hart, *Empire and Revolution*, 25–31; Valerio-Jiménez, *River of Hope*, 247–60; Kelley, *River of Lost Dreams*, 72–78.
8. Beckert, *Empire of Cotton*, ix–xxii, 242-246; Leigh, *Trading with the Enemy*, 1–14; James Oakes, *The Ruling Race: A History of American Slaveholders* (New York: Alfred A Knopf, 1982), xi–xiii, 225–27; Baptist, *Half Has Never Been Told*, xvi–xxvii; Alan L. Olmstead and Paul Webb Rhode, *Creating Abundance: Biological Innovation and American Agricultural Development* (New York: Cambridge University Press, 2008), 98–133.
9. Foner, *Free Soil, Free Labor, Free Men*, ix–xxxix, 310; Brian Schoen, *The Fragile Fabric of Union: Cotton, Federal Politics, and the Global Origins of the Civil War* (Baltimore: Johns Hopkins University Press, 2009), 201–59.
10. Annual reports on shipping and navigation, trade and commerce, agriculture, and population and industries from the port of Galveston, pp. 48–83, FO 701/28, National Archives of the UK.
11. Beckert, *Empire of Cotton*, 246–48; John D. Pelzer, "Liverpool and the American Civil War," *History Today* 40 (March 1990): 46–52.
12. Daddysman, *Matamoros Trade*, 22–25, 30–33; Rodman L. Underwood, *Waters of Discord: The Union Blockade of Texas during the Civil War* (Jefferson, NC: McFarland, 2003), 63–65; Cerutti, *Burguesía*,

capitales e industria, 74–87; Mario Cerutti and Miguel Gonzalez-Quiroga, "Guerra y Comercio En Torno al Río Bravo (1855–1867). Línea Fronteriza, Espacio Económico Común," *Historia Mexicana* 40, no. 2 (Winter 1990): 217–97; Mario Cerutti and Miguel A. González-Quiroga, *El Norte de México y Texas, 1848–1880: Comercio, Capitales y Trabajadores En Una Economía de Frontera* (México, DF: Instituto Mora, 1999), 51–75, 134–42.

13. Letter regarding the sale of bonds for the purchase of cotton, February 1863, box 2014/022-1, folder 2, Texas Governor Pendleton Murrah Records, Archives and Information Services Division, Texas State Library and Archives Commission (hereafter cited as Governor Murrah Records).
14. Gibbs to Murrah, February 19, 1864, box 2014/022-1, folder 36, Governor Murrah Records.
15. Special Order no. 97, Article XIV, April 20, 1864, box 2014/022-2, folder 62, Governor Murrah Records.
16. Daddysman, *Matamoros Trade*, 107–9; Thompson, *Tejano Tiger*, 139–41; Amberson, J. McAllen, and M. McAllen, *I Would Rather Sleep in Texas*, 185–89.
17. Debbie M. Liles and Angela Boswell, eds., *Women in Civil War Texas: Diversity and Dissidence in the Trans-Mississippi* (Denton: University of North Texas Press, 2016); Clara Sue Kidwell, *The Choctaws in Oklahoma: From Tribe to Nation, 1855–1870* (Norman: University of Oklahoma Press, 2007), 32, 47, 57–58; Cerutti and Gonzalez-Quiroga, "Guerra y Comercio," 383.
18. Henry Baumberger to Dearest Relatives and Friends, Aug. 24, 1863, folder 7, HB Letters.
19. Amberson, J. McAllen, and M. McAllen, *I Would Rather Sleep in Texas*, 199.
20. Henry Baumberger to Dear Relatives and Friends, Jan. 23, 1861, folder 6, HB Letters.
21. *Tri-Weekly Telegraph* (Houston, TX), vol. 29, no. 26, ed. 1, Friday, May 15, 1863, University of North Texas Libraries, Portal to Texas History, accessed October 15, 2019, https://texashistory.unt.edu, crediting Dolph Briscoe Center for American History.
22. Thompson, *Tejano Tiger*, 123–24.
23. *Weekly Telegraph* (Houston, TX), vol. 27, no. 35, ed. 1, Wednesday, November 13, 1861; Joseph E. Chance, *José María de Jesús Carvajal: The Life and Times of a Mexican Revolutionary* (San Antonio: Trinity University Press, 2006), 173; Kearney and Knopp, *Boom and Bust*, 120–23.
24. *Daily True Delta*, published as *The Daily True Delta* (New Orleans), vol. 25, no. 21, December 12, 1861.

25. *Weekly Telegraph*, (Houston, TX), vol. 27, no. 39, ed. 1, Wednesday, December 11, 1861.
26. Lucius Avery, US Vice Consul Matamoros, "Memorial of Leopold Schlinger, September 26, 1869, box 2.35/A72b, Leopold Schlinger Family Papers, 1833–1877, Dolph Briscoe Center for American History, University of Texas at Austin (hereafter cited as LSF Papers).
27. Erhard Deposition, March 17, 1869, Santos Coy Deposition, September 24, 1869, Schlinger Deposition, April 2, 1862, Box 2.35/A72b, LSF Papers.
28. Vale to Stillman, April 11, 1863, CSBP, MS Am 800.27 (21)-(39).
29. Morell to Stillman, May 27, 1861, Letters from various others to Charles Stillman, February 1862, CSBP.
30. Dewey, *Pesos and Dollars*, 121–31.
31. Adams, *Conflict and Commerce on the Rio Grande*, 89–94; García, *Children of John Z. Leyendecker*, 7–13; Thompson, *Tejano Tiger*, 84–207; Thompson, *Warm Weather & Bad Whiskey*, 14–29; Cerutti and Gonzalez-Quiroga, "Guerra y Comercio," 291–94.
32. Major C. C. Sibley to Major F. J. Porter, March 11, 1861, in Russel A. Alger, ed., *The War of the Rebellion: A Compilation of the Official Records of the Union and Confederate Armies*, vol. 52 (Washington, DC: Government Printing Office, 1898), 134.
33. *Civilian and Gazette Weekly* (Galveston, TX), vol. 23, no. 52, ed. 1, Tuesday, April 2, 1861, University of North Texas Libraries, Portal to Texas History, accessed October 16, 2019, https://texashistory.unt.edu, crediting Dolph Briscoe Center for American History; *Standard* (Clarksville, TX), vol. 18, no. 13, ed. 1, Saturday, April 13, 1861, University of North Texas Libraries, Portal to Texas History, accessed October 16, 2019, https://texashistory.unt.edu, crediting Dolph Briscoe Center for American History; Thompson, *Tejano Tiger*, 78.
34. Thompson, *Tejano Tiger*, 123–34; Adams, *Conflict and Commerce on the Rio Grande*, 89–93.
35. Thompson, *Tejano Tiger*, 113, 187–88.
36. DeWitt actually wrote a letter to Leyendecker on a Sweet & Lacoste Co. flyer: Bart J. DeWitt to John Z. Leyendecker, April 24, 1863, box 2M314, JZL Papers; Roseann Bacha-Garza et al., eds., *The Civil War on the Rio Grande, 1846–1876*, 1st ed., Elma Dill Russell Spencer Series in the West and Southwest 46 (College Station: Texas A&M University Press, 2019), 165; Charles R Porter, *Spanish Water, Anglo Water: Early Development in San Antonio* (College Station: Texas A&M University Press, 2011), 102; Ralph A. Wooster, *Civil War Texas: A History and a Guide* (Austin: Texas State Historical Association, 1999), 33–34.

37. David Montejano, "Mexican Merchants and Teamsters on the Texas Cotton Road, 1862–1865," in *Mexico and Mexicans in the Making of the United States*, ed. John Tutino, History, Culture, and Society Series (Austin: University of Texas Press, 2012), 163–64.
38. DeWitt to Leyendecker, July 24, 1863, box 2M314, JZL Papers.
39. Porter, *Spanish Water, Anglo Water*, 102; Miguel Gonzalez Quiroga, "Los Inicios de la Migración Laboral Mexicana a Texas (1850–1880)," in *Encuentro en la Frontera: Mexicanos y Norteamericanos en un Espacio Común*, ed. Ramirez M. Ceballos (Mexico: COLEF, 2001), 357–58.
40. Charles Lege to Leyendecker, July 6, 1864, box 2M314, JZL Papers.
41. Jockusch & Co. to Leyendecker, May 31, 1865, box 2M314, JZL Papers; Lege to Leyendecker, May 31, 1865, box 2M314, JZL Papers.
42. Mora-Torres, *Making of the Mexican Border*, 50; Adams, *Conflict and Commerce*, 92–93; Thompson, *Tejano Tiger*, 164–66; Tyler, *Santiago Vidaurri*, 122–27.
43. Arthur J. Mayer, "San Antonio, Frontier Entrepot" (PhD diss., University of Texas at Austin, 1976), 477–83; Confederate States of America Quartermaster's Department records for Laredo, box 2M318, JZL Papers.
44. Graf, "Economic History of the Lower Rio Grande Valley," 489–90; Irby, *Backdoor at Bagdad*, 5–7.
45. Montejano, "Mexican Merchants and Teamsters," 159–66.
46. Cerutti, *Burguesía, capitales e industria*, 74–87; Tyler, *Santiago Vidaurri*, 50–51.
47. After the Civil War, San Román took over the Hernández Hermanos holdings in Matamoros: Ledger for Hernández Hermanos, Matamoros, January-August 1864, box 2G133, JSR Papers.
48. Mora-Torres, *Making of the Mexican Border*, 33–34, 92–93; Cerutti and González-Quiroga, "Guerra y Comercio," 245–47, 264–73.
49. Asa Pullen to José San Román, July 2, 1865, box 2G73, JSR Papers; E. M. Wheelock, *Reports of Cases Argued and Decided in the Supreme Court of the State of Texas During the Latter Part of the Second Annual Session of the Court, Commencing the First Monday of December 1871*, XXXVI (St. Louis: Gilbert Book Company: 1882), 602–18.
50. Pullen to San Román, July 2, 1865, box 2G73, JSR Papers; C. W. Whitis to San Román, Sep. 15, 1864, box 2G73, JSR Papers; José San Román Cash Book, May 1, 1858-May 31, 1865, p. 447, box 2G131, JSR Papers.
51. Morell to Stillman, Feb. 26, 1862, CSBP, MS Am 800.27 (21)-(39).
52. Hart, *Empire and Revolution*, 23–25; Hart, *Revolutionary Mexico*, 110–23; Cerutti and González-Quiroga, "Guerra y Comercio," 255–71.

53. Morell to San Román, Jan. 07, 1862, box 2G61, JSR Papers; Hart, *Revolutionary Mexico*, 110–15; Marilyn McAdams Sibley, "Charles Stillman: A Case Study of Entrepreneurship on the Rio Grande, 1861–1865," *Southwestern Historical Quarterly* 77, no. 2 (1973): 227–40; Montejano, "Mexican Merchants and Teamsters," 141–70.
54. Tindall and Shi, *America*, 766; Daddysman, *Matamoros Trade*, 165–68; Alger, *War of the Rebellion*, 228–29.
55. G. Coppell to Lord Lyons, Nov. 16, 1863, Matamoros Seizures, FO 5/1181, TNA; Henry Howard, *Report by Her Majesty's Agent of the Proceedings and Awards of the Mixed Commission on British and American Claims* (London: Harrison and Sons, 1874), 102–18.
56. Montejano, *Mexican Merchants and Teamsters*, 160; Joseph Railton to San Román, September 01, 1862, box 2G61, JSR Papers.
57. Linda K. Salvucci and Richard J. Salvucci, "The Lizardi Brothers: A Mexican Family Business and the Expansion of New Orleans, 1825–1846," *Journal of Southern History* 82, no. 4 (November 2016): 759–88; Thomas Courtland Manning, Francois-Xavier Martin, and Merritt M. Robinson, *Reports of Cases Argued and Determined in the Supreme Court of Louisiana and in the Superior Court of the Territory of Louisiana. [1809–1896]: 1846–1847*, vol. 21 (St. Paul: West Publishing Company, 1910), 281–91.
58. H. N. Caldwell to F. Lizardi and Co, Aug. 17, 1863; F. Lizardi and Co. to H. N. Caldwell, Aug. 18, 1863; F. Lizardi and Co to José San Román, Aug 21, 1863, in Matamoros Seizures, August 1864–November 1865, FO 5/1184, TNA; José San Román Cash Book, May 1, 1858–May 31, 1865, p. 333, box 2G131, JSR Papers; "Brig Dashing Wave v. The United States," in Stephen K. Williams, *Cases Argued and Decided in the Supreme Court of the United States, December Terms, 1865–1867* (Rochester: Lawyers' Cooperative Publishing Company, 1901), 621–25.
59. Beckert, *Empire of Cotton*, 149; Daddysman, *Matamoros Trade*, 156; Bill of Lading for the *Joven Rafael*, Oct. 14, 1864, and Bill of Lading for the *Angelita*, Oct. 15, 1864, box 2G73, JSR papers.
60. John Decker to San Román, Oct. 4, 1864, box 2G73, JSR Papers.
61. Laredo Archives, 1749–1838, reel 1, p.3, DeGolyer Library Microfilm, Southern Methodist University; *Camargo Church Marriage Records, 1764–1913: Grooms, Second Revision* (Corpus Christi: Spanish American Genealogical Association, 1995), 52; John Decker to San Román, Oct. 12, 1864, box 2G73, JSR Papers.
62. Before Mexico's independence, the Spanish called the town Revilla: Historia vol. 56, Nuevo Santander, Villa de Revilla, 410-423, AGM.
63. Thompson, *Tejano Tiger*, 85–87.

64. Henry Redmond to Charles Stillman, May 7, 1861, CSBP, MS Am 800.27 (4-20).
65. Thompson, *Tejano Tiger*, 91–94; Christopher L. Miller, Russell K. Skowronek, and Roseann Bacha-Garza, *Blue and Gray on the Border: The Rio Grande Valley Civil War Trail* (College Station: Texas A&M University Press, 2018), 137.
66. Henry Redmond to José San Román, Sep. 05, 1864, box 2G73, JSR Papers; US Dept. of Treasury, Impost Books.
67. Henry Redmond to José San Román, Sep. 18, 1864, box 2G73, JSR Papers; Norman L. McCarver, *Hearne on the Brazos* (San Antonio: Century Press of Texas, 1958), 22–23.

Notes for Chapter 6

1. Joseph Kleiber to Woodhouse, May 13, 1872, Letter book, box 2E293, Joseph Kleiber Papers, 1860–1877, Dolph Briscoe Center for American History, University of Texas at Austin (hereafter cited as JK Papers).
2. See chap. 4.
3. Monday and Vick, *Petra's Legacy*, 141–71; Montejano, "Mexican Merchants and Teamsters," 141–70; Kearney and Knopp, *Boom and Bust*, 143–59; William Cronon, *Nature's Metropolis: Chicago and the Great West* (New York: W. W. Norton, 1991), 296–303.
4. Kelley, *River of Lost Dreams*, 72–85; Jürgen Osterhammel, *The Transformation of the World: A Global History of the Nineteenth Century*, trans. Patrick Camiller, America in the World (Princeton, NJ: Princeton University Press, 2014), 126.
5. James Lewellyn Allhands, *Gringo Builders* (Joplin, MO; Dallas, TX: privately printed, 1931); James L. Allhands, *Uriah Lott* (San Antonio: Naylor, 1949).
6. Hart, *Empire and Revolution*, 104–30; Richard White, *Railroaded: The Transcontinentals and the Making of Modern America* (New York: W. W. Norton, 2011), 215–16; Bruce Cheeseman, *Perfectly Exhausted with Pleasure: The 1881 King-Kenedy Excursion Train to Laredo* (Austin: Book Club of Texas, 1992), 27.
7. Montejano, "Mexican Merchants and Teamsters," 141–70.
8. Joseph Kleiber to H. E. Woodhouse, May 13, 1872, box 2E293, typescript of letter book, JK Papers.
9. August Santleben, *A Texas Pioneer; Early Staging and Overland Freighting Days on the Frontiers of Texas and Mexico* (New York: Neale, 1910), 60–63.
10. Santleben, *Texas Pioneer*, 65.
11. Santleben, *Texas Pioneer*, 41–42.

12. H. A. Maltby and Somers Kinney, *Daily Ranchero* (Brownsville, TX), vol. 3, no. 36, ed. 1, Wednesday, December 11, 1867, University of North Texas Libraries, Portal to Texas History, accessed March 29, 2022, https://texashistory.unt.edu, crediting San Jacinto Museum of History; Montejano, "Mexican Merchants and Teamsters," 145–51; Miguel Gonzalez-Quiroga, "Mexicanos in Texas during the Civil War," in Emilio Zamora et al., eds., *Mexican Americans in Texas History: Selected Essays* (Austin: Texas State Historical Association, 2000), 57–62.
13. Edward Downey to Mifflin Kenedy, Oct. 9, 1867, box #007, folder Letters (1863–1867) "C," Kenedy Family Collection, South Texas Archives, James C. Jernigan Library, Texas A&M University–Kingsville (hereafter cited as Kenedy Family Collection).
14. Maltby and Kinney, *Daily Ranchero* (Brownsville, TX), vol. 3, no. 28, ed. 1, Friday November 22, 1867, accessed March 29, 2022.
15. Jerry Thompson and Lawrence T. Jones III, *Civil War and Revolution on the Rio Grande Frontier: A Narrative and Photographic History* (Austin: Texas State Historical Association, 2004), 132–34.
16. Robert Dalzell to Mifflin Kenedy, Oct. 21, 1877, box #022, folder Letters-1877, Kenedy Family Collection.
17. Kelley, *River of Lost Dreams*, 77; W. Armstrong Price, "Hurricanes Affecting the Coast of Texas from Galveston to Rio Grande," Technical Memorandum no. 78, Army Corps of Engineers, March 1956, A22–A23; Monday and Brannen, *Petra's Legacy*, 155–60.
18. Sibley, "Charles Stillman," 239–40; Amberson, J. McAllen, and M. McAllen, *I Would Rather Sleep in Texas*, 279; Monday and Brannen, *Petra's Legacy*, 145; John Mason Hart, "Stillman, Charles," *Handbook of Texas Online*, accessed May 17, 2022, https://www.tshaonline.org/handbook/entries/stillman-charles. The National City Bank of New York eventually evolved into Citi Bank, the modern banking behemoth.
19. Kleiber to Mussina, May 13, 1870, Letter book, box 2E293, JK Papers.
20. White, *Railroaded*, 93–130; Hart, *Empire and Revolution*, 33–39.
21. Richard J. Evans, *The Pursuit of Power: Europe 1815–1914*, Penguin History of Europe 7 (New York: Penguin Books, 2016), 152–53; Allan Brinkley, *The Unfinished Nation: A Concise History of the American People*, 7th ed. (New York: McGraw-Hill, 2014), 227.
22. Time book of the *Mustang*, 1864, Folder 6, Theodore M. Warner Collection, Margaret H. McAllen Memorial Archives, Museum of South Texas History, Edinburg, TX.
23. Kearney and Knopp, *Boom and Bust*, 142–43, 157–59.
24. Joseph Kleiber to Simon Mussina, May 13, 1870, Letter book, box 2E293, JK Papers.

25. Joseph Kleiber to Robert Leman, Nov. 11, 1870, Letter book, box 2E293, JK Papers.
26. Joseph Kleiber to Simon Mussina, May 13, 1870, Letter book, box 2E293, JK Papers.
27. W. H. Chatfield, *The Twin Cities of the Border (Brownsville, Texas and Matamoros, Mexico), and the Country of the Lower Rio Grande* (New Orleans: E. P. Brandao, 1893), 21; Kearney and Knopp, *Boom and Bust*, 157–59.
28. Dalzell to Kenedy, April 17, 1876, box #021, folder Letters-1876 to 1878 (Robert Dalzell), Kenedy Family Collection.
29. Frank Daniel Yturria, *The Patriarch: The Remarkable Life and Extraordinary Times of Francisco Yturria* (Brownsville: University of Texas at Brownsville and Texas Southmost College, 2006), 243–45; Monday and Vick, *Petra's Legacy*, 50, 145; Amberson, J. McAllen, and M. McAllen, *I Would Rather Sleep in Texas*, 356.
30. Quoted in Carl H. Moneyhon, *Texas after the Civil War: The Struggle of Reconstruction*, 1st ed., Texas A&M Southwestern Studies 14 (College Station: Texas A&M University Press, 2004), 121.
31. Carl H. Moneyhon, *Edmund J. Davis of Texas: Civil War General, Republican Leader, Reconstruction Governor* (Fort Worth: TCU Press, 2010), 46–60; Moneyhon, *Texas after the Civil War*, 119–22; González-Quiroga, *War and Peace on the Rio Grande*, 256–59; Monday and Vick, *Petra's Legacy*, 183–85.
32. Kleiber to E. J. Davis, July 7, 1871, Letter book, box 2E293, JK Papers.
33. Moneyhon, *Texas after the Civil War*, 122.
34. H. Howlett to Kenedy, May 26, 1871, Folder Letters, 1868–1875, Kenedy Family Collection.
35. Kleiber to Woodhouse, Sep. 3, 1870, Letter book, box 2E293, JK Papers.
36. Kleiber to F. Schlickum, June 24, 1870 and Kleiber to Schlickum, Sep 03, 1870, Letter book, box 2E293, JK Papers; Monday and Vick, *Petra's Legacy*, 183; Friedrich R Wollmershäuser, *Passengers Listed in the Allgemeine Auswanderungs-Zeitung, 1848–1869* [*Allgemeine Auswanderungs-Zeitung: Einträge Zu Passagieren, 1848–1869*] (Morgantown, PA: Masthof Press, 2014), 465; *Daily Ranchero* (Brownsville, TX), vol. 10, ed. 1, Saturday, September 10, 1870, University of North Texas Libraries, Portal to Texas History, accessed June 7, 2022, https://texashistory.unt.edu.
37. William Kelly to Kenedy, April 30, 1871, box #008, Letters, 1868–1875; Dalzell to Kenedy, Apr. 20, 1877, box #022, Letters-1877; Kenedy Family Collection.
38. Dalzell to Kenedy, Feb. 13, 1876, box #021, Folder Letters-1876–1878 (Robert Dalzell), Kenedy Family Collection.

39. James P. Baughman, "Morgan, Charles," *Handbook of Texas Online*, accessed May 18, 2022, https://www.tshaonline.org/handbook/entries/morgan-charles.
40. Kleiber to Woodhouse, Jan. 21, 1873, Letter book, box 2E293, JK Papers.
41. Philip Riden, "The Output of the British Iron Industry before 1870," *Economic History Review* 30, no. 3 (1977): 442; David Nasaw, *Andrew Carnegie* (New York: Penguin Books, 2006), 115–17; Evans, *Pursuit of Power*, 152–56.
42. B. O. Hicks to Kenedy, Sep. 30, 1874, box #017, Folder Letters 1871–July 1 to Sept. 30, Kenedy Family Collection.
43. Monday and Vick, *Petra's Legacy*, 190.
44. Mifflin Kenedy vs. The Rio Grande Rail Road Company and F. Armendaiz, Filed 13, Dec. 1875, box #017, Folder Rio Grande Rail Road Company, 1874, Kenedy Family Collection.
45. Kleiber to Woodhouse, April 17, 1872, Letter book, box 2E293, JK Papers.
46. Kearney and Knopp, *Boom and Bust*, 157–59; Yturria, *Patriarch*, 243.
47. Joseph Kleiber to Woodhouse, May 13, 1872, Letter book, box 2E293, JK Papers.
48. Lovenskiold to Kenedy, April 3, 1873; Lovenskiold to Kenedy, May 30, 1873, Folder Telegrams Relating to Settlement with Rio Grande RRC, 1870s, Kenedy Family Collection.
49. P. M. Spinelli to Kenedy, Sep. 17, 1874, Folder Letters July 1–Sept. 30, Kenedy Family Collection.
50. Brewster to Kenedy, Aug. 17, 1874, box #017 Folder Letters-1874-July 1–Sept. 30; Taylor to Kenedy, Oct. 1, 1874, Folder Letters-1874-Oct. 1–Dec. 31, Kenedy Family Collection.
51. Kleiber to Railton, Dec. 26, 1872, Letter book, box 2E293, JK Papers.
52. Kenedy to S. M. Swenson, Aug. 04, no year, box 22, Folder Letters-S. Powers-1877–1880, Kenedy Family Collection.
53. Kleiber to Woodhouse, Jan. 21, 1873, Letter book, box 2E293, JK Papers.
54. *The Manchester Commercial List, 1873–1874* (London: Estell, 1873), "Conditions, &c," n.p. "Changes, Amalgamations and New Firms," 24; Joseph Railton to San Román, September 01, 1862, box 2G61, JSR Papers.
55. Mifflin Kenedy vs. Rio Grande Railroad Company, Petition to set aside award damages, Aug. 13, 1878, Box #024, Folder Rio Grande Rail Road Company 1878, Kenedy Family Collection.
56. Stephen Powers to Kenedy, Sep. 9, 1879, Box #022, Folder Letters S. Powers-1877–1880, Kenedy Family Collection.

Notes for Chapter 6

57. Moneyhon, *Texas after the Civil War*, 198–99.
58. Dalzell to Kenedy, Oct. 21, 1878, Box #023, Folder Letters-1878, Kenedy Family Collection.
59. Dalzell to Kenedy, Nov. 10, 1878, Box #023, Folder Letters-1878, Kenedy Family Collection.
60. Thompson, *Cortina*, 29.
61. Allhands, *Uriah Lott*, 1–3; Monday and Vick, *Petra's Legacy*, 207–14.
62. Allhands, *Uriah Lott*, 6–9; A. A. Champion, "Papers and Personalities of Frontier Journalism," in *More Studies in Brownsville History*, ed. Milo Kearney (Brownsville, TX: Pan American University, 1989), 138–42.
63. Allhands, *Uriah Lott*, 11.
64. Cheeseman, *Perfectly Exhausted with Pleasure*, 11–35; J. L. Allhands, *Railroads to the Rio* (Salado, TX: Anson Jones Press, 1960), 17–32.
65. Monday and Vick, *Petra's Legacy*, 219.
66. White, *Railroaded*, 62–87, 230; Cheeseman, *Perfectly Exhausted with Pleasure*, 21–22; Brinkley, *Unfinished Nation*, 360.
67. Dull to Kenedy, Dec. 17, 1880, box #024, Folder Letters-July–December 1880, Kenedy Family Collection.
68. White, *Railroaded*, 203–16.
69. Hart, *Empire and Revolution*, 104–30; Adams, *Conflict and Commerce on the Rio Grande*, 107–14; White, *Railroaded*, 215–16.
70. Hart, *Empire and Revolution*, 123; Adams, *Conflict and Commerce on the Rio Grande*, 107–8.
71. Uriah Lott to Oscar Turner, Mar. 16, 1880, "San Antonio and Border Railroad Company," H.R. Rep. No. 756 Pt. 2, 46th Cong., 2nd Sess. (1880).
72. Allhands, *Uriah Lott*, 18–19; Adams, *Conflict and Commerce on the Rio Grande*, 106.
73. Translated contract from the Secretary of State of Mexico, 1880, Box #027, Folder Rio Grande Railroad Company, Kenedy Family Collection.
74. White, *Railroaded*, 195–96; Allhands, *Uriah Lott*, 20-21; Cheeseman, *Perfectly Exhausted with Pleasure*, 27.
75. Quoted in Yturria, *Patriarch*, 245.
76. Allhands, *Gringo Builders*, 110–12.
77. Allhands, *Gringo Builders*, 112–13.
78. Dictation from Mifflin Kenedy, Corpus Christi, Nueces County: 1889, BANC MSS P-O 133:9, Bancroft Library, University of California.
79. J. H. Stephens to Kenedy, Aug. 3, 1880, Box #027, Folder Letters-Jan–June 1880, Kenedy Family Collection.

Notes for Epilogue

1. Bowman, *Blood Oranges*, 1–13; Arreola and Curtis, *Mexican Border Cities*, 3–13; "QuickFacts, San Antonio city, Texas," *United States Census Bureau,* accessed July 29, 2022, https://www.census.gov/quickfacts/fact/table/sanantoniocitytexas/POP010220; "Área Metropolitana de Monterrey, la segunda más poblada de México," *Telediario,* accessed July 29, 2022, https://www.telediario.mx/local/area-metropolitana-de-monterrey-la-segunda-mas-poblada-de-mexico.
2. Dickson, "Speculations of John Charles Beales," 122–23.
3. Frederick Jackson Turner, *The Frontier in American History* (New York: Henry Holt, 1921), 4.
4. Claudia Hazlewood, "Kennedy, William," *Handbook of Texas Online,* accessed March 13, 2020, http://www.tshaonline.org/handbook/online/articles/fke25.
5. Montejano, "Mexican Merchants and Teamsters," 158–61; Salmón, "San Roman, Jose."
6. Kleiber to Joseph San Roman, Aug. 08, 1874, box 2E293, Typescript of letter book, JK Papers; John H. Hunter, "Kleiber, Joseph," *Handbook of Texas Online,* accessed March 12, 2020, http://www.tshaonline.org/handbook/online/articles/fkl08.
7. Thompson, *Warm Weather & Bad Whiskey*, 1–12, 29, 33–42; García, *Children of John Z. Leyendecker*, 32.
8. Dewey, *Pesos and Dollars*, 115–21; Valerio-Jiménez, *River of Hope,* 269–74.
9. Rufus Kay Wyllys, "The French of California and Sonora," *Pacific Historical Review* 1, no. 3 (1932): 351–53.
10. George Catlin, "Notes for the Emigrant to America to Accompany… the United States Land Company," Galveston Correspondence with Foreign Office, FO 701/30, TNA; Richard H. Ribb, "Catlin, George," *Handbook of Texas Online,* accessed March 04, 2020, http://www.tshaonline.org/handbook/online/articles/fca94.

Bibliography

Archival Sources

Corpus Christi Public Library, Corpus Christi, TX
    Wagner Research Papers
Daughters of the Republic of Texas Library, San Antonio, TX
    Bustillo Family Papers, 1772–1936
    Henry Baumberger Letters, 1856–1867
DeGolyer Library, Southern Methodist University, Dallas, TX
    Despatches from United States Consuls in Matamoros, Mexico, 1826–1906
    Laredo Archives, 1749–1838
    Vander Staten Family Papers
Dolph Briscoe Center for American History, University of Texas at Austin, Austin, TX
    Archivo General de Mexico, 1538–1849
    Broadside Collection
    Gilbert Kingsbury Papers
    John Charles Beales Papers, 1832–1855
    John Zirvas Leyendecker Papers, 1842–1979
    José San Román Papers, 1823–1934
    Joseph Kleiber Papers, 1860–1877
    Leopold Schlinger Family Papers, 1833–1877
    Matamoros Archives
Houghton Library, Harvard University Library, Cambridge, MA
    Charles Stillman Business Papers, 1847–1884
Mary and Jeff Bell Library, Texas A&M University–Corpus Christi, Corpus Christi, TX
    Conrad Blucher Surveying Collection
Museum of South Texas History, Edinburg, TX
    Port of Brownsville Documents
    Theodore M. Warner Collection

The National Archives of the United Kingdom, Kew, London, England
    Foreign Office, General Correspondence, Mexico, 1822–1905
    Matamoros Fire Claims
South Texas Archives, James C. Jernigan Library, Texas A&M University–Kingsville, Kingsville, TX
    Kenedy Family Collection
Special Collections, University of Texas at Arlington, Arlington, TX
    Rare Map Collection
Texas State Library and Archives, Austin, TX
    Texas Governor Pendleton Murrah Records
    Texas Secretary of State Colonization Records
The United States National Archives, Fort Worth, TX
    Department of Treasury Impost Books
University of California Berkeley, Bancroft Library
University of Texas Rio Grande Valley Special Collections and Archives, Edinburg, TX
    Camargo Archives Collection
    Mier Archives Collection

Published Primary Sources

Adams, Ephraim Douglass. "British Correspondence concerning Texas, XV." *Southwestern Historical Quarterly* 19, no. 1 (July 1915): 91–93.
Adams, Ephraim Douglass. *British Diplomatic Correspondence Concerning the Republic of Texas, 1838–1846*. Austin: Texas State Historical Association, 1918.
Alger, Russel A., ed. *The War of the Rebellion: A Compilation of the Official Records of the Union and Confederate Armies*. Vol. 52. Washington, DC: Government Printing Office, 1898.
Barker, Nancy Nichols, and A. Dubois de Saligny. *The French Legation in Texas*. Austin: Texas State Historical Association, 1971.
Berlandier, Jean Louis. *Journey to Mexico during the Years 1826–1834*. Vols. 1–2. Austin: Texas State Historical Association and Center for Studies in Texas History, 1980.
Bollaert, William. *William Bollaert's Texas*. Edited by W. Eugene Hollon and Ruth Lapham Butler. Norman: University of Oklahoma Press, 1956.

Camargo Church Marriage Records, 1764–1913: Grooms, Second Revision. Corpus Christi: Spanish American Genealogical Association, 1995.

Clay, Henry. *The Works of Henry Clay Comprising his Life, Correspondence and Speeches.* Edited by Calvin Colton. Vol. 3. New York: G. P. Putnam's Sons, 1904.

Fish, Hamilton. *Treaties and Conventions Concluded between the United States of America and Other Powers since 1776.* Washington, DC: Government Printing Office, 1871.

Francis, Samuel W. *Biographical Sketches of Distinguished Living New York Physicians.* New York: G. P. Putnam & Son, 1867.

Gammel, H. P. N. *The Laws of Texas, 1822–1897.* 10 vols. Austin: Gammel, 1898.

Hecke, J. Valentin. *Reise Durch Die Vereinigten Staaten Von Nord-Amerika in Den Jahren 1818 Und 1819: Nebst Einer Kurzen Uebersicht Der Neuesten Ereignisse Auf Dem. Und West-Indien.* Berlin: H. Ph. Petri, 1821.

Holley, Mary Austin. *Texas: Observations, Historical, Geographical and Descriptive, in a Series of Letters.* Baltimore: Armstong & Plaskitt, 1833.

Houston, Sam. *The Writings of Sam Houston, 1813–1963.* Edited by Eugene C. Barker. Vol. 2 Austin: University of Texas Press, 1939.

Howard, Henry. *Report by Her Majesty's Agent of the Proceedings and Awards of the Mixed Commission on British and American Claims.* London: Harrison and Sons, 1874.

Joseph San Romons and William Armstrong, Administrators of James B. Armstrong vs. The United States, December 18, 1860. In Congressional Series of United States Public Documents, United States Congressional Serial Set, vol. 1109. Washington, DC: US Government Printing Office, 1861.

Kennedy, William. *Texas: The Rise, Progress, and Prospects of the Republic of Texas.* 2nd ed. 2 vols. London: R. Hastings, 1841.

Leech, D. D. T. *List of the Post-Offices in the United States: With the Names of the Postmasters on the 1st of April, 1859; Also, the Laws and Regulations of the Post Office Department with an Appendix Containing the Names of the Post Offices Arranged by States and Counties.* Washington, DC: John C. Rives, 1859.

Ludecus, Eduard. *John Charles Beales's Rio Grande Colony: Letters by Eduard Ludecus, a German Colonist, to Friends in Germany in 1833–1834, Recounting His Journey, Trials, and Observations in Early Texas.* Translated by Louis E. Brister. Austin: Texas State Historical Association, 2008.

The Manchester Commercial List, 1873–1874. London: Estell, 1873.

Mier y Terán, Manuel de. *Texas by Terán: The Diary Kept by General Manuel de Mier y Terán on His 1828 Inspection of Texas*. Edited by Jack Jackson. Translated by John Wheat. With botanical notes by Scooter Cheatham and Lynn Marshall. 1st ed. Jack and Doris Smothers Series in Texas History, Life, and Culture 2. Austin: University of Texas Press, 2000.

Nicholls, Sir George. *A History of the Scotch Poor Law, in Connexion with the Condition of the People*. London: Knight, 1856.

Price, W. Armstrong. "Hurricanes Affecting the Coast of Texas from Galveston to Rio Grande." Technical Memorandum no. 78. Army Corps of Engineers, March 1956.

Santleben, August. *A Texas Pioneer; Early Staging and Overland Freighting on the Frontiers of Texas and Mexico*. New York: Neale, 1910.

Smither, Harriet, and Adolphus Sterne. "Diary of Adolphus Sterne." *Southwestern Historical Quarterly* 30, no. 2 (1926): 139–55.

Solms-Braunfels, Carl. *Voyage to North America, 1844–45: Prince Carl of Solms's Texas Diary of People, Places, and Events*. Translation and notes by W. M. Von-Maszewski. Denton: German-Texan Heritage Society and University of North Texas Press, 2000.

Swartwout, Samuel, James Morgan, Feris A. Bass, and B. R. Brunson. *Fragile Empires: The Texas Correspondence of Samuel Swartwout and James Morgan, 1836–1856*. 1st ed. Austin: Shoal Creek Publishers, 1978.

Testimony taken by the Special Committee on Texas Frontier Troubles. Resolution of the House of Representatives, report no. 343. Washington, DC: Government Printing Office, 1876.

Tilden, Bryant Parrot. *Notes on the Upper Rio Grande, explored in the months of October and November 1846 on board the US Steamer Major Brown, Commanded by Capt. Mark Sterling of Pittsburgh*. Philadelphia: Lindsay & Blakiston, 1847.

Walker, A. S. *The Texas Reports: Cases Argued and Decided in the Supreme Court of the State of Texas*. Vol. 74. Austin: State of Texas, 1890.

Weeks, William F. *Debates of the Texas Convention*. Houston: J. W. Cruger, 1846.

Wollmershäuser, Friedrich R. *Passengers Listed in the Allgemeine Auswanderungs-Zeitung, 1848–1869 [Allgemeine Auswanderungs-Zeitung: Einträge Zu Passagieren, 1848–1869]*. Morgantown, PA: Masthof Press, 2014.

Woodward, John. *An Abstract of the Constitutions, Laws, and Other Documents Having Reference to and Including the Empresario Grants and Contracts Made by the State of Coahuila y Texas to and with John Charles Beales; Also Deeds of the Same from Him to John Woodward; to* which is Appended and Argument Sustaining the Rights and Titles of John Woodward. New York: Narine and Co., 1842.

Books and Articles

Acuna, Rodolfo F. *Occupied America: The Chicano's Struggle toward Liberation*. San Francisco: Harper & Row, 1972.

Adams, David B. "Embattled Borderland: Northern Nuevo León and the Indios Bárbaros, 1686–1870." *Southwestern Historical Quarterly* 95, no. 2 (October 1991): 205–20.

Adams, David Bergen. *Las colonias tlaxcaltecas de Coahuila y Nuevo León en la Nueva España: un aspecto de la colonización del norte de México*. 1st ed. Saltillo, Coahuila: Archivo Municipal de Saltillo, 1991.

Adams, David Wallace, and Crista DeLuzio, eds. *On the Borders of Love and Power: Families and Kinship in the Intercultural American Southwest*. Berkeley: University of California Press, 2012.

Adams, John A. *Conflict and Commerce on the Rio Grande: Laredo, 1755–1955*. College Station: Texas A&M University Press, 2008.

Adelman, Jeremy, and Stephen Aron. "From Borderlands to Borders: Empires, Nation-States, and the Peoples in between in North American History." *American Historical Review* 104, no. 3 (June 1999): 814–41.

Allhands, James Lewellyn. *Gringo Builders*. Joplin, MO; Dallas, TX: privately printed, 1931.

Allhands, James Lewellyn. *Railroads to the Rio*. Salado, TX: Anson Jones Press, 1960.

Allhands, James Lewellyn. *Uriah Lott*. San Antonio: Naylor, 1949.

Alonzo, Armando C. *Tejano Legacy: Rancheros and Settlers in South Texas, 1734–1900*. 1st ed. Albuquerque: University of New Mexico Press, 1998.

Amberson, Mary Margaret McAllen, James A. McAllen, and Margaret H. McAllen. *I Would Rather Sleep in Texas: A History of the Lower Rio Grande Valley and the People of the Santa Anita Land Grant*. Austin: Texas State Historical Association, 2003.

Anderson, Gary Clayton. *The Conquest of Texas: Ethnic Cleansing in the Promised Land, 1820–1875*. Norman: University of Oklahoma Press, 2005.

Anderson, Gary Clayton. *The Indian Southwest, 1580–1830: Ethnogenesis and Reinvention*. Civilization of the American Indian Series 232. Norman: University of Oklahoma Press, 1999.

Anna, Timothy E. *The Fall of the Royal Government in Mexico City*. Lincoln: University of Nebraska Press, 1978.

Arreola, Daniel D., and James R. Curtis. *The Mexican Border Cities: Landscape Anatomy and Place Personality*. Tucson: University of Arizona Press, 1993.

Ateş, Sabri. *The Ottoman-Iranian Borderlands: Making a Boundary, 1843–1914*. New York: Cambridge University Press, 2013.

Bacha-Garza, Roseann, Christopher L. Miller, Russell K. Skowronek, Gary W. Gallagher, and Christopher L. Miller, eds. *The Civil War on the Rio Grande, 1846–1876*. 1st ed. Elma Dill Russell Spencer Series in the West and Southwest 46. College Station: Texas A&M University Press, 2019.

Baptist, Edward E. *The Half Has Never Been Told: Slavery and the Making of American Capitalism*. New York: Basic Books, 2014.

Barclay, David E. "Political Trends and Movements, 1830–1850: The *Vormärz* and the Revolutions of 1848–1849." In *Germany 1800–1870*, edited by Jonathan Sperber, 46–68. Oxford: Oxford University Press, 2004.

Barker, Eugene C. "The Annexation of Texas." *Southwestern Historical Quarterly* 50, no. 1 (1946): 49–74.

Barker, Eugene C. "Land Speculation as a Cause of the Texas Revolution." *Quarterly of the Texas State Historical Association* 10, no. 1 (1906): 76–95.

Barker, Eugene C. *The Life of Stephen F. Austin, Founder of Texas, 1793–1836: A Chapter in the Westward Movement of the Anglo-American People*. Nashville: Cokesbury Press, 1925.

Barker, Eugene C. *Mexico and Texas, 1821–1835*. Dallas: P. L. Turner, 1928.

Barker, Eugene C. "Notes on the Colonization of Texas." *Southwestern Historical Quarterly* 27, no. 2 (October 1923): 108–19.

Barker, Nancy N. "Dubois De Saligny." *Handbook of Texas Online*. Accessed May 30, 2019. http://www.tshaonline.org/handbook/online/articles/fdu02.

Barr, Juliana. *Peace Came in the Form of a Woman: Indians and Spaniards in the Texas Borderlands*. Chapel Hill: University of North Carolina Press, 2007.

Baughman, James P. "Morgan, Charles." *Handbook of Texas Online*. Accessed May 18, 2022. https://www.tshaonline.org/handbook/entries/morgan-charles.

Bayly, C. A. *The Birth of the Modern World, 1780–1914: Global Connections and Comparisons*. Blackwell History of the World. Malden, MA: Blackwell, 2004.

Bazant, Jan. *A Concise History of Mexico from Hidalgo to Cárdenas, 1805–1940*. Cambridge: Cambridge University Press, 1977.

Beckert, Sven. *Empire of Cotton: A Global History*. New York: Vintage Books, 2014.

Beckert, Sven. *The Monied Metropolis: New York City and the Consolidation of the American Bourgeoisie, 1850–1896*. New York: Cambridge University Press, 2001.

Beckert, Sven, and Christine Desan, eds. *American Capitalism: New Histories*. New York: Columbia University Press, 2018.

Beecher, Jonathan. *Victor Considerant and the Rise and Fall of French Romantic Socialism*. Berkeley: University of California Press, 2001.

Berlandier, Jean Louis. *Journey to Mexico during the Years 1826–1834*. Vol. 2. Austin: Texas State Historical Association and Center for Studies in Texas History, 1980.

Bernecker, Walther L. "Between European and American Dominance: Mexican Foreign Trade in the Nineteenth Century." *Itinerario* 21, no. 3 (1997): 115–41.

Biesele, Rudolph Leopold. *The History of the German Settlements in Texas, 1831–1861*. Austin: Von Boeckmann-Jones, 1930.

Bolton, Herbert Eugene. "Tienda de Cuervo's Ynspeccion of Laredo, 1757." *Quarterly of the Texas State Historical Association* 6, no. 3 (January 1903): 187–203.

Bowman, Timothy Paul. *Blood Oranges: Colonialism and Agriculture in the South Texas Borderlands*. 1st ed. Connecting the Greater West Series. College Station: Texas A&M University Press, 2016.

Braudel, Fernand. *The Mediterranean and the Mediterranean World in the Age of Philip II*. Vol. 1. New York: Harper & Row, 1972.

Brinkley, Alan. *The Unfinished Nation: A Concise History of the American People*. 7th ed. New York: McGraw-Hill, 2014.

Brister, Louis E. "Eduard Ludecus's Journey to the Texas Frontier: A Critical Account of Beales's Rio Grande Colony." *Southwestern Historical Quarterly* 108, no. 3 (January 2005): 368–85.

Britten, Thomas A. *The Lipan Apaches: People of Wind and Lightning*. Albuquerque: University of New Mexico Press, 2011.

Brooks, Charles E. *Frontier Settlement and Market Revolution: The Holland Land Purchase*. Ithaca, NY: Fall Creek Books, 2012.

Brooks, James. *Captives & Cousins: Slavery, Kinship, and Community in the Southwest Borderlands*. Chapel Hill: University of North Carolina Press, 2002.

Browning, Robert M., Jr. *Lincoln's Trident: The West Gulf Blockading Squadron during the Civil War*. Tuscaloosa: University of Alabama Press, 2014.

Burkholder, Mark A., and Lyman L. Johnson. *Colonial Latin America*. 6th ed. New York: Oxford University Press, 2008.

Calomiris, Charles W., and Larry Schweikart. "The Panic of 1857: Origins, Transmission, and Containment." *Journal of Economic History* 51, no. 4 (December 1991): 807–34.

Camargo, Julio A. "Contribution of Spanish-American Silver Mines (1570–1820) to the Present High Mercury Concentrations in the Global Environment: A Review." *Chemosphere* 48, no. 1 (2002): 51–57.

Campbell, Randolph B. *An Empire for Slavery: The Peculiar Institution in Texas, 1821–1865*. Baton Rouge: Louisiana State University Press, 2009.

Campbell, Randolph B. *Gone to Texas: A History of the Lone Star State*. 3rd ed. New York; Oxford: Oxford University Press, 2018.

Campbell, Randolph B. *Sam Houston: And the American Southwest*. 3rd ed. Library of American Biography. New York: Pearson Longman, 2007.

Cantrell, Gregg. *Stephen F. Austin, Empresario of Texas*. New Haven, CT: Yale University Press, 1999.

del Carmen Velázquez, María. *El Marqués de Altamira y Las Provincias Internas de Nueva España*. 1st ed. Vol. 81. Mexico DF: Colegio de Mexico, 1976. www.jstor.org/stable/j.ctv2868cb.

Carr, Raymond, ed. *Spain: A History*. New York: Oxford University Press, 2000.

Castañeda, Carlos E. *Our Catholic Heritage in Texas, 1519–1936*. Austin: Von Boeckmann-Jones, 1936.

Cerutti, Mario. *Burguesía, capitales e industria en el norte de México: Monterrey y su ámbito regional (1850–1910)*. México, DF: Alianza Ed, 1992.

Cerutti, Mario, and Miguel A. González-Quiroga. *El Norte de México y Texas, 1848–1880: Comercio, Capitales y Trabajadores En Una Economía de Frontera*. 1st ed. San Juan, Mixcoac, México, DF: Instituto Mora, 1999.

Cerutti, Mario, and Miguel Gonzalez-Quiroga. "Guerra y Comercio En Torno al Río Bravo (1855–1867). Línea Fronteriza, Espacio Económico Común." *Historia Mexicana* 40, no. 2 (Winter 1990): 217–97. https://www-jstor-org.proxy.libraries.smu.edu/stable/25138354.

Champion, A. A. "Papers and Personalities of Frontier Journalism." In *More Studies in Brownsville History*, edited by Milo Kearney, 138–42. Brownsville, TX: Pan American University at Brownsville, 1989.

Chance, Joseph E. *José María de Jesús Carvajal: The Life and Times of a Mexican Revolutionary*. San Antonio: Trinity University Press, 2006.

Chandler, Alfred D. *The Visible Hand: The Managerial Revolution in American Business*. Cambridge: Belknap Press, 1977.

Chatfield, W. H. *The Twin Cities of the Border (Brownsville, Texas and Matamoros, Mexico), and the Country of the Lower Rio Grande*. New Orleans: E. P. Brandao, 1893.

Cheeseman, Bruce. *Perfectly Exhausted with Pleasure: The 1881 King-Kenedy Excursion Train to Laredo*. Austin: Book Club of Texas, 1992.

Chipman, Donald E., and Harriett Denise Joseph. *Notable Men and Women of Spanish Texas*. 1st ed. Austin: University of Texas Press, 1999.

Chowning, Margaret. *Wealth and Power in Provincial Mexico: Michoacán from the Late Colony to the Revolution*. Stanford, CA: Stanford University Press, 1999.

Collingham, H. A. C., and R. S. Alexander. *The July Monarchy: A Political History of France, 1830–1848*. New York: Longman, 1988.

Costeloe, Michael P. *Bonds and Bondholders: British Investors and Mexico's Foreign Debt, 1824–1888*. Westport, CT: Praeger, 2003.

Costeloe, Michael P. "To Bowl a Mexican Maiden Over: Cricket in Mexico, 1827–1900." *Bulletin of Latin American Research* 26, no. 1 (2007): 112–24.

Costeloe, Michael P. *Bubbles and Bonanzas: British Investors and Investments in Mexico, 1821–1860*. Lanham, MD: Lexington Books, 2011.

Costeloe, Michael P. "William Bullock and the Mexican Connection." *Mexican Studies/Estudios Mexicanos* 22, no. 2 (August 2006): 275–309.

Cowan, Helen I. "Charles Williamson and the Southern Entrance to the Genesee Country." *New York History* 23, no. 3 (July 1942): 260–74.

Crapol, Edward P. "John Tyler and the Pursuit of National Destiny." *Journal of the Early Republic* 17, no. 3 (1997): 467.

Crimm, A. Carolina Castillo. *De León, a Tejano Family History*. Austin: University of Texas Press, 2003.

Cronon, William. *Nature's Metropolis: Chicago and the Great West*. New York: W. W. Norton, 1991.

Crook, Cornelia E. *Henry Castro*. San Antonio: St. Mary's University Press, 1988. Daddysman, James W. *The Matamoros Trade: Confederate Commerce, Diplomacy, and Intrigue*. Newark: University of Delaware Press, 1984.

Darwin, John. *Unfinished Empire: The Global Expansion of Britain*. New York: Bloomsbury Press, 2013.

Davis, Charles G. "Fort Chadbourne." *Handbook of Texas Online*. Accessed June 21, 2019. http://www.tshaonline.org/handbook/online/articles/qbf08.

Davis, Graham. *Land! Irish Pioneers in Mexican and Revolutionary Texas*. 1st ed. Centennial Series of the Association of Former Students, Texas A&M University 92. College Station: Texas A&M University Press, 2002.

Davis, Jack E. *The Gulf: The Making of an American Sea*. New York: W. W. Norton, 2018. Ebook.

DeLay, Brian. *War of a Thousand Deserts: Indian Raids and the U.S.-Mexican War*. New Haven, CT: Yale University Press, 2008.

De León, Arnoldo. *They Called Them Greasers: Anglo Attitudes Toward Mexicans in Texas, 1821–1900*. Austin: University of Texas Press, 1983.

De León, Arnoldo, and Kenneth L. Stewart. *Tejanos and the Numbers Game: A Socio-Historical Interpretation from the Federal Censuses, 1850–1900*. Albuquerque: University of New Mexico Press, 1989.

Dewey, Alicia M. *Pesos and Dollars: Entrepreneurs in the Texas-Mexico Borderlands, 1880–1940*. College Station: Texas A&M University Press, 2014.

Diamond, William. "Imports of the Confederate Government from Europe and Mexico." *Journal of Southern History* 6, no. 4 (November 1940): 470–503.

Diaz, George T. *Border Contraband: A History of Smuggling across the Rio Grande*. Austin: University of Texas Press, 2015.

Douglass, William A., and Jon Bilbao. *Amerikanuak: Basques in the New World*. Basque Series. Reno: University of Nevada Press, 1975.

Elliott, John Huxtable. *Empires of the Atlantic World: Britain and Spain in America, 1492–1830*. New Haven, CT: Yale University Press, 2007.

Estep, Raymond. "Exter, Richard." *Handbook of Texas Online*. Accessed September 07, 2018. http://www.tshaonline.org/handbook/online/articles/fex03.

Evans, Richard J. *The Pursuit of Power: Europe, 1815–1914*. Penguin History of Europe 7. New York: Penguin Books, 2016.

Evans, Sterling, ed. *Farming across Borders: A Transnational History of the North American West*. College Station: Texas A&M University Press, 2017.

Fehrenbach, T. R. *Fire and Blood: A History of Mexico*. 1st Da Capo Press ed., updated ed. New York: Da Capo Press, 1995.

Foner, Eric. *Free Soil, Free Labor, Free Men: The Ideology of the Republican Party before the Civil War*. Oxford; New York: Oxford University Press, 1995.

Fowler, Will. *Santa Anna of Mexico*. Lincoln: University of Nebraska Press, 2007.

Frye, David L. *Indians into Mexicans: History and Identity in a Mexican Town*. 1st ed. Austin: University of Texas Press, 1996.

Gallis, Michael, Gary Moll, and Heather Millar. "People–Nature: The Human Network." *ArcNews Online* (Summer 2007). Accessed May 17, 2024.

https://www.esri.com/news/arcnews/summer07articles/people-nature.html

García, Félix. *The Children of John Z. Leyendecker: A Brief Genealogical Sketch* Laredo: Felix Garcia, 1984.

Garrison, George P., ed. *Diplomatic Correspondence of the Republic of Texas*. Vol. 2, part 3. Washington, DC: Government Printing Press, 1911.

Garza, Joseph Rafael de la, Jerry D. Thompson, and Manuel Yturri Castillo. *Tejanos in Gray: Civil War Letters of Captains Joseph Rafael de La Garza and Manuel Yturri*. 1st. ed. Fronteras Series 9. College Station: Texas A&M University Press, 2011.

Gerhard, Peter. *The North Frontier of New Spain*. Princeton, NJ: Princeton University Press, 1982.

Gilbert, Minnie. "The Valley's Earliest Pioneers." In *Roots by the River*, 9–14. Canyon, TX: Staked Plains Press, 1978.

Goldberg, P. Koujianou, and R. Hellerstein. "A Structural Approach to Identifying the Sources of Local Currency Price Stability." *Review of Economic Studies* 80, no. 1 (January 2013): 175–210. https://academic.oup.com/restud/article-lookup/doi/10.1093/restud/rds015.

González-Quiroga, Miguel Ángel. "Conflict and Cooperation in the Making of Texas-Mexico Border Society, 1840–1880." In *Bridging National Borders in North America: Transnational and Comparative Histories*, edited by Benjamin Heber Johnson and Andrew R. Graybill, 33–52. Durham, NC: Duke University Press, 2010.

González-Quiroga, Miguel Ángel. "Los Inicios de la Migración Laboral Mexicana a Texas (1850-1880)." In *Encuentro en la Frontera: Mexicanos y Norteamericanos en un Espacio Común*, edited by Ramirez M. Ceballos, 345–72. Mexico: COLEF, 2001.

González-Quiroga, Miguel Ángel. "Mexicanos in Texas during the Civil War." In *Mexican Americans in Texas History: Selected Essays*, edited by Emilio Zamora, Cynthia Orozco, Rodolfo Rocha, and Texas State Historical Association, 57–62. Austin: Texas State Historical Association, 2000.

González-Quiroga, Miguel Ángel. *War and Peace on the Rio Grande Frontier, 1830–1880*. New Directions in Tejano History 1. Norman: University of Oklahoma Press, 2020.

Graf, Leroy P. "Colonizing Projects in Texas South of the Nueces, 1820–1845." *Southwestern Historical Quarterly* 50, no. 4 (April 1947): 431–48.

Green, Stanley. *Border Biographies*. 2nd ed. Vol. 1. Laredo: Texas A&M International University Border Studies Center, 1993.

Greenberg, Amy S. *Manifest Destiny and American Territorial Expansion: A Brief History with Documents.* Boston: Bedford/St. Martin's, 2012.

Greenberg, Amy S. *A Wicked War: Polk, Clay, Lincoln, and the 1846 US Invasion of Mexico.* 1st ed. New York: Alfred A. Knopf, 2012.

Guizot, François, William Hazlitt, and Larry Siedentop. *The History of Civilization in Europe.* Indianapolis: Liberty Fund, 2013.

Guldi, Jo, and David Armitage. *The History Manifesto.* Cambridge: Cambridge University Press, 2014.

Haeger, John D. *The Investment Frontier: New York Businessmen and the Economic Development of the Old Northwest.* Albany: State University of New York Press, 1981.

Hämäläinen, Pekka. *The Comanche Empire.* New Haven, CT: Yale University Press, 2008.

Hämäläinen, P., and S. Truett. "On Borderlands." *Journal of American History* 98, no. 2 (September 2011): 338–61.

Hammett, A. B. J. *The Empresario, Don Martin DeLeon: The Richest Man in Texas.* Kerrville, TX: Braswell, 1971.

Hamnett, Brian R. "Mercantile Rivalry and Peninsular Division: The Consulados of New Spain and the Impact of the Bourbon Reforms, 1789–1824." *Ibero-Amerikanisches Archiv* 2, no. 4 (1976): 273–305.

Hart, John M. *Empire and Revolution: The Americans in Mexico since the Civil War.* Berkeley: University of California Press, 2002.

Hart, John M. *Revolutionary Mexico: The Coming and Process of the Mexican Revolution.* Berkeley: University of California Press, 1987.

Hart, John Mason. "Stillman, Charles." *Handbook of Texas Online.* Accessed May 17, 2022. https://www.tshaonline.org/handbook/entries/stillman-charles.

Haynes, Sam W. *Soldiers of Misfortune: The Somervell and Mier Expeditions.* Austin: University of Texas Press, 1997.

Haynes, Sam W. *Unfinished Revolution: The Early American Republic in a British World.* Charlottesville: University of Virginia Press, 2011.

Haynes, Sam W. *Unsettled Land: From Revolution to Republic, the Struggle for Texas.* 1st ed. New York: Basic Books, 2022.

Hazelton, John. "Nuestra Senora de los Dolores Hacienda." *Handbook of Texas Online.* Accessed June 03, 2019. http://www.tshaonline.org/handbook/online/articles/uen02

Hazlewood, Claudia. "Kennedy, William." *Handbook of Texas Online.* Accessed March 13, 2020. http://www.tshaonline.org/handbook/online/articles/fke25.

Henderson, Mary Virginia. "Minor Empresario Contracts for the Colonization of Texas, 1825–1834." Pts. 1 and 2. *Southwestern Historical Quarterly* 31, no. 4 (April 1928): 295–324; 32, no. 1 (July 1928): 1–28.

Henkin, David M. *The Postal Age: The Emergence of Modern Communications in Nineteenth-Century America*. Chicago: University of Chicago Press, 2006.

Herzog, Tamar. *Defining Nations: Immigrants and Citizens in Early Modern Spain and Spanish America*. New Haven, CT: Yale University Press, 2003.

Hill, Lawrence Francis. *José de Escandón and the Founding of Nuevo Santander, a Study in Spanish Colonization*. Columbus: Ohio State University Press, 1926.

Hinojosa, Gilberto Miguel. *A Borderlands Town in Transition: Laredo, 1755–1870*. College Station: Texas A&M University Press, 1983.

House, E. *A Narrative of the Captivity of Mrs. Horn, and her Two Children, with Mrs. Harris, by the Camanche Indians, after they had Murdered their Husbands and Traveling Companions*. St. Louis: C. Keemle, 1839.

Howe, Daniel Walker. *What Hath God Wrought: The Transformation of America, 1815–1848*. Oxford History of the United States. New York: Oxford University Press, 2007.

Hunter, John H. "Kleiber, Joseph." *Handbook of Texas Online*. Accessed March 12, 2020. http://www.tshaonline.org/handbook/online/articles/fkl08.

Hutchison, I. G. C. "Workshop of Empire: The Nineteenth Century." In *Scotland: A History*, edited by Jenny Wormald, 207–40. New York: Oxford University Press, 2005.

Irby, James A. *Backdoor at Bagdad: The Civil War on the Rio Grande*. El Paso: Texas Western Press, 1977.

John, Richard R. *Spreading the News: The American Postal System from Franklin to Morse*. Cambridge, MA: Harvard University Press, 1998.

Johnson, Walter. *Soul by Soul: Life inside the Antebellum Slave Market*. Cambridge, MA: Harvard University Press, 1999.

Kearney, Milo, and Anthony K. Knopp. *Boom and Bust: The Historical Cycles of Matamoros and Brownsville*. Austin: Eakin Press, 1991.

Kelley, Pat. *River of Lost Dreams: Navigation on the Rio Grande*. Lincoln: University of Nebraska Press, 1986.

Keyes, Clinton W. "The Greek Letter of Introduction." *American Journal of Philology* 56, no. 1 (1935): 28. https://www.jstor.org/stable/289706?origin=crossref.

Kidwell, Clara Sue. *The Choctaws in Oklahoma: From Tribe to Nation, 1855–1870*. Norman: University of Oklahoma Press, 2007.

Konishi, Shino. "J. C. Byrne, Entrepreneurial Imperialism and the Question of Indigenous Rights." *Journal of Imperial and Commonwealth History* 48, no. 6 (2020): 981–1010.

Kuethe, Allan J., and Kenneth J. Andrien. *The Spanish Atlantic World in the Eighteenth Century: War and the Bourbon Reforms, 1713–1796*. Cambridge: Cambridge University Press, 2014.

Kurlansky, Mark. *Salt: A World History*. New York: Penguin Books, 2002.

Landa, Janet Tai. *Trust, Ethnicity, and Identity: Beyond the New Institutional Economics of Ethnic Trading Networks, Contract Law, and Gift-Exchange*. Economics, Cognition, and Society. Ann Arbor: University of Michigan Press, 1994.

Latour, Bruno. *Reassembling the Social: An Introduction to Actor-Network-Theory*. Oxford: Oxford University Press, 2007.

La Vere, David. "The Caddo Chiefdoms of Texas." In *Major Problems in Texas History: Documents and Essays*, edited by Sam W. Haynes and Cary D. Wintz, 41–46. 2nd ed. Boston: Cengage Learning, 2017.

La Vere, David. *The Texas Indians*. 1st ed. Centennial Series of the Association of Former Students, Texas A&M University 95. College Station: Texas A&M University Press, 2004.

Lee, Sidney, ed. *Dictionary of National Biography*. Vol. 46. New York: MacMillan, 1896.

Leigh, Philip. *Trading with the Enemy: The Covert Economy during the American Civil War*. Yardley, PA: Westholme, 2014.

Lewis, James E., Jr. *The Burr Conspiracy: Uncovering the Story of an Early American Crisis*. Princeton, NJ: Princeton University Press, 2017.

Liles, Debbie M., and Angela Boswell, eds. *Women in Civil War Texas: Diversity and Dissidence in the Trans-Mississippi*. Denton: University of North Texas Press, 2016.

Liss, Peggy K. *Atlantic Empires: The Network of Trade and Revolution, 1713–1826*. Baltimore: Johns Hopkins University Press, 1983.

Maggor, Noam. *Brahmin Capitalism: Frontiers of Wealth and Populism in America's First Gilded Age*. Cambridge, MA: Harvard University Press, 2017.

Manning, Thomas Courtland, Francois-Xavier Martin, and Merritt M. Robinson. *Reports of Cases Argued and Determined in the Supreme Court of Louisiana and in the Superior Court of the Territory of Louisiana. [1809–1896]: 1846–1847*. Vol. 21. St. Paul: West Publishing Company, 1910.

Marichal, Carlos. *Bankruptcy of Empire: Mexican Silver and the Wars between Spain, Britain, and France, 1760–1810*. Cambridge Latin American Studies 91. New York: Cambridge University Press, 2007.

Martin, Robert S. "Maps of an Empresario: Austin's Contribution to the Cartography of Texas." *Southwestern Historical Quarterly* 85, no. 4 (April 1982): 371–400.

Mauro, Frédéric. "Le Développement Économique de Monterrey (1890–1960)." *Caravelle* 2, no. 1 (1964): 35–126.

McCarver, Norman L. *Hearne on the Brazos.* San Antonio: Century Press of Texas, 1958.

McEnroe, Sean F. *From Colony to Nationhood in Mexico: Laying the Foundations, 1560–1840.* Cambridge; New York: Cambridge University Press, 2014.

McWilliams, Carey. *North from Mexico: The Spanish Speaking People of the United States.* New York: Monthly Review Press, 1948.

Mendoza, Alexander. "'For Our Own Best Interests': Nineteenth-Century Laredo Tejanos, Military Service, and the Development of American Nationalism." *Southwestern Historical Quarterly* 115, no. 2 (October 2011): 125–52.

Miller, Christopher L., Russell K. Skowronek, and Roseann Bacha-Garza. *Blue and Gray on the Border: The Rio Grande Valley Civil War Trail.* College Station: Texas A&M University Press, 2018.

Miller, Edward L. *New Orleans and the Texas Revolution.* 1st ed. College Station: Texas A&M University Press, 2004.

Monday, Jane Clements, and Frances Brannen Vick. *Petra's Legacy: The South Texas Ranching Empire of Petra Vela and Mifflin Kenedy.* College Station: Texas A&M University Press, 2007.

Moneyhon, Carl H. *Edmund J. Davis of Texas: Civil War General, Republican Leader, Reconstruction Governor.* Fort Worth: TCU Press, 2010.

Moneyhon, Carl H. *Texas after the Civil War: The Struggle of Reconstruction.* 1st ed. Texas A&M Southwestern Studies 14. College Station: Texas A&M University Press, 2004.

Montejano, David. *Anglos and Mexicans in the Making of Texas, 1836–1986.* 1st ed. Austin: University of Texas Press, 1987.

Montejano, David. "Mexican Merchants and Teamsters on the Texas Cotton Road, 1862–1865." In *Mexico and Mexicans in the Making of the United States,* edited by John Tutino, 141–70. History, Culture, and Society Series. Austin: University of Texas Press, 2012.

Moorehead, Max L. *The Presidio: Bastion of the Spanish Borderlands.* Norman: University of Oklahoma Press, 1975.

Mora-Torres, Juan. *The Making of the Mexican Border.* Austin: University of Texas Press, 2001.

Morgenthaler, George J. *Promised Land: Solms, Castro, and Sam Houston's Colonization Contracts.* 1st ed. Sam Rayburn Series on Rural Life 19. College Station: Texas A&M University Press, 2009.

Moseley, Edward Holt. "The Public Career of Santiago Vidaurri, 1855–1858." Diss., University of Alabama, 1963.

Nance, Joseph Milton. *After San Jacinto: The Texas-Mexican Frontier, 1836–1841*. Austin: University of Texas Press, 1963.

Nasaw, David. *Andrew Carnegie*. New York: Penguin Books, 2006.

Newcomb, W. W., Jr. *The Indians of Texas from Prehistoric to Modern Times*. Austin: University of Texas Press, 1961.

Newton, Ada L. K. "The Anglo-Irish House of the Rio Grande." *Pioneer America* 5, no. 1 (1973): 33–38.

Oakes, James. *The Ruling Race: A History of American Slaveholders*. New York: Alfred A Knopf, 1982.

Oberste, William H. *Texas Irish Empresarios and Their Colonies*. 2nd ed. Austin: Von Boeckmann-Jones, 1973.

Offutt, Leslie Scott. "Defending Corporate Identity on New Spain's Northeastern Frontier: San Esteban de Nueva Tlaxcala, 1780–1810." *Americas* 64, no. 3 (January 2008): 351–75.

Offutt, Leslie Scott. "Puro Tlaxcalteca? Ethnic Integrity and Consciousness in Late Seventeenth-Century Northern New Spain." *Americas* 75, no. 1 (2018): 27–46.

Offutt, Leslie Scott. *Saltillo, 1770–1810: Town and Region in the Mexican North*. Tucson: University of Arizona Press, 2001.

O'Hara, Matthew D. *A Flock Divided: Race, Religion, and Politics in Mexico, 1749–1857*. Durham, NC: Duke University Press, 2010.

Olmstead, Alan L., and Paul Webb Rhode. *Creating Abundance: Biological Innovation and American Agricultural Development*. New York: Cambridge University Press, 2008.

Opie, John. *Ogallala: Water for a Dry Land*. 3rd ed. Lincoln: University of Nebraska Press, 2018.

Osante, Patricia. *Orígenes Del Nuevo Santander (1748–1772)*. 1st ed. Serie Historia Novohispana 59. Ciudad Victoria, México: Universidad Nacional Autónoma de México, Instituto de Investigaciones Históricas, Universidad Autónoma de Tamaulipas, 1997.

Osante, Patricia. "Un Proyecto de Antonio Ladrón de Guevara para las poblaciones de Nuevo Santander, 1767." *Estudios de Historia Novohispana* 49, no. 1 (2013): 170–91.

Osterhammel, Jürgen. *The Transformation of the World: A Global History of the Nineteenth Century*. Translated by Patrick Camiller. America in the World. Princeton, NJ: Princeton University Press, 2014.

Pelzer, John D. "Liverpool and the American Civil War." *History Today* 40 (March 1990): 46–52.

Poovey, Mary. "Risk, Uncertainty, and Data: Managing Risk in Twentieth-Century America." In Beckert and Desan, *American Capitalism*, 221–35.

Porter, Amy M. *Their Lives, Their Wills: Women in the Borderlands, 1750–1846*. Women, Gender, and the West. Lubbock: Texas Tech University Press, 2015.

Porter, Charles R. *Spanish Water, Anglo Water: Early Development in San Antonio*. College Station: Texas A&M University Press, 2011.

Powell, Philip Wayne. *Mexico's Miguel Caldera: The Taming of America's First Frontier, 1548–1597*. Tucson: University of Arizona Press, 1977.

Prucha, Francis Paul. *American Indian Policy in Crisis: Christian Reformers and the Indian, 1865–1900*. Norman: University of Oklahoma Press, 1976.

Ramírez, Axel. *Chicanos, el orgullo de ser: memoria del encuentro Chicano México 1990*. México: Universidad Nacional Autónoma de México, 1992.

Rao, Gautham. *National Duties: Custom Houses and the Making of the American State*. Chicago: University of Chicago Press, 2016.

Regele, Lindsay Schakenbach. *Manufacturing Advantage: War, the State, and the Origins of American Industry, 1776–1848*. Baltimore: Johns Hopkins University Press, 2019.

Reid, Stuart. *The Secret War for Texas*. 1st ed. Elma Dill Russell Spencer Series in the West and Southwest 28. College Station: Texas A&M University Press, 2007.

Reséndez, Andrés. *Changing National Identities at the Frontier: Texas and New Mexico, 1800–1850*. New York: Cambridge University Press, 2005.

Reséndez, Andrés. *A Land So Strange: The Epic Journey of Cabeza de Vaca*. New York; London: Basic Books, 2009.

Reséndez, Andrés. *The Other Slavery: The Uncovered Story of Indian Enslavement in America*. Boston: Houghton Mifflin Harcourt, 2016.

Ribb, Richard H. "Catlin, George." *Handbook of Texas Online*. Accessed March 04, 2020. http://www.tshaonline.org/handbook/online/articles/fca94.

Riden, Philip. "The Output of the British Iron Industry before 1870." *Economic History Review* 30, no. 3 (1977): 442.

Rister, Carl Coke. *Comanche Bondage: Dr. John Charles Beales's Settlement of La Villa de Dolores on Las Moras Creek in Southern Texas of the 1830's*. Glendale, CA: A. H. Clark, 1955.

Roberts, Alasdair. *America's First Great Depression: Economic Crisis and Political Disorder after the Panic of 1837*. Ithaca, NY: Cornell University Press, 2012.

Rockman, Seth. *Scraping By: Wage Labor, Slavery, and Survival in Early Baltimore*. Studies in Early American Economy and Society from the Library Company of Philadelphia. Baltimore: Johns Hopkins University Press, 2009.

Rodríguez O., Jaime E. *"We Are Now the True Spaniards": Sovereignty, Revolution, Independence, and the Emergence of the Federal Republic of Mexico, 1808–1824*. Stanford, CA: Stanford University Press, 2012.

Rodriguez, Sarah K. M. "'The Greatest Nation on Earth': The Politics and Patriotism of the First Anglo American Immigrants to Mexican Texas, 1820–1824." *Pacific Historical Review* 86, no. 1 (February 2017): 50–83.

Rothman, Adam. *Slave Country: American Expansion and the Origins of the Deep South*. Cambridge: Harvard University Press, 2005.

Ruef, Martin. *Between Slavery and Capitalism: The Legacy of Emancipation in the American South*. Princeton, NJ: Princeton University Press, 2014.

Ruiz de Gordejuela Urquijo, Jesús. *Vasconavarros En México*. Grandes empresarios. México DF: LID, 2012.

Sahlins, Peter. *Boundaries: The Making of France and Spain in the Pyrenees*. Berkeley: University of California Press, 1991.

Sakolski, Aaron Morton. *The Great American Land Bubble; the Amazing Story of Land-Grabbing, Speculations, and Booms from Colonial Days to the Present Time*. New York: Harper and Brothers, 1932.

Salinas, Martin. *Indians of the Rio Grande Delta: Their Role in the History of Southern Texas and Northeastern Mexico*. 1st ed. Texas Archaeology and Ethnohistory Series. Austin: University of Texas Press, 1990.

Salmón, Roberto Mario. "San Roman, Jose." *Handbook of Texas Online*. Accessed March 12, 2020. http://www.tshaonline.org/handbook/online/articles/fsa16

Salvucci, Linda K., and Richard J. Salvucci. "The Lizardi Brothers: A Mexican Family Business and the Expansion of New Orleans, 1825–1846." *Journal of Southern History* 82, no. 4 (November 2016): 759–88.

Saragoza, Alex M. *The Monterrey Elite and the Mexican State, 1880–1940*. Austin: University of Texas Press, 1988.

Schaefer, David R. "Resource Characteristics in Social Exchange Networks: Implications for Positional Advantage." *Social Networks* 33, no. 2 (May 2011): 143–51.

Schermerhorn, Calvin. *The Business of Slavery and the Rise of American Capitalism, 1815–1860*. New Haven, CT: Yale University Press, 2015.

Schoen, Brian. *The Fragile Fabric of Union: Cotton, Federal Politics, and the Global Origins of the Civil War*. Baltimore: Johns Hopkins University Press, 2009.

Scott, Florence Johnson. *Historical Heritage of the Lower Rio Grande: A Historical Record of Spanish Exploration, Subjugation and Colonization of the Lower Rio Grande Valley and the Activities of José Escandón, Count of Sierra Gorda together with the Development of Towns and Ranches Under Spanish, Mexican and Texas Sovereignties 1747–1848*. Rio Grande City, TX: La Retama Press, 1965.

Scott, Florence Johnson. *Royal Land Grants North of the Río Grande, 1777–1821: Early History of Large Grants Made by Spain to Families in Jurisdiction of Reynosa Which Became a Part of Texas After the Treaty of Guadalupe Hidalgo, 1848*. Rio Grande City, TX: La Retama Press, 1969.

Scott, James C. *The Art of Not Being Governed: An Anarchist History of Upland Southeast Asia*. New Haven, CT: Yale University Press, 2009.

Scoville, Joseph Alfred. *The Old Merchants of New York City*. 5 vols. New York: Thomas R. Knox, 1885.

Sibley, Marilyn McAdams. "Charles Stillman: A Case Study of Entrepreneurship on the Rio Grande, 1861–1865." *Southwestern Historical Quarterly* 77, no. 2 (1973): 227–40.

Sims, Harold. *The Expulsion of Mexico's Spaniards, 1821–1836*. Pitt Latin American Series. Pittsburgh: University of Pittsburgh Press, 1990.

Smith, Mitchell. "The 'Neutral' Matamoros Trade, 1861–1865." *Southwest Review* 37, no. 4 (Autumn 1952): 319–24.

Spain, Jonathan. "Ellice, Edward (1810–1880)." *Oxford Dictionary of National Biography*. Oxford: Oxford University Press, 2013. Accessed December 06, 2018. http://www.oxforddnb.com/view/10.1093/ref:odnb/9780198614128.001.0001/odnb-9780198614128-e-8651.

Spicer, Edward Holland. *Cycles of Conquest: The Impact of Spain, Mexico, and the United States on Indians of the Southwest, 1533–1960*. Tucson: University of Arizona Press, 1962.

Staples, Anne. "Mexican Mining and Independence: The Saga of Enticing Opportunities." In *The Birth of Modern Mexico, 1780–1824*, edited by Christon I. Archer, 151–64. Wilmington, DE: Scholarly Resources, 2003.

Teja, Jesús F. de la, Paula Mitchell Marks, and Ronnie C. Tyler. *Texas: Crossroads of North America*. Boston: Houghton Mifflin, 2004.

Terrell, John J. *Biennial Report of the Commissioner of the General Land Office of the State of Texas.* Austin: Gammel-Statesman, 1905.

Thompson, Jerry D. *Cortina: Defending the Mexican Name in Texas.* College Station: Texas A&M University Press, 2013.

Thompson, Jerry D. *Tejano Tiger: José de Los Santos Benavides and the Texas-Mexico Borderlands, 1823–1891.* Fort Worth: TCU Press, 2017.

Thompson, Jerry D. *Warm Weather & Bad Whiskey: The 1886 Laredo Election Riot.* El Paso: Texas Western Press, 1991.

Thompson, Jerry D., and Lawrence T. Jones. *Civil War and Revolution on the Rio Grande Frontier: A Narrative and Photographic History.* Austin: Texas State Historical Association, 2004.

Tindall, George Brown, and David E. Shi. *America: A Narrative History.* 5th ed. New York: Norton, 1999.

Torget, Andrew J. *Seeds of Empire: Cotton, Slavery, and the Transformation of the Texas Borderlands, 1800–1850.* Chapel Hill: University of North Carolina Press, 2015.

Tortella Casares, Gabriel, and Farid el-Khazen. *The Development of Modern Spain: An Economic History of the Nineteenth and Twentieth Centuries.* Translated by Valerie J. Herr. Cambridge, MA: Harvard University Press, 2000.

Turner, Frederick Jackson. *The Frontier in American History.* New York: Henry Holt, 1921.

Tutino, John. *Making a New World: Founding Capitalism in the Bajío and Spanish North America.* Durham, NC: Duke University Press, 2011.

Tyler, Ronnie C. "Santiago Vidaurri and the Confederacy." *Americas* 26, no. 1 (1969): 66–76.

Tyler, Ronnie C. *Santiago Vidaurri and the Southern Confederacy.* Austin: Texas State Historical Association, 1973.

Underwood, Rodman L. *Waters of Discord: The Union Blockade of Texas during the Civil War.* Jefferson, NC: McFarland, 2003.

Valerio-Jiménez, Omar S. "Neglected Citizens and Willing Traders: The Villas Del Norte (Tamaulipas) in Mexico's Northern Borderlands, 1749–1846." *Mexican Studies/Estudios Mexicanos* 18, no. 2 (August 2002): 251–96.

Valerio-Jiménez, Omar S. *River of Hope: Forging Identity and Nation in the Rio Grande Borderlands.* Durham, NC: Duke University Press, 2013.

Vigness, David M., ed., trans. "Nuevo Santander in 1795: A Provincial Inspection by Félix Calleja." *Southwestern Historical Quarterly* 75, no. 4 (April 1972): 461–506.

Wagner, Peter. *Modernity: Understanding the Present*. Malden, MA: Polity, 2012.
Walsh, Casey. *Building the Borderlands: A Transnational History of Irrigated Cotton along the Mexico-Texas Border*. College Station: Texas A&M University Press, 2008.
Wasserman, Mark. *Everyday Life and Politics in Nineteenth Century Mexico: Men, Women, and War*. 1st ed. Diálogos. Albuquerque: University of New Mexico Press, 2000.
Waugh, Julia Nott. *Castro-Ville and Henry Castro, Empresario*. San Antonio: Standard Press, 1934.
Weaver, Bobby D. *Castro's Colony: Empresario Development in Texas, 1842–1865*. 1st ed. College Station: Texas A&M University Press, 1985.
Weber, David J. *Bárbaros: Spaniards and Their Savages in the Age of Enlightenment*. New Haven, CT: Yale University Press, 2005.
Weber, David J. *The Mexican Frontier, 1821–1846: The American Southwest under Mexico*. 1st ed. Histories of the American Frontier. Albuquerque: University of New Mexico Press, 1982.
Weber, David J. *The Spanish Frontier in North America*. New Haven, CT: Yale University Press, 1992.
Weddle, Robert S. *San Juan Bautista: Gateway to Spanish Texas*. Austin: University of Texas Press, 1968.
White, George W., Joseph P. Dymond, Elizabeth Chacko, Justin Scheidt, and Michael Bradshaw. *Essentials of World Regional Geography*. 3rd ed. New York: McGraw Hill, 2014.
White, Richard. *The Middle Ground: Indians, Empires, and Republics in the Great Lakes Region, 1650–1815*. 16th pr. Cambridge Studies in North American Indian History. Cambridge: Cambridge University Press, 2006.
White, Richard. *Railroaded: The Transcontinentals and the Making of Modern America*. New York: W. W. Norton, 2011.
Williams, Elgin. *The Animating Pursuits of Speculation: Land Traffic in the Annexation of Texas*. New York: Columbia University Press, 1949.
Williams, Stephen K. *Cases Argued and Decided in the Supreme Court of the United States, December Terms, 1865–1867*. Rochester: Lawyers' Cooperative Publishing Company, 1901.
Wilson, H. *Trow's New York City Directory*. New York: John F. Trow, 1859.
Wilson, Walter E. *Civil War Scoundrels and the Texas Cotton Trade*. Jefferson, NC: McFarland, 2020.
Winichakul, Thongchai. *Siam Mapped: A History of the Geo-Body of the Nation*. Honolulu: University of Hawaii Press, 1997.

Wooster, Ralph A. *Civil War Texas: A History and a Guide.* Austin: Texas State Historical Association, 1999.

Wright, Carroll D. *Comparative Wages, Prices, and Cost of Living.* Boston: Wright & Potter, 1889.

Wyllys, Rufus Kay. "The French of California and Sonora." *Pacific Historical Review* 1, no. 3 (1932): 337–59.

Yturria, Frank Daniel. *The Patriarch: The Remarkable Life and Extraordinary Times of Francisco Yturria.* Brownsville: University of Texas at Brownsville and Texas Southmost College, 2006.

Zahra, Tara. *The Great Departure: Mass Migration from Eastern Europe and the Making of the Free World.* New York: W. W. Norton, 2016.

Unpublished theses and dissertations

Adams, Larry Earl. "Economic Development in Texas during Reconstruction, 1865–1875." PhD diss., University of North Texas, 1980.

Brookins, Julia Akinyi. "Immigrant Settlers and Frontier Citizens: German Texas in the American Empire, 1835–1890." PhD diss., University of Chicago, 2013.

Cardenas, Mario Alberto. "José De Escandón, the Last Spanish Conquistador: A Study of Royal Service and Personal Achievement in 18th Century New Spain." Master's thesis, Texas A&M University–Kingsville, 1999.

Cunningham, Debbie S. "The Exploration and Preliminary Colonization of the *Seno Mexicano* Under Don José de Escandón (1747–1749): An Analysis Based on Primary Spanish Manuscripts." PhD diss., Texas A&M University, 2010.

Dickson, Lucy Lee. "Speculations of John Charles Beales in Texas Lands." MA thesis, University of Texas, 1941.

Garza, Juanita Elizondo. "Indian and Spanish-Mexican Cultural Influence in the Lower Rio Grande Valley." MA thesis, Pan American University, Edinburg, 1984.

Graf, Leroy P. "The Economic History of the Lower Rio Grande Valley, 1820–1875." PhD diss., Harvard University, 1942.

Kline, Kristen D. "Gulf Trade Networks and Family Ties: French Migration via New Orleans to the Lower Rio Grande Valley, 1848–1881." Master's thesis, University of Texas–Rio Grande Valley, 2019.

Mayer, Arthur J. "San Antonio, Frontier Entrepot." PhD diss., University of Texas at Austin, 1976.

Newspapers

Charleston Courier
Civilian and Gazette Weekly
Corpus Christi Star
Daily Picayune (New Orleans)
Daily Ranchero
Daily True Delta
New York Commercial Advertiser
New York Times
Republic of the Rio Grande and Friend of the People
Standard
Telegraph and Texas Register
Tri-Weekly Telegraph

Index

A

Adams-Onís Treaty, 48
alcalde, 62–63, 147
alcohol, 104, 113
Alleyton, TX, 131, 137
American system, 48, 89
Anglo-Americans, 2, 4, 6, 11, 66, 70, 95–96, 99–100, 107, 111–12, 114
anti-Semitism, 127, 134
Apache, 18–19, 26, 38, 44–45, 59, 65, 112
Aransas Bay, TX, 57, 65
archives, 74, 161, 175
Armstrong, James B., 105–7
Atlantic, 2–3, 5, 7, 9–10, 45–46, 67, 97–98, 103–4, 111–12, 122–23, 126–28, 139, 141–42, 154, 176
  trade, 10, 17, 91, 97–98, 103, 139, 142, 147, 154, 160, 165
Attrill, Henry, 138, 143, 145
August, Karl, 55
Austin, Moses, 47
Austin, Stephen F., 47, 50, 63
Austin, TX, 74, 83, 150, 155, 158, 162, 164, 167, 175, 177
Auzas, France, 114
ayuntamiento, 62

B

Baden, Germany, 77–78
Bagdad, Mexico, 139, 141–42, 153
Ballí, José María de, 35
Ballí, Salomé, 105
Baltimore, MD, 50, 52, 117
Barbé-Marbois, Francois, 82
Barron-Forbes, 167
Basque, Spain, 100, 110
Battle of San Jacinto, 70
Baumberger, Henry, 132, 137
Bavaria, Germany, 77–78
Beales Colony, 43–65
Beales, John Charles, 11, 43, 49
Becher, F. M., 55
beef, 25, 37, 139, 168
Benavides, Cristóbal, 116, 120, 135
Benavides, José, 115
Benavides, María Andrea, 115–16
Benavides, María Tomasa, 115
Benavides, Santos, 114–16, 121, 135, 147
Bichotte, Francois, 108
Bilbao, Spain, 100, 110, 175
Bloom, Conrad, 108
Bollaert, William, 88–89
Bordeaux, Spain, 75
borderlanders, 1–11, 15–41, 43–47, 49, 54–59, 65–77, 79–83, 85–91, 95–109, 111, 117–18, 121–23, 125–27, 129–30, 132–34, 136–43, 145, 147, 149–71, 173–77
borderlands, 1–11, 15–41, 43–47, 49, 54–59, 65–77, 79–83, 85–91, 95–109, 111, 117–18, 121–23, 125–27, 129–30, 132–34, 136–43, 145, 147, 149–71, 173–77
borderlands entrepreneurs, 2–6, 8–11, 44–46, 66, 68–91, 96–97, 99, 123, 127, 150–51, 154–55, 159–61, 165–66, 171, 173–77
Bourbon Reforms, 16–17
Bourbon, Spain, 16–17, 21
Bourgeois d'Orvanne, Alexander, 68, 72
Braunschweig, Germany, 55
Brazos de Santiago, TX, 152
Brazos Manufacturing Company, 147
Brazos River, 47, 160
British Foreign Office, 1, 80, 89, 174
Brownsville, TX, 102–4, 106, 108, 110–12, 125–26, 131, 136–37, 140, 142, 150–56, 158, 161–63, 165, 167, 170

239

Buffalo Bayou, 131
Burgundy, France, 75
Burr, Aaron, 53
Burr Conspiracy, 53
Buzcarrones, Bernardo Vidal, 30–31

C

Caballero and Company, 103
Caldwell, H. N., 144
Calle Comercio, 101
Calleja, Félix María, 38–39, 41
Camargo, Mexico, 9, 24, 29, 31, 34, 36, 40–41, 107, 137–38, 145–46, 169
camino de viborero, 39
Camino Real, 32–33, 50, 98
Canada, 81, 86
Caribbean, 9, 143
Carlist wars, 100
carters, 130, 132, 152
Carvajal, José María Jesús, 133, 142
Cass, Lewis, 122
Catholic, 74, 115–16, 134
Catholicism, 114–15
Catlin, George, 177
cattle, 24–25, 28–29, 31, 34–35, 38, 157, 161, 166, 168, 173, 175
cattle rustling, 157
Celaya, Simón, 103–4, 161, 170
Cerralvo, Mexico, 169
Chandler, Alfred, 5
Charles X, 72
chattel slavery, 69–70, 87
Cherokee, 48
Chicago and Alton Railroad, 165
Chicago, IL, 150
Choctaw, 132
Christianize, 18
Ciudad Guerrero, Mexico, 146
Ciudad Victoria, Mexico, 109, 131
Civil War, 11, 107–8, 118, 125–26, 128–29, 136, 141, 145, 150–51, 153, 157
civilization, 77
Clay, Henry, 89
clerks, 2, 4
Clichy-la-Garenne, France, 73

Coahuila, Mexico, 48, 50, 65
Coahuila y Texas, 43, 48, 63, 65
Coahuiltecans, 19, 35, 38
Coke, Richard, 164
colonialism, 13, 20, 41
colony, 7, 11, 16, 20–22, 33–34, 36–37, 41, 43–72, 80, 82–84, 88–91, 174, 177
Comanche, 10, 18–19, 30, 37–40, 44–46, 59–60, 64–65, 68, 74–75, 84, 112–13, 130, 132, 135
Comanche Empire, 10, 37–38, 40, 46, 68, 74
comercio libre, 16
commerce, 2, 6, 22, 26, 28, 36, 38–41, 73, 75, 96, 99, 173, 175
Commercial and Agricultural Bank of Galveston, 107
Confederacy, 123, 125–26, 129, 132, 138, 140, 157
Conquistadora, 28
consul, 2, 80, 83–84, 87, 90, 108, 117–19, 122–23, 143, 170, 174
corn, 31–32, 44, 60, 118–21, 129, 173
Corpus Christi, San Diego, and Rio Grande Narrow Gauge Railroad Company (CCRR), 166–70
Corpus Christi, TX, 9, 98, 120–22, 151, 161–62, 165–66, 168–70, 176–77
Cortina, Juan Nepomuceno, 126, 132–33, 146
Cortinista, 140
cotton, 8, 11, 51–53, 84, 90, 108–9, 125–47, 151–52, 154, 157, 163, 173, 175
Crawford, Joseph, 1–2
Crédit Mobilier, 166
Cuba, 103
Cuellar, Agapita, 146
Cuellar, Teodoro, 146
cultural boundaries, 4
currency, 25, 101, 107, 117, 125, 136–37, 140
customs, 8, 21, 75, 98, 109, 121, 146
Czech, 7

Index   241

D

Daily Ranchero, 153
Dalzell, Robert, 162
Dashing Wave, 143–45
Davis, Edmund J., 157–58, 164
debt peonage, 22
Decker, Cecilia, 145
Decker, John, 107, 145–46
Deffendorfer, R., 158
de la Barrera y Garza, Tomás Sanchez, 32
de la Serna, Jesús, 133
Delmas, Theophile, 105
Denver and Rio Grande Railway, 170
DeWitt, Bart, 117, 119, 136
DeWitt, Catherine, 117
Díaz, Porfirio, 151, 161, 167, 172
Diaz, Refugia, 146
Dolores colony, 11, 44, 63, 82
Don Fernandez, 110
Dosal, Manuel, 109
Downey, Ed, 162
Dubois de Saligny, Jean Pierre Isidore Alphonse, 71
Duchy of Nassau, 112
Ducos, Armand, 68–69, 72–73, 76–77, 81, 90
Dull, J. J., 167

E

Eagle Pass, 9, 141, 152
Earl of Durham, 81
Edwards, Benjamin, 48
Edwards, Haden, 48
Egerton, William Henry, 51–52, 60, 62–64
ejido, 34
Ellice, Edward, 85–86
empresario, 45, 47–52, 54, 56, 62–63, 65–70, 73, 78–80, 83–85, 87, 89–90
empresario system, 47–48, 51, 66, 68
Engineers Association of Scotland, 84
English, 43–44, 55, 57, 60, 62, 64–66, 91, 100–101, 122, 125, 137–38, 141–42, 177
Escandón, José de, 10, 15, 19, 22, 35, 91, 111, 173, 177

Espiritu Santo grant, 163
ethnic boundaries, 4
European-born entrepreneurs, 2–11, 66, 71, 91, 96–97, 99–100, 105–8, 110–11, 113, 123, 127–28, 149–50, 154–55, 159–60, 171, 175–77
Europeanize, 22
European merchants, 1, 4, 76, 96, 99, 122–23, 127, 134, 140, 150, 174
Europeans, 2–8, 10–11, 15, 43, 45–46, 49, 60–61, 66, 68–70, 74, 82–83, 86, 97, 122–23, 173–75
Evans, Richard, 155
exchange, 4, 7–8, 17, 31, 95–97, 100–101, 111, 113, 118–22, 136, 138, 145, 147, 174–75
Exchange Hotel, 101
Exter, Richard, 49–50, 52

F

failure, 33, 35, 41, 45, 50, 62, 66, 90–91, 142, 145, 171, 174, 177
farming, 23, 61, 83
F. de Lizardi Company, 144–45
F. Groos and Company, 152
filibusters, 133
Fitzpatrick, Richard, 122–23
flour, 31, 60, 120, 138
Fort Brown, TX, 106–7, 155
Fort Chadbourne, TX, 113
Fort Duncan, TX, 169
Fort McIntosh, TX, 98, 112–14, 121, 135, 138, 169
Fort Ringgold, TX, 106
Franciscans, 18
Fredericksburg, TX, 113, 116
Fredonian Republic, 48
free labor, 128
French, 20–22, 66–83, 85, 87–91, 101, 103, 105, 107, 109, 117–23, 125–28, 133, 140, 142, 176–77
French Intervention, 126, 128
friction of distance, 28
frontier, 5–7, 10, 15–16, 18, 20–26, 31, 38–41, 46, 49, 54, 66, 173–74, 177

G

Galvan, Jeremiah, 157, 164–65
Galveston Bay and Texas Land
  Company, 7, 53
Galveston, Houston, and San Antonio
  Railroad, 165
Galveston, TX, 7, 71, 73, 80, 83, 87,
  115, 129, 162, 165
García, Benito, 115
German, 2, 7, 55–57, 62, 77–80, 88, 90,
  108, 113, 115–17, 119–20, 122,
  176–77
Gilded Age, 7, 171
globalization, 3, 7, 96–97, 122, 176–77
Goliad, TX, 57–58
Gomila, M. J., 154, 158, 164, 170
Gould, Jay, 167, 169
Grant, James, 50–52, 164
Great Northern Railroad Company, 169
Grieve, James H., 84
Guadalajara, Mexico, 25
Guadalupe, 105
Guerrero, Cipriano, 133
Guilbeau, Francois, 117–22
Guizot, François, 73, 76–77
Gulf of Mexico, 9, 17, 30, 70, 72, 103,
  111, 144, 153, 159, 162

H

Hamilton-Gordon, George
  (Lord Aberdeen), 83
Hapsburgs, 21
Hasslauer, Victor, 108
Havana, Cuba, 103–4
Hernandez, Mariano, 109–10
Hernández y Hermanos, 140
Hewetson, James, 49
hide, 8, 25, 31, 113, 118–22, 129,
  147, 151
hierarchies, 4
Hinojosa, Juan, 35
Hispanicize, 18
Horn, John, 56
Horn, Sarah, 54–56, 58
House of Commons, 85–86
Houston, Sam, 68–70, 73, 77, 83

I

identity, 6, 142, 155, 176
Illinois Central Railroad, 165
Indian, 16, 20–21, 26, 30, 36, 40, 44, 60,
  64, 74–75, 84, 111–13
Indigenous, 1–2, 10, 15–18, 20–22,
  25–26, 30, 35–37, 40–41, 46,
  60, 65–66, 98–99, 132, 157,
  173–74
indio, 15, 18, 22, 29, 34
indios bárbaros, 15, 18, 22, 34
infrastructure, 16, 25, 28, 33, 38–39, 41,
  72, 177
Ireland, 80–81, 85
Irish, 7, 43, 49, 57, 62, 64, 120, 138, 157
iron ore, 51

J

Jacksonian democracy, 4
Jones, Anson, 79, 102, 131
July Monarchy, 72, 76

K

Karankawa, 20
Kenedy, Miflin, 102–3, 106–7, 137–38,
  149–72, 175–76
Kennedy, William, 69, 80–91, 174, 177
King, Kenedy, and Company, 105–7,
  149–52, 156–57, 160, 162, 169–70
King Ranch, 167
King, Richard, 137, 151, 153, 155–59,
  161, 163, 165–66, 168, 170,
  175–76
kinship, 5, 21, 40, 100, 104–5, 111,
  115–17, 122
Kiowas, 40
Kleiber, Joseph, 142, 152, 155–58,
  161–63, 175
Knight, Frank, 5

L

Lacoste, Jean B., 137–38, 143
Ladrón de Guevara, Antonio, 33
Lafitte, Jean, 76
LaFon, Ramon, 76

Index 243

Lamar, Mirabeau, 74
Laredo, TX, 9, 32, 40–41, 46, 97–99,
    110–22, 135–39, 146, 151, 153,
    161, 166–67, 169–70, 176–77
La Sal del Rey, 24
Las Moras Creek, 44, 51–52, 60–62
Latour, Bruno, 7
Lauregue, Vicente, 109
Laureles ranch, 161–62
Lavaca Bay, 74
Law of April 6, 1830, 45, 49, 53
Law of Nations, 126
Le Courrier du Rio Grande, 165
Lege, Charles, 137
Leyendecker, John Z., 97, 111–22,
    135–39, 143, 145, 147, 176–77
Liberal Party, 85
Linnville, TX, 74
Llamas, José de Ossorio de, 35
London, England, 69, 80, 87–88, 104,
    144, 167
Lott, Uriah, 151, 165–67, 169–70
Lovenskiold, 162
Ludecus, Eduard, 54–56, 61–62, 64

M

Madero, Evaristo, 120, 138, 152
man of progress, 51
manifest destiny, 77
markets, 4–5, 7, 10, 46, 50, 97, 100–101,
    103–4, 111, 118, 120, 122
Marqués de Altamira, 22–23
Marqués de las Amarillas, 29
Martin, Raymond, 114
Matamoros, Mexico, 1–2, 55–56, 63–65,
    74, 96–99, 101–3, 109–11,
    122–23, 126–27, 130–31, 133,
    137–47, 153–54, 156–57, 169–70
Maximilian, 127
McGloin, James, 49
McMullen, John, 49
Medina River, 73
merchants, 1–2, 4–5, 16, 39, 55, 71–72,
    75–76, 88–89, 95–101, 104–5,
    108–10, 114, 122–23, 127–28,
    133–34, 136–42, 145, 150, 152

mestizo, 29
Mexican, 1–2, 7, 9–11, 39–41, 44–56,
    60, 62–71, 86, 95–103, 107–10,
    112, 126–27, 130–34, 137–40,
    142–43, 145–47, 151–52,
    154–55, 167–70, 173–75
Mexican National Railway, 168, 170,
    173, 175, 177
Mexico, 1–2, 7–10, 16–18, 41, 43–54,
    56–57, 59–60, 62–72, 75–77,
    86–88, 95, 97–99, 103, 109–11,
    125–26, 128–33, 137–45,
    151–55, 167–70, 172–73
Mexico City, Mexico, 36, 39, 48–50, 54,
    133, 168
Michoacán, 49
Mier, Mexico, 48
Mier y Terán, Manuel, 48
Milam, Benjamin, 50
Milmo, Patricio, 120, 138, 140,
    142–43, 145
misinformation, 69, 91
mission system, 18, 21–22
Mississippi River, 46, 150
Missouri Pacific Railroad, 167, 170
modernity, 5, 75, 93, 127, 150, 154, 161
Monclova, Mexico, 63
monopoly, 15, 102, 105–6, 112, 146,
    150–51, 154, 156, 158, 160, 171
Montemorelos, Mexico, 109
Monterrey, Mexico, 9, 29, 31, 33, 108–10,
    120, 123, 125–27, 130–31,
    138–42, 152, 168–69, 173
Morell, Joseph, 125, 128, 134, 142
Morgan, Charles, 159
Morgan, J. P., 167
Morgan Line, 159–60
mulattoes, 48
Murrah, Pendleton, 130
Mussina, Simon, 154, 156

N

Nacogdoches, TX, 48
Nahuatl, 18, 23
National City Bank of New York, 154
nation-state, 75, 98

Native American, 4, 113
network, 6–8, 10–11, 16, 36, 50, 72–73, 91, 93–123, 134–40, 142, 145–47, 154–55, 159–60, 168, 177
New Mexico, 17–18, 20, 53–54, 72, 109, 120, 144, 159, 162, 167
New Orleans, LA, 55–56, 83, 100–101, 103–4, 114, 119–21, 143–44, 159, 162, 165–66
New Spain, 15–18, 20–26, 29, 32, 35, 37–38, 40–41, 109, 173
New York City, NY, 43, 54–55, 104, 118, 142, 151, 167
Nueces River, 18, 26, 43, 49–51, 68, 70, 88
Nueces Strip, 26, 45, 51, 54, 70–71, 74, 78, 86, 132, 173
Nuevo Laredo, Mexico, 9, 99, 119, 121–22, 131, 138–39, 146–47, 168
Nuevo León, Mexico, 22–24, 26–27, 29, 32, 120, 125–26, 137–38, 173
Nuevo Santander, 27–30, 33–36, 38

O

Oak Creek, 113–14, 117
Ochoa, Antonio, 146
Olmos, Andrés de, 18
Orinoco River, 83
ownership, 4, 34–35, 46, 158, 170

P

pacification, 16, 166–67, 170
Palacio, Juan Armando de, 35
Palmer-Sullivan Group, 170
Panic of 1837, 52, 69–70, 77, 83
Panic of 1857, 118, 129
Panuco River, 18
Paraje del Gato, 135
Paredes, Pedro, 26
parliament, 80, 85
Parras, Mexico, 50
patio process, 25
Pearsall, Thomas, 169
Pepin, Victor, 62
Philadelphia, PA, 117
Piedras Negras, Mexico, 9, 131, 138, 141
political boundaries, 75
Poor Laws, 85

Porfiriato, 7
postmaster, 121, 146, 162, 176
Power, James, 49
Power, Thomas A., 54, 57
Preau and Couturie Company, 119
presidio, 18, 20–22, 60, 65, 70, 73, 77, 83, 167, 169
Presidio del Rio Grande, 60
Prince Carl of Solms, 79
Pringle, Thomas, 87
Pringle, William, 87
Protestant, 49, 134
Pullen, Asa, 141

Q

Quartermaster Department, 106–7
Querétaro, 18, 20, 22

R

Railton, Joseph, 143, 162–63
Railton and Sons, 143, 159, 162–63
Raleigh Letter, 89
ranching, 25, 32, 114, 166
Realitos, TX, 169
Reconstruction, 150–51, 158, 164, 172
Redmond, Henry, 146–47
Reds and Blues, 164
Refugio, TX, 49, 135
regidor, 62
Republicans, 164
Republic of Texas, 11, 66–73, 75–91
Revilla, Mexico, 29, 31, 41
Reyes, María Guadalupe, 51
Reynosa, Mexico, 9, 24, 31, 35–36, 40–41, 133, 169
Rhineland, 77
Rhine River, 77
Rio Grande and Texas Land Company, 53–54, 63, 82
Rio Grande borderlands, 1–11, 15–19, 21–25, 27–46, 54–55, 65–66, 68–72, 74–75, 77, 82–83, 86–91, 95–98, 100–102, 104–6, 121–23, 125–27, 136–38, 140–43, 149–71, 173–77
Rio Grande City, TX, 106–8, 110, 145–46

Index

Rio Grande Railroad Company (RGRRC), 155–65, 169–70, 172, 175
Rio Grande River, 26, 43, 50–51, 61, 68, 70, 73, 77, 160
  Lower Rio Grande, 2, 6–7, 10, 20, 24, 30, 37, 41, 96, 99–100, 102–3, 106, 153, 157, 160, 171, 177
Robson, Robert, 84
Rockefeller, William, 167
Roma, TX, 9, 110, 122, 134, 153
Rullmann, A., 67–68

S

Saint-Denis, Louis, 20–21
Salado Creek, 86
Salmon, Francis, 53
salt, 24–25, 28–29, 31–32, 37
Saltillo, Mexico, 29, 33
San Antonio and Border Railroad Company, 169
San Antonio Road, 98
San Antonio, TX, 9, 26, 32, 47, 50, 58–59, 62, 73, 79, 86, 88, 98, 108, 113, 117–20, 127, 131–32, 137, 139, 152, 165, 169–70, 173
Sánchez, Petra, 115
Sánchez, Tomás, 115
Sanders and Company, 134
San Fernando, Mexico, 60, 64
San Juan Bautista, 20
San Luis Potosí, Mexico, 23, 25, 74, 168
San Román, Augustin, 103
San Román, José, 96, 100, 103, 122, 140, 144, 147, 149, 154, 163, 175
Santa Anna, 65, 69–70
Santa Fe, NM, 47, 71–72, 76, 88
Santa Gertrudis ranch, 161
Santleben, August, 152
Saxe-Weimar, Germany, 55
Schlickum, Ferdinand, 158
Schlinger family, 133
Scotland, 80, 84–86
Scott, Tom, 167
Seno Mexicano, 17–23, 25–28, 31, 33
settler, 13, 16–17, 20, 23–25, 28–36, 44–45, 62, 87, 126
Seven Years' War, 71

Shawnee, 59–61
sheep, 85, 152
Sibley, C. C., 135
Sierra Gorda, Mexico, 22
Sierra Madre, Mexico, 44
Sigondis, Lepine de, 177
silver, 24–25, 103, 137, 140–41, 170
Sir William Peel, 143, 145
slavery, 69–70, 87, 128
slave system, 128
Smith, Ashbel, 79
Society for the Protection of German Immigrants, 77–79
Soto, Fortunato, 50
Soto la Marina, Mexico, 27–28, 30–31, 37
Soto y Saldaña, María Dolores, 49
South Carolina, 54, 122
Southern, 52–53, 128–29
Southern Democrats, 151
South Texas, 114, 128, 130, 132, 157–58, 161–62, 169, 177
Spain, 2, 8–10, 15–18, 20–26, 29, 31–32, 34–38, 40–41, 47–48, 100, 173
Spanish, 2–4, 7, 10, 15–41, 100–101, 103, 105, 109–11, 113, 116, 140–41, 154, 157–58, 173, 175
Spanish Empire, 2, 15–17, 22, 28, 37–38, 40
speculators, 4, 44–46, 49–54, 65–66, 69, 76, 80, 84, 95, 101, 144
Spinelli, P. M., 162
Stephens, J. H., 171
Stillman, Charles, 102, 104, 108, 125, 134, 142, 146, 153–54, 156, 168
Stillman, James, 105, 154, 156, 167–70
Stillman syndicate, 104–7, 111, 156–57
St. Louis, MO, 150
Stuyvesant, Peter Gerard, 53
sugar, 90
Swan, 105
Swartwout, Samuel, 53
Switzerland, 132

T

Tamaulipas, Mexico, 110, 125–26, 133–34, 146
Tampico, Mexico, 1, 18, 33

09–10, 123, 140
...
...
–45, 48–49, 52–54, 56–59,
    63, 65–75, 77–91, 102, 113–15,
    117, 125–26, 128–41, 146–47,
    151–54, 156–58, 161–62, 164,
    166–70, 172–74, 176–77
annexation, 67, 69, 75, 89–90, 95
southern, 153
Texas Cotton Bureau, 136
textile, 8, 52, 85, 103, 107, 109, 122,
    126–30, 140, 147, 152
Thorn and McGrath, 100–101, 103–4
Tienda de Cuervo, José, 29
Tlaxcalans, 23
tobacco, 16, 103–4, 110, 139
transatlantic, 7, 97, 103, 105, 141,
    143–45, 154, 159, 163, 175
transnational, 95–123, 129, 132, 143,
    168–70, 172–73
Treaty of Amity, Commerce, and
    Navigation, 99
Treaty of Guadalupe Hidalgo, 10, 98,
    125, 129
Treviño, Albino, 114
Treviño, Josefa, 114, 116
Treviño, Manuel, 108
Treviño, Tomás, 114
Turner, Frederick Jackson, 174
Tweed, Robert, 104

U

Union, 125–30, 132, 136–37, 139–40,
    142–44, 146, 155, 166
Union Pacific Railroad, 166
United States, 7–8, 10–11, 47–49,
    52–53, 66–67, 69–70, 74–75,
    81–83, 89–90, 95, 98–99,
    103–4, 113–14, 120, 123,
    128–30, 142–44, 161–62,
    167–70, 172–73
US Army, 95, 98–99, 103, 113
US South, 53, 128

United States Land Company, 177
US-Mexico borderlands, 7, 9, 11, 96–97,
    105, 123
US-Mexico War, 7, 9, 11, 95–97, 100,
    104–5, 109, 111–14, 121, 142

V

Vale, John, 134
Vásquez, Rafael, 86
Velasco, TX, 71
Veracruz, Mexico, 26, 144
Vidaurri, Santiago, 120, 126, 135,
    137–38, 140, 142

W

wage system, 22
Wales, 85
War of Reform, 126
War of the Spanish Succession, 21
Werbiski, Alexander, 158
whiskey, 113, 166
Whitis, C. W., 141
Whitmonday, 116
Whitsunday, 116
Williamson, Charles, 53
wine, 75, 103, 118–19, 139
Woll, Adrián, 86–87
Woodhouse, H. E., 156, 158–59, 163,
    170
wool, 25, 31, 55, 138, 151
Wulff, Anton, 113, 116–19

Y

Young, John, 105–6
Yturria, Francisco, 102, 156, 170
Yucatán, Mexico, 25, 95, 153

Z

Zacatecas, Mexico, 25, 65
Zapata County, TX, 146
Zapata, Octaviano, 132
zona libre, 110